10th Edition

Neighbor Law

Fences, Trees, Boundaries & Noise

Attorneys Emily Doskow & Lina Guillen

W

TENTH EDITION	JULY 2020
Editor	LINA GUILLEN
Cover Design	SUSAN PUTNEY
Production	SUSAN PUTNEY
Proofreader	SUSAN CARLSON GREENE
Index	UNGER INDEXING
Printing	BANG PRINTING

ISBN: 978-1-4133-2772-4 (pbk)
ISBN: 978-1-4133-2773-1 (ebook)

Please note

We believe accurate, plain-English legal information should help you solve many of your own legal problems. But this text is not a substitute for personalized advice from a knowledgeable lawyer. If you want the help of a trained professional—and we'll always point out situations in which we think that's a good idea—consult an attorney licensed to practice in your state.

Acknowledgments

Credit for *Neighbor Law* goes to Cora Jordan, who was the original author of the first through fifth editions. We are indeed fortunate to have reaped the benefit of her expansive knowledge of the legal and emotional issues faced by neighbors across the country.

I also want to thank the dedicated research team at Nolo, including Jessica Gillespie and Chris Barta for their thoughtful and expert assistance on this edition and in making sure we provide our readers with accurate legal information.

—Lina Guillen

About the Authors

Emily Doskow is a practicing attorney and mediator who has worked with families in the Bay Area for more than 18 years. She is the author of *Nolo's Essential Guide to Divorce* and the coauthor or editor of many Nolo titles.

Lina Guillen earned her law degree from the University of California, Hastings College of the Law. She is an experienced trial attorney, with over 15 years of practice in a wide range of legal matters. She is also the coauthor of *Divorce and Money* (Nolo) and has been quoted in several publications including the *New York Times, U.S. News,* and *Real Simple* magazine.

Foreword

Like it or not, we're all neighbors—and we ought to get better at it. With good neighborly relations, you can live more safely, comfortably, sociably, and happily. Human beings, after all, are not solitary creatures like cats; we're a sociable species, made for each other's company. And in a period of our history when many of us live alone, or are single parents, a lack of good neighborly relations is likely to make life lonely, dangerous, and expensive. The best periods of my own life have been when I lived on small streets where everybody knew everybody. We looked after each other's kids; we sometimes shared potluck suppers; we picked up each other's papers and mail; we loaned each other tools—and returned them immediately, knowing the ill will generated by irresponsible borrowing habits.

Good neighbors share other things too: wisdom, time, vegetables, old car parts, you name it. They also share surveillance of their neighborhood. Neighborhood Watch programs are wonderful not only because they deter criminals, but because they get people together in the process of drawing up a neighborhood map and picking a block captain. Often they go on to have block parties and clean-up days, and work together to get the attention of city hall. But even citizens who know each other just informally and therefore tend to keep an eye on the street and on each other's yards and houses are an enormously more effective force against crime than the police can ever be. They make it possible for small children's lives to be freer of constant parental supervision; they can keep some rein on obstreperous teenagers.

Being neighborly doesn't mean poking your nose into your neighbor's life or business (unless you're asked, of course, and even then, you should be cautious). There's a fine practical line about privacy and noninterference that people have to learn to recognize. One of the best neighbors I ever had put this in a wonderfully wise way. We were confronting at the time a neighbor who had serious mental difficulties; she had, in fact, just come out of the mental hospital. She began tossing bottles off her porch to smash on the street at 2 a.m., while playing loud music through her open door, and one day she threatened some children with a hammer. For my neighbor George, that crossed the line. "What people do in their houses is their own business," he said, "but when they come down on the street, it's everybody's business." (We organized a sizable neighborhood delegation to call on the woman's psychiatrist and discuss the problem, and got it resolved.)

The magnificent positive potential of good neighborly relations, of course, is too seldom uppermost in our minds. We all tend to concentrate on the plentiful horror stories about neighbor conflicts. But it seems to be wiser to expect decent relationships with your neighbors; there is something about the very expectation that makes it more likely to happen. To be sure, there are in this world people so antagonistic, spiteful, bothersome, irresponsible, or otherwise impossible to live near that no amount of rational foresight, flexible negotiation, or even outright capitulation can bring their neighbors peace. Faced with such a situation, you have only the two alternatives of moving (which I would recommend) or trying to make their lives even more intolerable than yours, so that they move; this will not improve your character, and it probably won't work either. Luckily, such extremes are rare. The ordinary run of neighbors presents an ordinary range of human delightfulness and orneriness; and most people share a quite natural desire to live in a state of reasonable peace with their neighbors.

This desire is far more likely to prove effective if you know not only the commonsense human rules of treating other people decently, but also the specific laws that govern how neighbors (when push comes to legal shove) must treat each other. In neighborly relations, as in any other area of life, only an idiot goes to the law when friendly—or even not so friendly—negotiation and compromise are likely to solve a problem. Indeed, applying the law may "settle" a question between neighbors but in the process permanently embitter not only the contestants but other people who live nearby as well. It is also, of course, costly and chancy and likely to bring out the worst in everyone.

But knowing the law can help all concerned to arrange reasonable solutions to neighborly problems in informal channels, either personally or through mediation. People sometimes behave with great certainty that the law is on their side and are surprised to find the situation is more complicated. What, for example, do you think you can legally do to a neighbor's tree branch that overhangs your property, or with the fruit hanging on it? As I was astounded to learn, different legal rules apply; you had better know them before you get out your saw—or, more wisely still, discuss the situation with the neighbor before even thinking about the saw. Or suppose a neighbor's teenager is using a garage for rock band rehearsals; what exactly can you do about it, short of cutting the electrical wires?

This book lays out calmly and sensibly what everybody needs to know about such legalities of neighborhood life. If you tend to be a little hot-headed, it will cool you off. If you tend to give in on things too easily, it will strengthen your resolve. Read it and use it, remembering that what we all really need in our dealings with neighbors is not legal triumph or revenge but sanity, fairness, and peace of mind.

Ernest Callenbach
Berkeley, California

Table of Contents

Introduction: Neighbors and Legal Questions

Lost is our old simplicity of times,
The world abounds with laws, and teems with crimes.

—*Pennsylvania Gazette*
February 8, 1775

For most of us, the word "neighbor" carries almost as much baggage as the term "Mom" and considerably more than "apple pie." We give to it a nostalgic quality, similar to a Norman Rockwell painting. We long for the good old days, for simpler times, for safe streets and porch swings, for a setting when people were really neighborly. We watch old reruns of Lucy, Desi, Fred, and Ethel. On Sunday mornings, we escape to the comic strips and check up on our old friends Dagwood and Herb, and Loweezy and Elviney at the gossip fence. Many of us believe that if we could just turn back the clock our problems with neighbors would disappear.

When we think this way, we are overlooking an important factor—human nature. Disputes between neighbors are older than any laws ever passed. They concern space, property, money, and human personalities. When we remember the pleasant past of riding bicycles on shady streets, we often forget that there was usually one spot on the block that our mothers warned us away from, the home of the neighborhood grouch.

The shrinking space of today's world exacerbates our problems, as does the transiency of society. Often, we simply don't know our neighbors and are too busy and too tired to make the effort. Congestion and fear of crime tend to make us isolate ourselves. The basic problems, however, are far from new. The Hatfields and McCoys were not products of the 21st century.

Much of the law—statutes and court decisions—addressing neighbor disputes is quite old. Courts were faced with these dilemmas and published decisions as far back as the 13th century. In the United States, most state statutes on the subject were in place in the 1800s. Laws providing protection for tree owners, for example, were adopted by state legislatures as the country was expanding.

Consider the times and the importance of having neighbor questions resolved. A settler who went out to string boundary fences had at least two major concerns: water and timber. If he put his fence in the wrong place, taking a few acres of his neighbor's trees, the stage was set for a legal battle.

These were not just problems of the wild west. They had to be resolved in every region for property owners, whether they were farmers, ranchers, merchants, or small homesteaders. The tree and fence laws in Vermont, for example, are similar to those in the southern and western states.

Relatively few neighbor disputes reach the courts today. There are several reasons for this. Many of the laws are long settled and disputes are resolved early on. And today when a subdivision springs up, the boundary lines are set by licensed surveyors. When property changes hands, a title company insures the buyer and the title. If a difficulty arises, the new owner can usually go to the insurance company rather than to court.

One obvious reason that neighbors don't take quarrels to court (except small claims court) is the enormous cost. An argument over a tree is often simply not worth the high fees charged by lawyers. It is one thing to hate the roots from your neighbor's tree that clutter your yard, and quite another to put out $5,000 and several years in court to try to change the situation.

Lawyers and judges don't like neighbor quarrels because they are destructive, ongoing, and congest already overloaded court dockets. Experience has shown that even after a court rules in favor of one party, the neighbors will find something else to fight about.

What we do see today is neighbors taking their disagreements instead to the increasingly popular forum of small claims court. The proceedings are much less expensive and are accessible to almost anybody. No lawyers are necessary, and disputes are settled quickly after the judge listens to each side of the story. There is a limit on the amount of money a person can sue for in this court, somewhere between $2,500 and $10,000, with a few lower and higher limits.

Even small claims court judges, however, dread fighting neighbors. Do not be surprised if you take your neighbor to small claims court and find yourself directed to mediation. This is a process in which you and your neighbor work out your own problems and reach an agreeable settlement, aided by a trained, impartial mediator. Mediation, with or without court involvement, is an extremely effective method of resolving arguments between neighbors. We discuss it in detail later in this book.

Most of us go along day to day being cordial, never mentioning that a problem exists, except behind the neighbor's back. Sometimes, only to ourselves, do we admit that we despise the dadburned tree or ugly fence or barking dog. Often, the offending person is never even aware of a problem. We don't dislike the neighbor, we don't want to cause a hassle, and we are unsure of where we stand with the law. We don't know what to do about the situation, so we do nothing.

For those neighbors who rush to call the police or think that court is the only answer, this book offers some alternatives. And for those silent neighbors with problems, we hope it will help them assert their legal rights.

Get Updates and More Online

When there are important changes to the information in this book, we'll post updates online, on a page dedicated to this book:

www.nolo.com/back-of-book/NEI.html

You'll find other useful information there, too, including author blogs, podcasts, and videos.

Tackling a Neighbor Problem

Nothing so needs reforming as other people's habits.

—Mark Twain

We don't have the pleasure of choosing our neighbors—they simply come with the territory. What a great joy it is to move into a strange city or new area and be warmly welcomed by a courteous and thoughtful person who lives next door. And what a terrible disappointment when instead, the next-door neighbor is thoughtless or given to some activity that is a constant annoyance.

In today's society, the limited space between properties magnifies even a small annoyance. Especially if it occurs every day, what starts out as a bother can turn into a nightmare for a neighbor. And sadly, neighbors (even those who are the cause of the problem) sometimes retaliate when they feel threatened or disturbed, fueling what can escalate into open warfare.

Specific types of common neighbor disagreements are covered in separate chapters of this book. To begin with, however, this chapter contains a step-by-step guide to negotiating a resolution to any type of neighbor trouble.

Get Prepared

Instead of plunging into a neighbor quarrel, you can take preliminary actions on your own that, in the long run, will make you more effective in your efforts to truly resolve the problem.

Learn the Law

The law offers protection from a neighbor's disturbing activities. Local laws and subdivision rules prohibit almost anything one neighbor can do that would seriously annoy another. And when there isn't a relevant law, you can bring a nuisance lawsuit against a neighbor who unreasonably interferes with the use and enjoyment of your property.

When you find yourself on the receiving end of a neighbor annoyance, you will strengthen your position by finding and reading the relevant law. If the offender realizes the conduct that disturbs you also violates the law, you may have found the key to ending the conflict. (Chapter 18 explains how to find local ordinances and other laws that may bear on the situation.)

Local Laws (Ordinances)

Many of the everyday activities that could disturb a neighbor are regulated by city or county ordinances. Especially when citizen involvement is high in a community, what bothers residents the most finds its way into a local ordinance. Uncut weeds, dogs roaming at large, even old cars up on blocks may all be against the law.

Whatever your particular concern, always check your local ordinances thoroughly. Your city or town may have posted its ordinances on the Internet. This is worth checking, especially if you live in a large community. Or go to the public library or the county law library (usually located in or next to the courthouse), read them yourself, and make copies of anything that you think is pertinent. (Chapter 18 has more on looking up local laws.)

Once you have a copy of an ordinance that addresses the problem, your troubles may be almost over. The neighbor probably has no idea that what he or she is doing is actually against the law. In most circumstances, just presenting a copy of the relevant ordinance will resolve the problem.

Changing Local Laws

If the problem is not covered by the law, consider trying to garner support from your neighbors and getting one passed. Talk to a member of the city council or county board of supervisors about your chances of enacting a needed ordinance.

Residential Zoning Rules

In most residential areas, zoning laws allow only single-family dwellings. This means that the investor who purchases property down the street and then turns it into an apartment house for partying college students may be violating the zoning laws.

Zoning laws may also prohibit running a business at home that attracts customers and creates traffic in a residential area. These can prohibit, among others, home-based beauty parlors, typing services, child care centers, art studios, tax preparers, and car mechanics. The neighbor who has a yard sale once a year is not really in business (although some towns require a permit), but the one who has an active website displaying products or opens the garage door every Saturday morning for a sale is probably violating the law.

Before you complain about a possible zoning violation, always check the zoning map at city hall. The neighbor creating a problem might be located just over the zoning line, in an acceptable district for the activity. Also be aware that, in some circumstances, cities have the power to zone land that lies just beyond their boundaries. In Illinois, for example, towns may zone land that lies up to one-and-a-half miles outside their boundaries.

Subdivision Rules

If you live in a subdivision, condominium, or planned unit development, you are likely to be subject to property regulations called covenants, conditions, and restrictions (CC&Rs). These CC&Rs are normally contained in a separate document that is referred to in each property owner's deed. The homeowners' association office can give you a copy of the CC&Rs if you need one.

Although you can still use a local ordinance to help you in most of these communities and subdivisions, the CC&Rs are often much stricter and more detailed than local laws. They restrict all types of activity on the property—for instance, some don't allow the use of outdoor clotheslines, and others prohibit installing a basketball hoop on the garage. When the property is subject to these extensive restrictions, just about anything one person could do to annoy another will probably be addressed.

In areas that have these regulations, a disturbed neighbor can inform the homeowners' association of a violation of the rules. Depending on the particular structure of the association, the complaint process will be more or less formal. The association will notify the person accused of the violation and demand conformity to the regulations. It may sanction the person by suspending privileges—for instance, the use of a tennis court or a swimming pool.

Some associations have the power to sue a member of the group to conform. One neighbor can also sue another to enforce the restrictions, but the lawsuit must be in regular court (not small claims court) and will be expensive.

Additional Rights If You're a Tenant (or Your Neighbors Are)

If you rent an apartment or a house—or if your neighbors do—you may have additional avenues for relief from neighbor problems.

Your right to quiet enjoyment. All tenants have at their disposal a very powerful legal tool, quaintly called the "covenant of quiet enjoyment." In a nutshell, this means that the landlord may not create, tolerate, or maintain any conditions that make it impossible for you to enjoy the peace and quiet of your rented home. Common violations of the covenant include allowing incessant, raucous parties, failing to deal with drug dealing on or near the property, and tolerating home businesses (such as a driveway auto repair operation) that create noise, pollution, crowds, or any condition making it unreasonably difficult for you to live in peace. Even if your lease or rental agreement doesn't specify that the landlord must abide by this covenant, state law does. Whether you are faced with a noise problem, a nasty animal, a neighbor who hogs the laundry facilities, or even one running an obnoxious home business, you can insist on your right to quiet enjoyment.

In practice, the covenant of quiet enjoyment means that your landlord has to make sure that all tenants act in ways that don't unreasonably interfere with each other's rights to peace and quiet. The landlord can, and must, evict tenants who refuse to stop unreasonably disturbing others. Smart landlords drive this point home by including a clause in leases or rental agreements in which tenants promise not to conduct any activity that would disturb others.

Problems with tenants in your building. Let's start with the most common situation: You're a tenant and are bothered by noise and disturbances coming from residents of your own building.

As a first step, talk to your neighbor about all tenants' rights to quiet enjoyment. If the lease or rental agreement includes a clause repeating this guarantee, remind the neighbor about it. If you don't know the neighbor, write a note and attach the agreement to it. Sign it and slip it under the door.

No response? Obtain the support of other annoyed tenants. A neighbor loathed by the entire building may mend ways. If polite attempts to work things out fail, it's time to involve the landlord or the building manager. A wise landlord doesn't want an unhappy group of residents and will force the problem neighbor to abide by the agreement or terminate the tenancy.

If the landlord refuses to help, you may be able to break your lease and move out without future liability for rent. Or, you may want to stay and sue the landlord in small claims court, asking for a rent reduction that represents the diminished value of your rental.

Problems with tenant-neighbors on separate properties. If your problem is with a neighbor who rents from someone other than your landlord, your landlord has no control over the situation. Only the tenant's own landlord can enforce the covenant of quiet enjoyment. The most that your landlord can do is to appeal to the neighboring tenant and landlord for some cooperation or, if this fails, take stronger measures as described in the rest of this chapter.

Approach your landlord and explain the situation, asking for help with the next-door tenant and landlord. A conscientious landlord will try to remedy the situation, knowing that unhappy tenants in the building spell vacancies ahead. If it doesn't help, you probably cannot break a lease and move out without negative consequences.

Problems of homeowners with neighboring rental properties. If you're a homeowner with a rental property next door and the tenants are creating a disturbance, what are your options?

First, you'll want to contact the tenants and ask for their cooperation. If that fails, get in touch with the landlord or property manager and ask that they intercede on your behalf. Their influence may be sufficient, especially if the tenants are month-to-month renters whose tenancy can be terminated with relatively short notice (most states require 30 days). If you get nowhere, you'll have to approach the problem as you would any neighbor issue.

State Laws (Statutes)

Some situations that affect neighbors are regulated by state laws. If you think that your neighbor is breaking the law, you may well find the answers in your state statutes. Common state statute topics relevant to neighbor relations include:

- adverse possession
- boundary fences
- damage to trees
- disorderly conduct
- easements
- nuisance
- right to farm
- spite fences, and
- trespass.

State statutes can be found in a large public library, a county or university law library, or on the Internet. (See Chapter 18 for more on legal research.)

Open the Lines of Communication

How fortunate neighbors are when they know and respect each other so well that they can easily discuss and solve any problems that arise. For many of us, this is not the reality of our lives. But most people can still lay the groundwork that will make things easier should a dispute occur.

Long before you complain, before you even have a problem, get out there and meet your neighbors. The long-range benefit of being able to call someone by name, of creating even the tiniest bit of goodwill, is enormous when a problem arises. This is something every one of us should do and do it now.

Many people simply don't have the time or the inclination to be friendly with their neighbors. But it is not necessary to socialize with someone in order to make conversation possible. A simple introduction followed by a cordial "good morning" or "hello" on a regular basis will put you on the right footing and make communication easier.

This approach is in your own best interest and will make you a better neighbor. Just knowing something about your neighbors can help avoid conflict. If the person next door is a nurse working the night shift and sleeping during the day, you want to know this to avoid creating problems yourself. Knowing the neighbor is a no-lose situation—over time, it can also have the pleasant result of building real community in your neighborhood.

Never Be Hasty

When an annoyance first occurs, there are several reasons for not diving into the water too soon. Acting in anger, whether it's racing over in your bathrobe and slippers, screaming through the telephone, or bringing in the police without warning, reveals your own lack of control and guarantees disastrous resentment.

But even more important, you need to know just how serious the problem is—whether it will be ongoing, occasional, or a single disturbance. You need more facts and therefore more time.

Suppose a new neighbor moves in and immediately throws a rowdy party that is still going strong at 2 a.m. You rush over, bristling with outrage, and try to stop the party. Later, you learn that the affair was a giant housewarming or an annual birthday party and that this person is a quiet, model neighbor the rest of the time. What have you done? You've spoiled your future relationship—and you've also made it harder to gather a few friends yourself.

This same rule of wait-and-see applies when a barking dog appears on the scene. Maybe the neighbor is dogsitting for one night, or trying a new dog outside and will learn without your help that it doesn't work. Stereo suddenly blasting? The neighbor could have invested several thousand dollars in a new system and wants to be enveloped in it just once for the experience. Screaming fight next door? Well, people fight occasionally and in the heat of the battle, they forget about the neighbors.

Keep a Log

The most effective way to remain in control when faced with a neighbor problem is to sit down and describe on paper what is happening. This simple act will distance you from your anger and help you manage the situation. Writing down your concerns will tell you how serious the problem is and how often you are being disturbed.

List what has happened and when. This record will help later when approaching the neighbor, talking to the authorities, or going to court. Even if it means putting up with the problem for a time while you accomplish this, you will have exhibited your own tolerance and discipline and be in a better position to take action.

Know Who Is Responsible

When the peace of the neighborhood is suddenly shattered and you don't know your neighbors, the easiest reaction can be to simply call the cops to investigate the disturbance. This approach has several disadvantages.

An anonymous phone call or report to the authorities can make the situation much worse. The neighbor at fault won't know who the accuser is and so can't explain or even apologize. The neighbor will feel defensive, isolated, and suspicious of everybody—a bad neighbor. You may succeed in stopping a problem for the time being, but the same problem or others will almost certainly surface again.

Try to find out who the offending neighbor is and deal directly with the person responsible. The long-term results will be more desirable.

Knowing who is responsible also includes more than finding out who is committing the offense. If the problem neighbor is a tenant who turns out to be uncooperative, the landlord may well be the person who can remedy the situation. This can be true for many problems, including noise, property deterioration, and tree and boundary disputes.

Is a Picture Worth a Thousand Words?

It may be tempting to photograph, videotape, or record your neighbor's "misdeeds" as soon as the troubles begin. There are arguments for and against this tactic, however, and you should consider carefully before you proceed.

On the one hand, if your neighbor is unaware of the problem, or flat out denies it after you've already attempted to explain the situation, then it may be a great help to show a picture of the way her trees block your view or play a tape recording of her puppy's daily barking fit. Furthermore, if you are unable to successfully resolve the dispute in face-to-face conversations and decide to take your neighbor to small claims court, documentation of the problem will certainly help your case.

On the other hand, think of how you would feel if your neighbor suddenly started taking pictures of you or your property. Would you feel harassed, as if your privacy had been violated? Would you feel angry and less interested in trying to calmly resolve the dispute? Would you call the police?

Putting a camera between you and your neighbor may block communication when it is needed most to keep a quarrel from escalating. If you do decide to take photographs or video, stay on your own property when you do it.

Find Out Who Else Is Affected

If you are being seriously disturbed by a neighbor, chances are you are not alone. A noise problem, for example, likely affects several neighbors. You may find that other concerns also bother more than one neighbor. Neglected property, noxious fumes, blocked views, even an unclear boundary line can be a problem in common. Contacting others who are adversely affected and having them join you in your efforts can be very wise. It strengthens your position and also dilutes the possibility of hostility or retaliation.

Approach the Neighbor

Complaining to a neighbor is never easy. In fact, it can be so intimidating that people put up with terrible problems for years just to avoid confrontation. However, by being prepared and using common sense, you can make the task less unpleasant and much more productive.

Assume the Neighbor Doesn't Know

Most neighbors do not intentionally set out to create problems. The very last person to know that someone is disturbed is usually the one causing the disturbance. It is sometimes amazing how dog owners really don't hear their dogs bark. The neighbor who plays "Yankee Doodle Dandy" each night at megavolume just when your head hits the pillow may actually believe it helps everyone get to sleep. And some people are just plain thoughtless and have to be told that a problem exists.

Even if you are almost positive that the neighbor knows and doesn't care about an annoyance, when you approach that neighbor, assume the neighbor wants and needs to be told. It can't hurt and may help.

Expect a Complaint Against You

Whenever you approach a neighbor with a grievance, be ready for a complaint against you; the neighbor may desperately grab for one. Never forget that you may actually be at fault for some minor irritation at the present time or in the past and not know it. Your neighbors may be leaving their dog—who could sing bass in the choir—under your window at night because they're angry about your tree's annual shower of debris but too timid to speak up. Ask yourself how you would like to be approached if you were responsible for a problem.

Choose Neutral Ground

Observe the neighbor's habits (but don't be a stalker). What time does she get home from work? Does he water his yard at a certain hour? When does the trash go out? How about shopping trips or doing laundry?

What you're looking for is a common ground, a place to meet that is not exactly your territory and not your neighbor's. A parking lot, sidewalk, laundry room, or the boundary of properties are all possibilities. Choosing a neutral spot for your chat creates a more equal footing and can head off territorial defensiveness.

Talk About Something Else First

Try bringing up a subject of common interest. "Do you think it will ever rain?" "Do you think the city will pass that parks referendum?" "How about those Raiders?" Get the conversation going before you plunge into a complaint. Once you are talking, you can gently shift into the problem.

Introduce the Problem as a Common Concern

Imagine the perfect scenario. You and the neighbor are out side by side on the boundary watering your parched plants and complaining about the weather together. You look up at the neighbor's monster tree loaded with dead menacing limbs and innocently ask, "Aren't you afraid some of those big limbs are going to come down?" You've asked for an opinion on a topic of mutual interest instead of stating, "By golly, I hate that tree of yours; do something about it or else."

How about, "Now that the weather is warmer and the windows are all open, do you think we should all turn down our TVs a little?" Or, "The walls in this building are so thin that the sound passes straight through them. Is there anything you can think of that we could do about it?"

With conversation first, common interests, and neutral ground, the neighbor may help solve the problem and you may find you have avoided any confrontation at all.

Phone or Visit the Neighbor

If for some reason you can't use neutral ground, you can still attempt a tactful phone call, using some of the tips above. Be sure to show your own consideration by calling at a convenient time, say early evening. The neighbor will be more responsive and less defensive.

If you want to go over to the neighbor's house, again choose a reasonable time—a weekend afternoon, for example. If you have found others affected by the problem, consider going together. But don't bring a big gang that will immediately make the neighbor feel attacked. Be prepared for some defensiveness when you complain on the neighbor's own territory, and use common sense. Something as basic as what you wear can affect the outcome. Keep it casual. If you come calling dressed in a coat and tie and the neighbor is in casual at-home clothes, you may have unwittingly encouraged hostility.

State the Complaint

You may be forced to just come out and tell the neighbor that a problem exists and it needs correcting. Still, some approaches work better than others. Try, "I'm sure you would want to know that your stereo (or tree, or collection of old cars in the yard) is disturbing me." Explain why you are disturbed, for example that you couldn't sleep Tuesday, Thursday, and Saturday nights (remember your list), or you're afraid the tree will fall on your car, or you think the yard's condition lowers property values on the street.

Don't be afraid to say you are sorry, that you hate to complain. Most people really are sorry to have to complain and if you say it, then it's easier for the neighbor to also say it.

Have a solution to the problem already in your mind and offer it. For instance, "Would you please be willing to wear headphones or to keep the TV low after nine o'clock when I have to sleep?" "Would you be willing to trim this tree before it causes severe damage?" (Or possibly, "I'm willing to share the cost of trimming this tree.")

Complain in Writing

Sometimes it is necessary to complain in writing to someone as a first step. If you are too timid to face the neighbor directly or you don't feel you have established enough of a relationship to do so, you can state your complaint effectively in writing. When you have already spoken to the neighbor without success, you'll want to complain in writing as a next step. A diplomatic approach is still the best choice. A sample letter is shown below.

Sample Complaint Letter #1

April 5, 20xx

Dear Mr. Costas,

   I am sure you would want to know that your dog has kept me awake for three nights this week. Could you please put him in the house after 10 p.m. so that he won't disturb the neighborhood? Thank you very much.

Sincerely yours,

Alice Batter

Alice Batter
123 Oak Lane
Storyville, NY 00000

Take a deep breath and sign your name. If others are affected, get everybody you can to sign with you.

Present the Law

Most neighbors will attempt to correct a situation that is bothering someone without even thinking about the law. But when this is not the case, it is time to present a copy of the relevant law.

How you do this will depend on the individual circumstances. If the relationship is still cordial, you can again use the "I'm sure you would want to know" approach and then simply give the neighbor a copy of the law. When hostility has developed, enclose the law with a firm letter, like the one below.

Sample Complaint Letter #2

April 12, 20xx

Dear Mr. Hamur,

As I pointed out to you last week, your puppy has been digging up and ruining my vegetable garden. I have enclosed a copy of our local ordinance which prohibits dogs from running at large.

Please leash your dog when off of your property as required by the law. Otherwise, I will be forced to contact the authorities. Thank you.

Sincerely yours,

John Ono

John Ono
456 Maple Drive
Anytown, MN 00000

Keep the letter civil, keep a copy, and send it certified. You are creating a record to present to the authorities if you wish, and later if necessary, to a judge. (See Chapter 20.) You also want to make it clear that you mean business.

When a problem such as an encroaching tree or a danger to children is not directly addressed by a specific law, a preliminary letter to the neighbor written by an attorney on a legal letterhead might still head off more trouble and expense. Having the laws explained to the neighbor by an attorney may be worth the cost and could even end the dispute.

The Ultimate Quarrel

Neighbor quarrels can escalate into full-fledged violence and sometimes even murder, a warning to all of us about the importance of remaining calm and using clear communication and mediation if necessary (see Chapter 19) to nip neighbor disputes in the bud before they get out of control.

Disputes that end in violence can arise over something as trivial as "you blew your leaves onto my yard with your blower, which is really loud anyway!" But disagreements over boundary lines may be the most frequent source of neighbor disagreements that turn ugly. For example, in March of 2013, filmmaker John Upton—who lived in Encinitas, California—was shot and killed by his neighbor over a dispute regarding some trees located on a narrow 130-foot strip of land. The neighbor—Michael Vilkin—was found guilty of murder.[1]

In Carmel Valley, California, a 72-year old geophysicist named John Kenney shot his next-door neighbors, Mel and Elizabeth Grimes (married lawyers) after a long dispute over a few feet of land and years of simmering neighbor issues.[2] Kenney was found guilty of murder and sentenced to life in prison.

And finally, in Idaho, a man was found guilty of second degree murder after shooting and killing his neighbor, with whom he had a long-running boundary dispute. In a statement to the press after the verdict, the prosecutor in that case said, "No sliver of land is worth the life of [the victim]."[3]

These cases serve as a lesson about the strong emotions that often underlie "simple" neighbor quarrels. Such terrible conflicts ruin lives and should remind us to know the law where we live and be ready to compromise to avoid such situations.

Turn to the Authorities for Help

Sometimes all the courtesy and common sense in the world just don't work. Some neighbors can be thoughtless, nasty, and dangerous. If your efforts produce nothing but hostility, the time has arrived to seek help.

The proper authority, whether it is the police, a zoning board, a city health department, or another entity, should be more receptive to your complaint because of your own efforts. Tell them what you have done to try to solve the problem. Present a copy of the records you have kept. When several people are involved, get everyone to complain at once, and keep it up until you get some action.

When someone complains about the violation of an ordinance, the city or county can warn the person, issue a fine, or take measures to correct the problem. Sometimes, if the person is uncooperative, the city will fix the problem (for instance, cleaning up rubbish) and bill the person responsible. In serious situations, the city or county attorney can sue the person to force compliance with the law. Someone who wants to fight a citation for a violation can go to court. If the judge orders the person to comply, violation of the order can result in another fine and, in some circumstances, a jail sentence.

In addition to official channels for complaint, if you live in a larger town or city, you also have another avenue open to you. Very often, instead of calling the police, calling your local neighborhood mediation center will result in a much more desirable solution.

Try Mediation

If your neighbor thinks your complaints are unreasonable and does nothing to remedy the situation, you have a choice: Go to court or suggest mediation. Because most legal mechanisms will cost time, money, and any future good relationship, trying mediation first is a worthwhile effort to keep the dispute just between you and your neighbor and to arrive at your own solution.

In mediation, you work out your own agreement with the help of a trained and neutral third party (the mediator). One reason mediation between neighbors is so successful is because sometimes both neighbors simply need to have their say. Often, both have complaints about other issues. Once they are aired, a compromise involving everything in dispute is possible.

You can find a good mediator in just about any urban area. Many communities have free or low-cost neighborhood mediation centers designed to handle serious and not-so-serious neighbor disputes. (Chapter 19 has all the details.)

Take the Neighbor to Court

If you can't work things out with a neighbor or get help from the city, don't give up. When a neighbor does something that is unreasonable or unlawful that interferes with the use and enjoyment of your residence, you can sue the person for creating what is called a private nuisance. You can ask for money and in certain cases, you can also ask for a judge's order making the neighbor remedy the problem. Usually, you'll sue in small claims court. (See Chapter 20.)

Some states describe what constitutes a private nuisance in their statutes. For example, some states make someone who does anything at all to interfere with the use or enjoyment of a neighbor's property legally liable to the neighbor for a nuisance.

The laws in a few states require conduct to be unlawful (in violation of an ordinance, for example) or unreasonable before it is considered a nuisance. In these states, it can be a little harder for a neighbor to win a nuisance lawsuit, but most activities that seriously disturb a neighbor would be considered unreasonable.

Most states don't have a general nuisance statute; instead, they list certain activities that are legally considered nuisances—for example, having garbage on property or keeping anything that's a health hazard. An activity that's not on the list can still be a nuisance under the common law (laws that are entirely developed by the courts rather than the legislature) if it interferes with someone else's use of property.

Appendix B lists each state's definition of a nuisance. In states that require unreasonable conduct, ask yourself if what the person is doing would be considered by most people as an unreasonable use of property. If you are not sure that what the neighbor is doing is unreasonable, you probably have very weak grounds for a legal complaint.

What You Can Sue For

You can ask the court to award you money to compensate you for your annoyance and also to order the neighbor to stop the nuisance. For a court order to stop the problem, you will probably need to hire a lawyer and use regular (not small claims) court.

But for money alone, you can use small claims court, which is fast, and where you don't need a lawyer. You must ask for an amount that is within your state's small claims court limit—between $2,500 and $10,000 in most states.

How much money should you ask for? Approaching the problem on a daily basis is the easiest method. If you had to clean up your yard after your neighbor's dog once a day for ten days, $10 a day would be considered reasonable by most people. When the dog's mess harmed the lawn, you would include the cost of fixing it. If the problem is more serious, such as something that makes you ill, keeps you awake, or decreases your property value, you could easily ask for as much as $50 to $100 a day.

After you sue a neighbor successfully for creating a nuisance, if the neighbor doesn't remedy the situation, you can sue again and again until something is done.

Suing a Landlord

If the problem neighbor is a tenant, you can sue the tenant, but you can also sue the landlord for maintaining a nuisance on the property—that is, for allowing the tenant's activities. If a landlord is allowing noisy all-night parties or worse—drug dealing, for example—on the property, suing the landlord will bring the problem to the landlord's attention and should lead to a remedy for the problem.

Neighbors Banding Together

One of the most effective approaches to stopping a nuisance in a neighborhood is for all neighbors who are affected by the activity to sue at the same time. What may seem like a small sum of money multiplied by ten or 20 small claims awards gets the attention of the person responsible (including a landlord) and usually stops the activity.

Neighbors have organized and successfully brought these multiple lawsuits when faced with everything from teenagers drag-racing on residential streets to noise at a major airport. For example, a group of neighbors actually forced a policy change at the San Francisco International Airport by collectively and repeatedly suing in small claims court about the noise.[4] Other groups of neighbors have used small claims court to combat drug dealing on their streets. (See "Drug Dealers" in Chapter 17.)

What You Must Prove

When you sue for a nuisance, you must prove the following:
- The neighbor is doing something that seriously annoys you.
- The neighbor's acts diminish your ability to use and enjoy your property.
- The person you are suing is responsible (and, in some states, the conduct is unreasonable or unlawful).
- The amount of money you need to compensate you for the annoyance.

You must be prepared to show the judge what the harmful activity is, and exactly how it affects you. In a case of illegal activity such as drug dealing, a person may rightfully fear being sued himself for making such an accusation. When neighbors know illegal activity is going on but can't really prove it, they can instead, and just as successfully, complain to a court just about the noise, traffic, and disturbance created.

If the neighbor is violating any ordinance, take a copy of the law with you to hand to the judge. If your state has a general nuisance statute, have a copy of the statute. And although it is not usually necessary in small claims court, you can do a little legal research and find a similar court case from your state to bolster your complaint. (See Chapter 18.) ●

Endnotes

1 "How a Simple Dispute Between Two Neighbors Ended in Death," *ABC News*, July 24, 2014.

2 "Straying over the property line isn't always deadly, but it can be dangerous," *SFGate* (San Francisco, California), February 16, 2007.

3 "Man Guilty in Murder of Neighbor," *Daily Herald* (Everett, Wash.), October 6, 2005.

4 *San Francisco v. Small Claims Court*, 190 Cal.Rptr. 340 (Cal. App. 1983).

Noise

He is happiest, be he king or peasant, who finds peace in his home.

—Goethe

I t is 7 a.m. on a Saturday morning. After a long and hard week, you are enjoying one of the great pleasures in life—not setting the alarm clock. Then the noise starts. Your next-door neighbor fires up the chain saw. Or the neighbor across the street gets an early start with her power mower. Or the teenager upstairs turns on the boom box. And the dog down the street barks at any and all of it.

Whatever the intrusion, your plans for peace are shot. You cover your head with the pillow for a while and then give up. Not wanting to cause trouble, you begin the weekend irritable, tired, maybe even physically ill.

In case you think you are just being too sensitive, think again. The Health and Place Initiative (HAPI) is a group of Harvard experts investigating how to create healthier cities in the future. In its October 2015 research brief, "Noise, Health, and Place," HAPI looked at the impacts of noise.[1] The team found that short-term impacts of environmental noise may include annoyance, cognitive impairments, and disturbed sleep, while the long-term impacts include secondary effects from sleep disturbance, such as possible mental health issues, increased risk of injury, ischemic heart disease (also known as coronary artery disease) —caused by lack of oxygen/reduced blood flow to the heart—and an increased risk of heart attack

Noise is a very serious matter, and the time may come when you realize that you should have acted long ago to curb the situation. In California, if you sell your house, you must fill out a disclosure form for the new buyer, pointing out any problems. There is a blank to mark "yes" or "no" to the question: Neighborhood Noise Problems.[2] Then what do you do?

Laws Against Noise

You are protected from a noisy neighbor by local, and sometimes state, law. Additionally, rules in rental agreements and planned communities further restrict allowable noise. Noise regulations are enforced by the police, landlords, neighborhood associations, and the courts. And when you are affected by your neighbor's excessive noise, you can sue the neighbor for creating a private nuisance. You can ask a court for money damages and to have the noise stopped.

Local Noise Laws

The most effective weapon you have to maintain your peace and quiet is your local ordinance. Almost every community has a noise ordinance prohibiting excessive, unnecessary, and unreasonable noise. And most laws designate certain times as quiet times, such as nights and some hours on weekends. Some types of noise may be allowed at some times but not at others.

Certain necessary noises occur all of the time and we simply have to put up with them—for instance, noise from a heavy industry or from traffic on the freeway. But when we can control the noise, the ordinances apply. Running a power mower may be perfectly acceptable at 10 a.m. on Saturday, but not at 7 a.m., and turning up the volume on the TV or stereo may be okay at 5 p.m. but not at 2 a.m. when neighbors are trying to sleep.

A Look at the Law

If you are a reasonable person and your neighbor is driving you wiggy with noise, the neighbor is probably violating a noise law.

Many towns also have decibel level noise limits, and your town probably has electronic equipment for measuring the noise when a neighbor complains. A few cities have special noise units to enforce the laws and to free the police for other calls.

A typical noise ordinance, this one from Oxford, Mississippi, begins like this: "Creation of any unreasonably loud, disturbing and unnecessary noises in the city is hereby prohibited."[3] Some cities use the language "loud, raucous or nerve-wracking noise." San Francisco, California, prohibits "unwanted, excessive, and avoidable noise."[4]

Some sounds that bother us the most are placed in special categories that are either not allowed or have special rules. These noises are assumed to disturb people. For instance, most cities prohibit—either in their noise laws or vehicle laws—the honking of auto horns unless there is danger. This means that the daily early-morning tooting across the street for the carpool is a violation.

Dogs are usually singled out; sometimes they are allowed to bark for very short periods, say under ten minutes. The dog that barks only at intruders or a passing fire engine is probably within legal limits. But the neighbors down the block who allow their dog to howl all night are violating the ordinance. If you are having problems with a dog, or are a dog owner, see *Every Dog's Legal Guide,* by Mary Randolph (Nolo).

Motorcycles may be mentioned by name in an ordinance. In some locations, unnecessary running of the engine, for example, may be presumed to disturb a neighbor.

In addition to actual lists of troublesome noises, certain types of noise are sometimes included in the special categories. Examples are sounds of annoying pitch, such as a screech, and persistent or repetitive sounds, like the hum of a motor or the pounding of a hammer.

When Is Noise Unreasonable?

Most ordinances prohibit unreasonable noise, but they don't define it. The police—or later, a judge—may have to make the decision. But to be unreasonable, the noise should be—in the opinion of an average person—too loud, prolonged, or disturbing for the time of day. It usually boils down to common sense and to what most people consider unacceptable. For example, the child who practices the piano for an hour each day is certainly not a matter for the law. A roaring piano at 11 o'clock every night is. A rollicking party several times a year— probably acceptable. Every three days? No way.

Music can present special problems. Sometimes it is a matter of taste. What is pleasant to some ears quickly hits the discomfort level of others.

These unreasonable noise laws are enforced by the police (or other local government agencies) and the courts according to the effect of the noise on a normal, reasonable person. If you jump out of your skin at the slightest peep of a puppy, you may find no help from the law. Sometimes cities require that the noise disturb two or more persons before it can be stopped, to prevent complaints from excessively sensitive people.

If you are the only neighbor on the block who is being bothered by a noise everyone hears at the same level, you may be too picky. People usually know deep down whether they are being reasonable, and most people actually allow more noise in their lives than the law does.

The Bouncing Ball

A bouncing basketball isn't usually considered a noise problem, but two California lawyers went to court over one. One sued the other who was dribbling the ball in the driveway and disturbing him.

After several court proceedings, including a full-blown court trial, the case went all the way up to the California Court of Appeal, which found in favor of the basketball-playing neighbor. The court held that the noise from basketball play in the neighbor's backyard, at a reasonable time of day, for less than 30 minutes at a time, and no more than five times per week did not constitute unlawful harassment and would not cause a reasonable person to suffer substantial emotional distress.[5]

Decibel Level Laws

Many towns prohibit sustained noise that exceeds a certain decibel level. The decibel limits are set according to the time of day and the neighborhood zoning. For example, higher levels are allowed anytime in industrial areas. In residential areas, the limit is lower than the industrial limit during the daytime and much lower at night. There are exceptions for emergency situations, such as road repair. Also, some cities allow people to apply for a variance to the noise law—a permit to exceed the noise level for a certain period of time, for instance during major construction. You may also be able to get a permit for a one-time event.

Unless you are a sound engineer, the language of these statutes may mean nothing to you. It does mean something to the police or the special noise unit. They have a machine and know how to read the noise level.

Measuring the Noise Level Yourself

If you are curious about the noise level where you live, you can purchase a decibel level machine at an electronics store, for $35 and up. Taking your own reading may give you an indication of how severe a problem is, even though if you complain, the police will want to take their own measurements.

What happens under a decibel level ordinance is that a neighbor complains and the noise unit comes out. If the noise is still going on, the noise officer places the machine on an estimated property line and takes a reading. If the noise level coming into the other property is above a certain number, it violates the noise ordinance. However, the offending noise has to be measured against what is called the ambient level—the background noise level without that particular disturbance.

Finding the ambient level with a live band playing can be difficult. The noise units have become experts at finding comparison levels, and many people insist that this method is the fairest one of all in controlling noise. For apartment living, the decibel level is measured inside, and it is common for the levels allowed to be much lower.

Today's Reasonable Person

The reasonable person in today's society is a strange mixture of adaptation and resistance. Consider for a moment your everyday life in the city. You slip your car into rush-hour traffic in the morning with several thousand noisy, honking others. Huge trucks fill the lane beside you. Stereos blast the air. Road crews pound with heavy equipment.

On your lunch break, you zip over to the diner, waving at the fellow with the jackhammer, stopping to let a screaming police car go by. You don't talk at lunch because the din of voices and clatter is so loud that you can't be heard. When you return to the office, you step into the elevator filled with music, get off on your floor, and return to work in a room with 200 cubicles, or a steam press, or the drum of machinery. After work, back into the thundering traffic, and then finally home. Thirty minutes later a lone dog starts to bark. You tense, then bristle with the invasion.

What's going on here?

The human brain is an incredibly flexible machine. Several hundred years ago, this kind of constant noise would have been unthinkable. Now you and I, today's reasonable people, have created an amazing compromise. Some noises are tolerable and some are not. Noise in some places at some times is okay and not in others—definitely not at home.

We may not realize it, but we have set very strict limits and cannot bend at all under certain circumstances. Fifty years ago, if music from your neighbor's house drifted into your window, you might have not only tolerated it but tapped your toe to the rhythm. Today, you react with resentment and can't allow it. An argument can be made that the reasonable person today is much more sensitive to noise at certain times and in certain places than in years past. As the tolerance for noise increases on one end, it decreases on the other to prevent an overload. We are looking at a method of survival. The Saturday morning lawn mower is not just a bother to some people; it is a nightmare.

It is no wonder that our police can hardly keep up with noise complaints, and that neighbor-to-neighbor fuses are so short. What's the answer? Who knows? Awareness of the situation is a beginning.

Once the machine shows that the particular noise is above the allowed level, the person responsible will usually be warned. If the noise continues or is repeated, then the person will be cited and fined. Fines are often levied according to how many violations there have been—for instance, $100 for the first time, $200 the second, $300 the third.

When a town adopts the decibel level method, it usually keeps the unreasonable noise law too. When a town has both kinds of laws, either one may be used.

Times of Day

Most local ordinances include what could be called "quiet times." The noise level allowed is lower during these times, the hours when most of us try to sleep. An average ordinance prohibits loud noises between the hours of 11 p.m. and 7 or 8 a.m. on weekdays and 11 p.m. or midnight until 8 to 10 a.m. on Saturdays, Sundays, and holidays. Some cities set the evening hour as early as 9 p.m. or even 6 p.m.

What this really means is that if any noise is loud enough to keep a reasonable person awake during these hours, it is above the limit allowed. Towns that use a decibel system also lower the limit during these hours.

These quiet hours can vary from one residential area to another within the same city depending on the zoning for the particular spot. In a residential-only zone, for example, the morning hour may be 8 a.m. and in an industrial area 7 a.m.

Having quiet times listed does not mean that there are no noise restrictions at other times. A blasting boom box can be a violation at any time. What it does mean is that you have the right to expect not to be disturbed during the quiet hours. If your neighbor starts up his chain saw at 6 a.m. on a Sunday, he is probably breaking the law. In suburban areas, the lines between different towns may meander around and different restrictions may apply from one block to the next. It's a good idea to know not only your own ordinance but those in areas that can affect you.

EXAMPLE: Bill and Barbara liked to stay out late and party every Saturday night and sleep in on Sunday mornings. Every Sunday morning, the church down the street pealed its large bell at 9 a.m. It was the only noise for the whole morning, but it meant waking up at nine. Bill read his local ordinance and saw that the quiet time lasted until 10 a.m. on Sundays. He was extremely uncomfortable complaining about a church, but he finally called the pastor. He then learned what real discomfort was when the pastor politely informed him that the church was located just two lots inside the next suburban town. Their quiet hours? 11 p.m. to 9 a.m. on Sunday.

Other Local Laws

Once in a while, a neighbor noise problem can be solved by using another local ordinance. For example, the neighbor who is running a little machine shop business in his back yard at night and on weekends may be violating a zoning ordinance. Any business conducted at home that creates customers and traffic probably doesn't fit residential-only zoning.

Other miscellaneous laws also have an effect on noise. Discharging firearms and shooting off firecrackers are forbidden by separate laws. Having too many animals on one property can violate another law. Even working on a broken car for too long may be prohibited.

Noises in some of these situations can be very annoying, yet don't quite fit the noise ordinance. To find out what other local laws might be applicable, read your particular ordinances. (See Chapter 18.)

State Laws

If a neighbor's noise is excessive and deliberate, it may be a violation of state laws against disturbing the peace or disorderly conduct. For example, New Mexico law says that anyone whose conduct is boisterous or unreasonably loud and tends to disturb the peace is guilty of a misdemeanor.[6] This means that the police can arrest anyone who is being unreasonably loud. Misdemeanors are minor criminal offenses usually punishable by fines and less than a year of jail time. And California has a criminal law that provides for a fine or jail or both for any person who willfully and maliciously disturbs another person by loud and unreasonable noise.[7] You can find out what state laws a neighbor may be violating by asking the police or researching the law. (See Chapter 18.)

Also, many states have noise control laws that address problems affecting us as a public, such as airport, heavy industry, and transportation noises. Some states have an office to receive complaints, and a staff that works with the federal government in its efforts to curb unnecessary noise. If a "big neighbor" is making your life miserable, you can find out from your city attorney's office how to proceed under these state provisions or look up your state's law. (See Chapter 18.)

Rental Agreements and Restrictive Covenants

If you live in a planned community or rent an apartment, you have extra remedies that may be available to you besides the town noise ordinances. You may not even need to ask for help from the city.

Renting: An Additional Weapon Against Noise

When your residence is a rented apartment in a large complex, you can be more vulnerable to noise. Problems arise not just because the walls can be a little thin, but also because you simply have more neighbors with whom you must contend. Sometimes the neighbor creating a problem is a complete stranger.

Many apartment dwellers seem to think they have given up a right to quiet, and they tolerate too much noise. They are afraid to be labeled as troublemakers and don't insist on their rights.

People who live next door to apartment complexes also sometimes take too much noise for granted.

If you are in either of these groups, you have a lot of avenues open to you to regain your quiet. Laws that prohibit unreasonable noise apply to apartments, as do decibel level laws (usually a lower level of noise is allowed within buildings than would be permissible outdoors). You can also sue the noisy neighbor for a private nuisance. But there is more. The person making the noise can be evicted, and you can sue the landlord. (See "Additional Rights If You're a Tenant," in Chapter 1.)

Standard rental and lease agreements contain a clause entitled "Quiet Enjoyment." In this clause you will find wording somewhat like this:

"Tenant(s) shall be entitled to quiet enjoyment of the premises. Tenant(s) shall not use the premises in such a way as to violate any law or ordinance, commit waste or nuisance, or annoy, disturb, inconvenience, or interfere with the quiet enjoyment of any other tenant or nearby resident."

If the neighbor's stereo is keeping you up every night, the tenants are probably violating the rental agreement. They can be evicted for the violation. Informing the neighbor of the lease restrictions may be all that is necessary. If that doesn't help, complaining to the landlord can be very effective.

Most apartment owners don't want problems among their tenants, and they won't put up with somebody who ignores the signed agreement and causes trouble. Especially if several tenants complain at the same time, the landlord will probably order the tenant to comply with the lease or face eviction.

The landlord also may know that a tenant's activity can form the basis for a lawsuit against the landlord. By allowing the situation on the property, the landlord is maintaining a private nuisance. If you have the same landlord, you may not want to sue, but you have the right to do so. If you are just a neighbor, going after the landlord can often solve the problem.

Planned Communities and Condos

When you buy a condominium or a house in a planned community, the deed often contains restrictions called restrictive covenants. These can range all the way from what color you can paint your fence to what activities are allowed on your property. You agree to the restrictions (called covenants, conditions, and restrictions, or CC&Rs) when you buy the residence.

Restrictions against excessive noise are quite common. The restrictions apply to you, your neighbors, and any tenants who are renting. What's more, they place responsibility for a tenant's actions on an owner. The owner is the one who agreed to the restrictions, and when a tenant breaks the rules, the owner can be disciplined and even sued to conform.

In planned communities and condos, the right to enforce the rules is usually placed in the hands of a residents' committee. Someone who violates the rules is sanctioned, for example, by having privileges to common areas (such as a swimming pool) revoked. These remedies are above and beyond the regular noise laws, which are also applicable to people in these locales. They provide another possible step to take before calling in the law. Some owners' associations have the power to sue members of the group to enforce the restriction. One neighbor can also sue another neighbor for violation of a restrictive covenant, but the time and expense probably won't be worthwhile unless the problem is very serious.

What to Do

There are two common reactions to noise coming from a neighbor. The first is a sense of helplessness and resignation. You hate the noise, but you do nothing. The second is anger. You lose your temper and call the cops. There are better ways to handle the situation—and middle ground to be found.

Approach the Neighbor

Discussing the problem with a neighbor is not easy. In fact, it can be very painful. But it is always the first step and, if done with respect and sensitivity, will hopefully be the last.

Often the neighbor is unaware of a problem (for instance, the dog barks only when nobody is home). Or the neighbor may just not realize that the noise is bothering someone else. An effective approach is to assume that the neighbor doesn't know, would like to be a good neighbor, and would like to be told. Before you complain behind the neighbor's back, and certainly before you think of calling the police, tell the neighbor. Step over there or pick up the phone and give communication a chance.

> **EXAMPLE:** When I began writing this chapter, the puppy belonging to my lovely new next-door neighbors decided, as if on cue, to serenade me. I had only met the neighbors once, and I could not believe what was happening. It was as if the puppy knew when I sat down to write. Every word was punctuated with a yelp. He barked until he became exhausted, slept for a while, and then started again. He barked only when the neighbors were not at home.
>
> Several days of this went by, much to the amusement of my family. It was not the least bit funny to me. I began to make mistakes in the text and had to rewrite whole paragraphs. For several nights, I looked at the telephone and cringed, wanting to call the neighbors but more strongly not wanting to call.
>
> I knew the dog's name and discovered if I yelled loudly enough at him, he would be quiet for a few minutes. My family became more amused. Now the neighborhood had turned into "bark, bark, yell; bark, bark, yell." I was becoming part of the problem.
>
> Finally, I had to call. How could I tell my readers to do something I couldn't do myself? The neighbors were horrified to learn that there was a problem and very apologetic. They placed the puppy inside and now I write this in silence.

This example is typical. Most of us really hate to complain. Yet look what happened. The dog isn't barking, the owners were grateful to be told, and the lines of communication are open. Once all of the apologies settle, these neighbors will probably be friends for years. All it took was one phone call.

Warn the Neighbor

When informing the neighbor of the problem doesn't work, the next step is to get a copy of your local noise ordinance at city hall, the public library, or from the Internet. (See Chapter 18.) Send a copy of the law to the neighbor accompanied with a letter like the following:

Sample Noise Complaint Letter

September 2, 20xx

Dear Mr. Thoughtless,

I have enclosed our local noise laws so that you may read them. You will see that playing your stereo so loudly is against the law. It is very disturbing to me. Please turn down the volume as I have asked you to do in the past. Otherwise, I will be forced to notify the authorities.

Sincerely yours,

Bob Bothered

Bob Bothered

Keep a copy of the letter because you may want it later if you sue the neighbor. (See "Sue for Nuisance," below.) Then see what happens. The neighbor may not know the law and finding out about it may put an end to the problem. Putting the complaint in writing also lets the neighbor know you mean business.

Bring in the Landlord

If you live in a rental unit or restricted housing area, send a copy of the lease agreement or special rules to the neighbor along with your written complaint. This can result in prompt action, especially if you suggest that your next complaint will be to the landlord or the neighborhood association. In an area with a homeowners' association, if a neighbor does not respond, notify the association.

If a tenant refuses to comply with your requests, report it to the landlord in writing. You are not a troublemaker. In fact, you are assisting the landlord in protecting his or her interests. A sample letter is below.

Sample Noise Complaint Letter to Landlord

> May 14, 20xx
>
> Dear Mr. Wilson:
>
> I live in Unit 5 of your Ridgeland Apartments complex. Mr. Jones in Unit 7 plays his stereo at such a loud volume that it is a serious disturbance to me. I have asked him several times to please turn it down and he has not responded. Last week, I sent him the enclosed letter pointing out to him that he was violating his lease.
>
> I regret having to bother you, but I know that you would want to be alerted to this situation so it can be corrected. Thank you for your cooperation.
>
> Sincerely yours,
>
> *Teri Tenant*
>
> Teri Tenant

Strength in Numbers

In dealing with a landlord or a hostile neighbor, one of the most effective things you can do is to get someone else to complain also. This is not nearly as hard as you might think. If you are being bothered, someone else probably is too. They are probably just waiting and hoping somebody will do something. They don't want to act alone either. The greater the number of people complaining, the faster the relief should be.

Suggest Mediation

When a neighbor is uncooperative, before you call the cops or rush to court, consider using mediation. You and the neighbor can sit down together with an impartial, unbiased mediator and resolve your own problems. Mediation services are available in most cities and often they are free or available at a nominal cost. You simply contact the mediation center, and most will then contact the neighbor for you.

In a noise dispute, you could not only try to settle the current problem but also work out an agreement that would avoid problems in the future. This is a much better solution than simply calling a police cruiser to the door, which will guarantee hard feelings from then on. And especially when there are more problems than just the noise, the neighbor may be delighted at a chance to be heard. If you value the neighbor relationship at all, or just want peace in the future, give mediation a try. (See Chapter 19.)

Call the Police

No response from the neighbor? Stereo turned up another notch? Now is the time to bring in the police. (If the problem is a barking dog, this may be the animal control officer in your town. And some cities have special noise units that respond to complaints. You can find out by calling the police office.) You are in a very different position than you were originally. You have tried to solve the problem yourself. You have done what you could on your own and even have a copy of a letter to prove it.

Of course you don't have to take all these steps before calling the law. But look at the difference between you, standing there with the written ordinance and the letter in your hand, and the thousands of people who call the cops over the slightest (and often most frivolous) matter. The police know the difference. They will know your complaint is serious and that you need help.

Try to notify the police while the noise is continuing. If they are using a decibel meter, they need to be able to measure the noise level to see if it is above the allowed limit.

Sue for Nuisance

Whenever someone else's unreasonable action interferes with your enjoyment of your property, that action creates what is called a private nuisance. If you are the one affected by the nuisance, by your neighbor's blasting stereo or howling dog, you can sue the neighbor and/or the neighbor's landlord. You can ask the court for money damages or to make the neighbor stop the noise (that is, to have the nuisance abated). For money damages alone, you can use small claims court; for a court order to stop the noise, you may have to sue in regular court. A few states limit what subjects can be addressed in small claims court. (See Chapter 20 for small claims limitations.)

What you really want is for the noise to disappear. However, having the neighbor ordered to pay you money can be amazingly effective in regaining your quiet. If the noise continues, you have a "continuing nuisance" and can sue again and again.

A lot of neighbors are using small claims court for noise situations. It's easy, inexpensive, and you don't need a lawyer.

To sue for private nuisance due to noise, this is what you need to show:

- There is excessive and disturbing noise.

- The person you are suing is either creating the noise or is the landlord and therefore responsible.

- Your enjoyment of your property is affected. (You don't have to own the property—you can be a tenant.)

- You have asked the person to stop the noise (a letter should be enough).

This can be shown by police reports, other witnesses, your own testimony, or even a recording.

The effect on you is called your damages. This may include loss of sleep, annoyance, or the inability to carry on normal activity without interference. You can ask for a reasonable dollar amount per day for damages. The amount you can sue for in small claims court is limited, usually between $2,500 and $15,000. (Chapter 20 lists each state's limit.) If you have been bothered for 20 days and want $20 a day for it, this would usually be considered reasonable and would be well within the limit. If the noise problem is really severe—keeping you from sleeping or working and making you completely frazzled—$100 a day wouldn't be too much to ask.

Once you have sued in small claims court, if the noise continues, you can sue again. Also, if other people are affected, get together with your neighbors. If ten people sue for $2,500 each, that's $25,000. Do it again—another $25,000. Sooner or later, the noise should stop. (For more on small claims court, see Chapter 20.)

If you choose to sue in regular court and hire a lawyer, get the attorney to write a threatening letter before you sue; that may be all that it takes. Sadly, some neighbors and landlords can be pretty rotten, and nothing short of a judge's order or high money damages will change the situation.

For example, consider one nasty neighbor and an owner attempting to rent his house next door. Every time a prospective tenant looks at the property, the neighbor revs up his huge motorcycle. When the police come out, all is quiet. Damages can mount up quickly for the owner of the house. For extreme situations like this, you will need an attorney.

Most noise problems between neighbors (and most neighbor disputes in general) can be solved by following a few simple guidelines:

- Know the law and stay within it.
- Be reasonably tolerant of your neighbors.
- Be assertive of your rights.
- Communicate with your neighbors—both the neighbor causing the problem and others affected by it.
- Ask the police for help when it is appropriate.
- Use the courts when necessary. ●

Endnotes

1 "Noise, Health, and Place," HAPI (2015).

2 Cal. Civ. Code § 1102.6(c).

3 Oxford, Miss., Mun. Code § 18-1.

4 San Francisco, CA, SFPC 29 § 2900.

5 *Schild v. Rubin*, 232 Cal. App. 3d 755 (1991).

6 N.M. Stat. Ann. § 30-20-1.

7 Cal. Penal Code § 415.

When a Tree Is Injured or Destroyed

Woodman, spare that tree!
Touch not a single bough!
In youth it sheltered me,
And I'll protect it now.

—George Pope Morris

We human beings exhibit some complicated, often conflicting, emotions over our trees. In the abstract, we understand our dependence on timber for shelter, comfort, even the daily newspaper, yet we are slowly comprehending the critical importance of standing forests to the environment. In our daily language, we have adopted the tree as a symbol—the tree of liberty, the tree of knowledge, and the old favorite, the family tree. We also seem to have a personal craving for trees. We bring them into our office buildings and shopping malls, tend little forests along city streets, and many of us fondly remember the excitement of childhood tree-planting ceremonies on Arbor Day.

But by far, the most powerful feelings emerge over the trees in our own yards—the trees we own. We plant, water, trim, even decorate them. We build treehouses and hang swings and birdfeeders in them. And we relax under them, relishing their shade and beauty. Most tree owners expect everybody else to love their trees. This, of course, is not always the case. The neighbor who lives downwind and has to rake up somebody else's leaves may despise the tree. And large trees can cause enormous problems—blocking views, producing invasive roots or dropping rotting fruit, and, especially if ill, threatening to fall on houses, cars, or people.

But one thing is certain: We take ownership and protection of our trees very seriously in this country, and this is reflected in the law. An annoyed neighbor who decides simply to get rid of someone else's tree and gets out a chainsaw can be in for some very nasty legal consequences.

Who Owns a Tree?

It is accepted law in all states that a tree whose trunk stands wholly on the land of one person belongs to that person. If the trunk stands partly on the land of two or more people, it usually belongs to all the property owners. (Special rules apply to such trees. See Chapter 6.)

Some states—California, for example—place this definition of ownership in their state statutes (laws passed by the state legislature). But even in states where the legislature has not done this, the rule is still the same under what we call the "common law," meaning case-by-case decisions made by the courts.

An Owner's Rights When a Tree Is Damaged

The basic rule is this: Someone who cuts down, removes, or hurts a tree without permission owes the tree's owner money to compensate for the harm done. The owner can sue to enforce that right.

To run afoul of the law, you do not have to chop down a tree. You can also get in trouble by damaging the health of someone else's tree. For example, you have the legal right to trim branches of a neighbor's tree that hang over your property. (See Chapter 4.) But seriously injuring the tree while doing the trimming can make you liable to the owner for the harm done. Or if you use a chemical in your own yard to destroy unwanted roots, and it seeps under to the neighbor's property and kills a tree standing there, you can be liable.

An owner can also recover damages for harm to shrubs, flowers, vines, and growing crops as well as trees. This means there is legal protection for a straggly little boxwood as well as a favorite old lilac bush.

For a tree owner to have a legal right to compensation for a damaged tree, there are two requirements:

- The owner's own property must be damaged. For instance, if a neighbor trims the part of your tree that is over the neighbor's yard making it look terrible, you have no right to recovery unless the portion on your property is damaged. (See Chapter 4.)

- The tree in question must not create an immediate danger to others. Unsound trees that threaten a neighboring property are not under the same legal protection as healthy trees. In some circumstances, for example, if a dead tree is about to fall, a neighbor can even enter an owner's property to prevent the harm. (See Chapter 5.)

It Wasn't Always This Way

Ascertaining ownership by looking at the trunk appears to reflect good plain common sense, but it has not always been the law. Years ago, there was a very different rule. It said that if the roots of a tree took nourishment from a neighboring land, sapping the strength of that land, then the neighbor also had part ownership of the tree.

As one might expect, judges began to have trouble with this. In 1836, a court in Connecticut discarded the rule, stating that it was impossible to apply because tree roots move around.[1] Other courts ruled the same way, and the law shifted to what we have today. Can you imagine the problems in our urban society if the nourishment test were still enforced?

What the Tree Owner Can Sue For

Someone who has lost a favorite tree because of a neighbor's actions can't get the only truly desirable outcome—to have the tree back. But if the person responsible for injuring or removing a tree won't make good the loss, and it isn't covered by insurance, the owner has the right to sue the tree chopper for money to compensate for the loss. Often the owner can sue in small claims court, with no need to hire an attorney.

A general principle is applied again and again in tree damage cases: If the person who hacked the tree did not do the harm intentionally, or made an honest mistake, the person will have to pay the owner only the amount of the owner's actual loss. If the offender didn't care or willfully entered the neighbor's property, penalties will be triggered. Often the penalty is two or three times the amount of the actual loss.

Let's take a moment to look at the three kinds of monetary awards (called damages) that may be available, depending on the circumstances and state law:

- **Compensatory (Actual) Damages:** The amount of the owner's actual loss due to the destruction of the tree.
- **Statutory Damages:** An extra amount of money, determined by state statute, that the person responsible pays to the owner. When damage to a tree was intentional, statutory damages are often three times the compensatory damages.
- **Punitive Damages:** A sum awarded by a judge or jury when the conduct of the person who damaged a tree was especially outrageous or malicious.

We discuss each of these kinds of damages below.

Criminal Penalties

A neighbor whose intent was to do harm and whose conduct was outrageous can be in for an enormously expensive lesson in neighbor law. Penalties for willful, malicious destruction of someone else's tree can include a fine and, in very extreme cases, even a jail term. See "Criminal Penalties," below.

Compensatory (Actual) Damages

Compensatory damages are intended to reimburse the owner for actual losses. Although it can be difficult to put a dollar value on the loss, this sum can be quite large when a mature tree is destroyed.

Here are the kinds of losses for which an owner can be compensated in a lawsuit over a damaged or destroyed tree.

Cost of Replacing the Tree

Some trees are small enough—usually, less than 12 inches in diameter—to be replaced at a nursery. In that case, the amount of actual damages would be the cost of having a new tree of similar size and type planted to replace the dead or damaged one. The cost of removing debris and cleanup would also be included.

The homeowner's insurance policy of the tree owner will commonly pay up to $500 to replace a tree, plus up to another $500 for cleanup. (See "What to Do If a Neighbor Damages Your Tree," below.)

> EXAMPLE: Boris is putting an addition on his house. He rents a bulldozer and begins clearing the area. Accidentally, he flattens a young maple tree belonging to Fran next door. Embarrassed over his lack of bulldozing skill and genuinely sorry about the tree, he goes to Fran and offers to reimburse her for her damage. Fran orders a new tree of the same kind and size, has the old stump and debris removed and the new one planted. Boris pays the bill. Fran has been compensated for her actual damages by having the tree replaced.
>
> Had Boris not been so cooperative and had Fran sued him in small claims court, the judge would probably have ordered him to pay Fran the same cost for replacement, plus her costs in filing suit.

A landscaping business can help an owner replace much larger trees— even a 50-year-old oak. At a tree farm, a tree is carefully removed, roots and all, and shipped on a flatbed truck to its destination. There are some possible problems; some states prohibit the importation of live plants, and if the tree is too big, it may not be allowed on the highway. The cost is another barrier—it can be as much as $10,000 to $20,000.

Diminished Property Value

For various reasons, replacing a tree may be impossible. Then, the most significant consequence of the loss is the lowering in the value of the owner's property as a whole. The tree owner is entitled to compensation for the decrease in property value caused by the loss of the trees.

For a reliable estimate of the drop in property value, an owner generally needs an expert opinion. The best opinion to obtain is that of a licensed or consulting arborist. For several hundred dollars, an arborist will consider many factors, including the size of the tree, its type, its age, its condition, and the benefit it provided to the property. Special benefits the tree provided, such as lowering utility bills and serving as a windbreak, will also be taken into account.

And if you are replacing the tree with a smaller one, an arborist can tell you what the loss is when considering the time it will take before the new tree reaches full size. Arborists use an elaborate formula for assessing tree value that has been accepted in court.

Landscape architects, real estate appraisers, developers, consultants, and horticulturists can also estimate diminished property value. These experts assess the property's market value before and after the loss of the tree. A good real estate agent (not an appraiser) can also give you an accurate estimate of property value loss, but in many areas, real estate agents do not give official appraisals.

If you use any expert other than an arborist, be aware that you may have to figure out on your own any special losses you have, such as a loss of shelter that affected utility bills. Always ask an expert exactly what factors are being considered in an appraisal. If a tree lowered utility bills substantially, or its loss renders a patio unusable in summer heat, and these losses are not included, you need to take them into account. The same would be true when the tree served as a windbreak, blocked an unsightly view, produced fruit or nuts—anything that would be considered if an arborist had done the appraisal.

The cost of any expert opinion will probably run several hundred dollars. If you go to court, include this fee as an expense of the incident, and ask the judge to order the neighbor who caused the damage to pay it back to you.

Some judges simply accept expert opinions as adequate proof of a loss. Occasionally, the property is actually viewed by a judge or jury.

Aesthetic Loss and Mental Anguish

Some trees are simply more valuable to us emotionally than others. Courts in Louisiana have compensated tree owners for aesthetic loss and mental anguish.

In Louisiana, in 1984, a judge considered the aesthetic loss of a man whose row of trees was mistakenly cut down by a neighbor. Actual damages to the property were put at $1,487.50. The judge obviously did not feel that this amount fully compensated the neighbor. Commenting that the beauty would not be restored for many years, the judge ordered an extra $2,500 paid to him for his "loss of aesthetic value."[2]

Another case, again in Louisiana, resulted in an award for the tree owner's mental anguish. A house mover, needing more space to accomplish his task, proceeded to remove limbs from six pecan trees on the property of an extremely upset woman. The court found actual property damages of $117.36. Again, unhappy with the measly sum, the judge considered the agitation of the injured owner. He took into account that the pecan trees had been planted by her grandfather 60 years earlier and tended by her father, who had just died. She was awarded an extra $1,250 for mental anguish.[3]

Finding an Expert

To find a licensed arborist, do an Internet search for "arborist," "trees," or "landscape." You can also look for state government offices; look for a division of plant industries, department of forestry, state plant board, or landscape architects' board. Someone should be able to furnish you with a list of all licensed arborists for your area or tell you whom to call. The American Society of Consulting Arborists (301-947-0483, www.asca-consultants.org) makes referrals to consulting arborists; make sure they refer you to an arborist with experience appraising trees.

Courts in California have also compensated tree owners for aesthetic loss. In 2012, the California Court of Appeal confirmed that California courts may award damages for lost aesthetics and functionality when considering the diminished value of an injured tree. In this case, the lower court awarded the plaintiff tree owner $15,000 for the loss of aesthetics that occurred when her neighbor hired an unskilled worker to "trim" the plaintiff's cypress tree. Instead of simply trimming away the branches that hung over onto the defendant neighbor's yard, the worker used a chainsaw to hack away at the tree so badly that it was left "very odd looking … one-sided and very unaesthetic."[4]

It is too soon to tell how courts in other states will respond when asked to compensate tree owners for aesthetic loss and mental anguish. If the tree that has been lost was a huge, spreading oak housing wildlife, climbed by the children, or planted by a loved and departed spouse, courts may be receptive to the idea.

Out-of-Pocket Expenses

Money reasonably spent trying to save an injured tree or remove a dead one, or to cover the loss, can often be recovered as part of actual damages. This includes the cost of appraisals, cleaning up debris, and repairing the yard. If you missed time from work to cope with—or try to stop—the injury, or incurred medical bills because the incident made you ill, you can also sue for these costs, but you will have to convince the judge they really resulted from the tree problem. Some states also allow court costs and attorneys' fees to be awarded if a neighbor must sue over the loss.

The Importance of Court Precedents

Decisions made by courts are called the common law. Common law exists alongside and interprets statutes and ordinances, and it can stand alone in areas of the law that legislatures haven't addressed. Whenever a judge writes an opinion deciding a case, the opinion becomes part of the common law. This court-made law can become a "precedent," which serves as a guide to future courts faced with a similar situation.

If the decision was made by the highest court in a state (usually the state supreme court), that ruling binds the other courts in that state until time, custom, and social change lead the court to change the doctrine, or the law is changed by the legislature. If it was rendered by a lower state court, it is typically implemented, but not necessarily binding on courts in that state. Similarly, courts are not obligated to follow other states' court decisions, but judges are often influenced by them.

Adjustments to the Actual Loss

If an insurance company compensated the tree owner for part of the loss, the amount paid must be subtracted from the damages claimed (unless the company must be repaid; see "What to Do If a Neighbor Damages Your Tree," below). Once this adjustment is made, the remainder is the owner's actual loss.

Double or Triple Damages (Statutory Damages)

Almost every state has a statute that makes someone who deliberately (as opposed to accidentally) injures someone else's tree liable to the owner for two or three times the amount of actual monetary loss. These civil penalties, which protect the owners of trees by providing harsh deterrents to would-be trespassers or tree pirates, have been described by one judge as a punishment for stealing.[5] Although many of these laws were originally designed to protect the large timber grower, they are just as applicable to you and your next-door neighbor.

In California, for example, if you intentionally injure or remove timber, trees, or underwood, you are liable for triple the amount of actual damages to the owner. If you did not do the damage intentionally or you made a mistake, then the amount owed is twice the compensatory sum.[6] In Maine, if the damage was done intentionally, the law provides for triple damages to the owner, with minimum damages of $500.[7] If the damage was done by mistake, the owner can recover two times the damages, with minimum damages of $250.

A few states, such as Alabama, make the wrongdoer liable to the tree owner for a specific dollar amount for damage to a tree, depending on what type of tree it is.[8]

Your State's Law

Appendix A lists citations to every state's tree laws. To read your state law, go to a local library or use the Internet. Chapter 18 explains how to find a statute.

Whether or not someone who damages a tree is liable for double or triple damages under one of these statutes depends on the person's intent.

Someone who makes an honest mistake and injures another's trees is responsible at the least for reimbursing the owner for the actual damage. But in most states, if the destruction was unintentional, the person probably won't have to pay the double or triple damages that many statutes allow.

> **EXAMPLE:** While thinning out trees on his property, an Alabama man relied on a map that he honestly believed reflected his boundary lines. The map, however, was hopelessly out of date, and he removed trees that were actually on his neighbor's land. When the neighbor sued, the local court slapped him with actual damages of $2,500 for the trees, plus a penalty of $2,590. The penalty was authorized by the statute that penalized willful conduct that harmed another's trees. He appealed to the state supreme court, and the justices ruled that his honest mistake should not have triggered the second sum. The penalty portion was removed.[9]

On the other hand, a person who intentionally injures a neighbor's tree and is sued will probably end up paying double or triple the amount of actual damages to the owner.

> **EXAMPLE:** A determined tree cutter in California waited until the owner was out of town and then sneaked a tree service in and removed her offensive trees. The judge found that his action was willful and malicious, and that the unsuspecting woman was deprived of beauty, shade, and shelter. Verdict: Triple the amount of actual damages, as allowed by California statute.[10] Did the misguided man think that she wouldn't notice or just wouldn't care?

A very few states do not have statutes that protect injured tree owners. In those states, normally the owner can be compensated for actual damages only.

Punitive Damages

Punitive damages are an extra sum of money tacked on to an award in a civil lawsuit as a way of punishing the wrongdoer. As discussed above, many state statutes allow actual damages to be doubled or tripled if the court finds that a tree was intentionally damaged or removed; essentially, this allows for punitive damages.

Occasionally, however, extra punitive damages are added even above the statutory doubling or tripling of actual loss. This happens when the conduct of the person responsible for the harm is especially outrageous, reckless, or malicious.

Although most judges have the authority to award punitive damages, in a few states, small claims court judges cannot award them. Normally, you must request punitive damages separately from all other damages. If your neighbor acted maliciously or recklessly, they may well be appropriate.

> EXAMPLE: This case from Oregon gives us a real understanding of the legal terms "maliciously" and "recklessly." In this case, the defendant neighbors were sued for trimming the plaintiff neighbor's trees without her permission. On several occasions, the plaintiff and her husband clearly told the defendants that they did not want their trees trimmed. Despite this, the defendants hired a tree service that topped and trimmed the plaintiff's trees. In the process of the unauthorized tree trimming, the plaintiff's fence was broken, a post was knocked down, and tree limbs were left strewn about her yard. The plaintiff also submitted evidence to show that when she discovered the trees were being trimmed, she protested to the men doing the work, but the defendant neighbors ignored her and instructed the trimmers to go ahead with their work despite her protests. The Court found that the injury to the plaintiff's tree was malicious or committed so recklessly as to imply a disregard of social obligations. The court upheld the $2,750 punitive damages award.[11]

Criminal Penalties

In many states, intentionally harming someone else's trees is a criminal act. The person responsible for the damage can be arrested, fined, and jailed. For example, in California it is a misdemeanor punishable by a fine of not more than $1,000 or a sentence of not more than six months in the county jail or both.[12]

Michigan also makes the intentional destruction of a tree worth more than $200 a misdemeanor crime that can carry a punishment of up to one year in prison, a $2,000 fine (or payment of three times the value of the tree), or both. Depending on the value of the tree, and whether the person has committed previous injuries to trees, the offense may rise to a felony with a 10-year prison term and a $15,000 fine.[13]

These criminal penalties can be important in the timber industry and Christmas tree business, where tree loss can affect a person's livelihood. They are rarely used in residential situations, but if one neighbor deliberately inflicts great harm on another, criminal punishment may be warranted. And if your hostile neighbor storms onto your property with an ax and begins hacking away at a favorite tree, your first reaction would probably be to call the police. The criminal laws are also effective as a threat to a nasty neighbor who is eyeing the sacred oak in your yard that rains debris on his.

What to Do If a Neighbor Damages Your Tree

Okay, enough legal theory. Let's ground this discussion in the rich, thick dirt of real life. You come home from work one evening and find an empty spot in your yard (and in your heart). Your neighbor has taken his ax (and the law) into his own hands and killed your favorite maple. After the moaning, weeping, and wringing of hands, what do you do?

Document Your Loss

Get your camera and take photographs. Hopefully, you have "before" pictures of your house and yard, taken for insurance purposes; now you can compare them to the "after" snapshots. You can use the pictures to show your insurance company or, if necessary, a court what you have lost. They will help to show the diminished market value of the property.

If your tree can be replaced, obtain a written estimate of the cost. If it cannot, refer to the kinds of losses for which you're entitled to compensation ("What the Tree Owner Can Sue For," above). Convert what you think you have lost to a money amount. Keep all receipts and a detailed list of any costs you incur.

Talk to the Neighbor

If you know who did the deed and you are still on speaking terms, step over and ask what in the heck happened. There may have been an awful mistake or accident, and the neighbor could be waiting with tail between legs, ready to reach for the checkbook or call the insurance company (which may cover your loss).

Even if you don't know or like the neighbor, a short conversation probably won't make things worse. You really do want to know what happened—was it outright murder or the mistake of a new gardener? If the loss is small and a good relationship important, the problem may be solved over a cup of coffee.

Talk to Your Insurance Company

But what if the loss is large and your neighbor unrepentant, or you don't even know who's responsible? Promptly call your insurance company.

Most homeowners' policies cover the destruction of your property when caused by someone else, and a lot of policies specifically cover damage to trees. If your own company pays you, it may then turn around and sue the neighbor. If that tactic is successful, you might even have your deductible portion returned to you.

Many policies, however, only pay up to a certain dollar amount per tree, often $500. They may pay an additional sum up to $500 for cleaning up debris or removing the dead tree. Because most trees are worth more than $500, you can still demand or, if necessary, sue your neighbor for your actual loss.

If you sue successfully after your claim has been paid, you may have to reimburse the insurance company. For instance, if the company pays you $500 and you are later awarded $2,000 from the neighbor, unless you deducted the $500 from your damages, you have been paid twice, and $500 may have to go back to the insurance company.

Homeowners' insurance policies vary on whether they require an insured person to reimburse the company if the person is later awarded money for the same loss. Some write into the conditions of insurance that this is to be done unless the company issues a waiver before a lawsuit. Before you sue, check with your insurance agent to determine the procedure under your particular policy.

If the neighbor responsible for the harm is also insured, that insurance company might pay you. This method of recovery is preferable to the owner, because the coverage limit on the tree owner's policy doesn't apply. Under the liability portion of some policies, when the insured person damages someone else's property, unless the damage was done intentionally, the company will pay for all of the damage—anything the neighbor could be found legally liable for.

Call the Police (If Necessary)

You may want to report the loss to the police department if the damage was done intentionally or maliciously. Another reason for making a police report is to have additional evidence that the loss occurred, either for your or your neighbor's insurance company or for a possible later lawsuit. When you call your local police station, the dispatcher may send an officer over or ask you to come down to the station. The officer will ask you questions, possibly look at the damage, and fill out a form. In those states that make tree cutting a crime, you will be asked if you want to press charges, and the procedure will be explained to you. The police report itself will provide an official record of what happened when and what you have lost. If the police officer doesn't give you a copy, ask for one.

Get Copies of the Law

Presenting the neighbor with a copy of the relevant state statute might result in prompt action and prevent a lawsuit.

Look at the chart in Appendix A and see whether your state has a statute on tree damage. If so, write down the statute number. Many public libraries have copies of the state statutes and they may be on the Internet. Your local public law library, usually located inside or next to the county courthouse, will have them. Make several copies of your statutes on damage to trees.

If your state doesn't have a statute, you can use a court opinion as a guide if you like. To find one that applies to your situation, you will have to do some research in a law library or on the Internet. (See Chapter 18.)

Ask for What Is Due You

The next step is to write a letter to the person at fault. This may sound like a waste of time if you have already had a fruitless conversation, but often it is not. It is amazing how many people never get what is owed to them simply because they don't make a formal demand for it. Later, if you do end up in court, you will find that in some states you can't win without proving you sent a demand letter. The letter also tells the judge that you attempted to settle the problem before coming to court. If your loss can be replaced, write a letter like the one shown below.

Enclose a copy of the statute if you think it will help, even though you are not requesting the double or triple damages that may be allowed by your state's statute. When you are asking only for replacement value, seeing the law may scare the neighbor so badly that you receive a check the next day. Remember that it is a waste of time to sling insults, even if they are deserved. Be polite, be firm, and keep a copy of the letter. And give the person a reasonable amount of time to respond before you go running to the courthouse.

Sample Letter: Tree Replacement

26 Elm Drive
Happy Hollow, CA 94260

May 4, 20xx

Mr. Tom Turner
28 Elm Drive
Happy Hollow, CA 94260

Dear Mr. Turner,

   On April 30, you were responsible for the
destruction of my fifteen-foot maple tree. I have
consulted Nona's Nursery and enclose their estimate
of $600 for them to replace it with a similar tree.
Please send me a check for this amount.

   I am sure that you will wish to attend to this
matter as soon as possible. I expect to hear from you
within the next two weeks.

Sincerely yours,

Wilma Ward

Wilma Ward

Consider Mediation

If your efforts with the neighbor are not producing results, you may want
to suggest mediation—the process of sitting down with the neighbor
and a neutral third party to try to work out an agreement. Mediation is
inexpensive and keeps the neighbors in control of their own decisions. Many
communities even have free or low-cost neighborhood mediation services.

Mediation can be extremely effective when one neighbor owes money to another. Fear of the enormous expense in a tree damage case could be the reason for the neighbor's cutting off communication with you. If you are willing to be flexible, for instance by arranging several partial payments instead of one big sum, a mediated agreement is ideal. And if salvaging a good neighbor relationship for the future is important, even lowering your demands could be far preferable to a hostile and expensive lawsuit. (See Chapter 19 for more on the mediation process.)

Sue the Neighbor

If the loss is large, the act was intentional, and the neighbor is nasty, you may have no choice but to sue the neighbor for your loss. First, try a stiffer letter, like the one below, that lets the neighbor know your intentions.

The letter shows that you know the law and you mean business. You may well hear from the neighbor or her insurance company.

If your requests elicit no response, or the neighbor calls you and tells you where to go in an unfriendly manner, sit down and do some serious thinking. What do you really want: Another tree? Compensation? Revenge? How much time, energy, and money are you willing to commit to this dispute? Before you pick up the phone and call a lawyer, think again. Attorneys' fees can eat up a good part of any amount you win unless you are in a state that allows you to recover attorneys' fees in the lawsuit. And if you do hire a lawyer and file a formal lawsuit, you may be dealing with the tree drama for several years.

Fortunately, if you must sue, there is an alternative to hiring a lawyer that is easier, cheaper, and faster. You can use small claims court, without an attorney. The amount of money you can ask for is limited— usually from $2,500 to $15,000. It is sometimes wiser to just ask for the small claims court limit even if your loss is much larger. You won't have to pay attorneys' fees, and the case will be resolved much more quickly—you can get a new tree, plant it, and get on with your life. Note, however, that a few states limit actions in small claims court and do not allow tree damage cases. (See Chapter 20.)

Sample Demand Letter Before Lawsuit

14 Oak Lane

Neighborly, CA 95327

May 3, 20xx

Mrs. Alice Adams

16 Oak Lane

Neighborly, CA 95327

Dear Mrs. Adams,

On April 30, you were responsible for the wrongful and intentional destruction of my large redwood tree. I have researched the law and found that you are liable to me for three times the amount of my loss. You will see that this is correct by reading the enclosed state statute.

The tree is irreplaceable, and the market value of my property has been diminished because of your action. I have enclosed two separate appraisals of the property. They both estimate the diminished value at $3,000. Your legal liability to me under state law is therefore $9,000 ($3,000 x 3).

Please contact me immediately so that we may settle this matter. Otherwise, I will be forced to take legal action against you.

Sincerely yours,

Paul Palmer

Paul Palmer

Preventing Damage

A neighbor sometimes gives warning to a tree owner that harm is on its way. If your tree is dropping huge amounts of leaves on someone else's property, beginning to shade a treasured vegetable garden or, especially, starting to block an expensive view, be aware of it. The neighbor could be sending signals to you, ranging all the way from nasty looks and remarks about the tree to actual threats to chop it down. If you think the tree is in danger and you want to protect it, don't just sit there until the neighbor gasses up a chainsaw. Do something.

A Neighborly Approach

First, have a chat with the neighbor—and be ready to compromise. You may learn that your beloved tree is driving the neighbor absolutely crazy or actually harming the value of the neighboring property. Try to work out some solution you both can live with that will preserve the tree. For example, a good trimming may benefit both the tree and your neighbor's disposition. If you can't agree, this is a good time to suggest mediation. You may find out that the tree is only the most obvious of the problems that need to be talked out. (See Chapter 19 for information on mediation.)

If you still suspect trouble, make sure that the neighbor knows the law. Share your copy of this book or give the neighbor a copy of the statute. Make sure your neighbor knows what your rights are as an owner, and understands that you fully intend to enforce them.

A Legal Approach

Even knowing the law, some people may hate an offending tree so much that they still intend to chop it down. If you think that you are in immediate danger of losing a beloved tree to a neighbor, make it clear to the neighbor that you will call the police if the tree is harmed, and that you will sue for all that state law allows.

You may want to hire an attorney to write the neighbor a formal letter and follow up with a phone call. Many lawyers are very good at this type of approach, which normally isn't prohibitively expensive—probably

$200 or $300. However, if this approach only seems to confirm that the neighbor is bent on tree mayhem, you may want to hire a lawyer to ask a court for an emergency temporary restraining order (TRO) to prevent the neighbor from going ahead. A judge will consider the request promptly—within a day or so—and rule on it favorably if you can convince the judge that the neighbor really poses an immediate threat to the tree. If the judge issues a TRO and the neighbor violates it, the neighbor will be found in contempt of court and may land in jail or be fined.

The TRO is only temporary, however, and just a first legal step. It must later be replaced with a permanent order from the judge. If your neighbor decides to fight, your fairly simple dispute may escalate into legal warfare. You could be getting into a big, expensive mess to save your tree.

If there is a question about whose tree it really is—for instance, a threatened tree is close to the boundary line and your neighbor claims it's not on your side at all—you can file a lawsuit asking the court for "declaratory relief." This means a judge will determine who owns the tree. Again, keep in mind that this sort of legal approach will cost a lot of time and money. It is far better to make an earnest effort to work the problem out with the neighbor and avoid the courts. ●

Endnotes

1 *Lyman v. Hale*, 11 Conn. 177 (1836).

2 *Howes v. Rocquin*, 457 So. 2d 1220 (La. App. 1984).

3 *Harkness v. Porter*, 521 So. 2d 832, *writ denied*, 523 So. 2d 1323 (La. App. 1988).

4 *Rony v. Costa*, 210 Cal. App. 4th 746, 751 (2012).

5 *Hickox v. Vester Morgan, Inc.*, 439 So. 2d 95 (Ala. 1983).

6 Cal. Civ. Code § 3346.

7 Me. Rev. Stat. Ann. tit. 14, § 7552.

8 Ala. Code § 35-14-1.

9 *Vick v. Tisdale*, 56 Ala. App. 565, 324 So. 2d 279 (1975).

10 *Butler v. Zeiss*, 63 Cal. App. 73, 218 P. 54 (1923).

11 *Fisher v. Carlin*, 219 Or. 159 (1959).

12 Cal. Penal Code § 384a.

13 Mich. Comp. Laws Ann. § 750.382.

Encroachment:
Invading Branches and Roots

Man's liberty ends, and it ought to end, when that liberty becomes the curse of his neighbors.

—**Frederic W. Farrar**

Disputes between neighbors can arise when trees do what they do naturally and predictably: They grow. The tree owner may be blissfully unaware that the mighty oak has crept outward as well as upward, and that it now hangs over a neighbor's property. A tree owner who does notice may assume that the neighbor is delighted by the shade and beauty. This is often the exact situation before an unhappy disagreement and even a lawsuit between neighbors.

Frequently the problem is a matter of degree. A few limbs over the fence present no problem; several years later those same limbs, now huge and pressing against the garage, are indeed quite a problem. The same principle applies to debris raining down from above and roots creeping underneath. A little autumn shedding is acceptable, but not clogged gutters every few days, and definitely not broken pipes from aggressive roots.

The law often reflects these matters of degree. For a simple inconvenience, the neighbor is usually expected to take responsibility and trim away any branches or roots that are a bother. If the injury to the neighbor is more severe, the neighbor may be able to sue the tree owner.

But there are several strategies to deal with encroaching branches or roots that are far simpler (and cheaper) than going to court.

Looking for Help

You may not have to lift a finger to trim invading branches or roots. In some cases, notifying the city, a utility company, or a homeowners' association will bring prompt action.

Local Government

Cities routinely prune trees that are on city property or that might endanger city property. Just bringing the problem to the attention of the correct department may be all it takes to get the tree trimmed.

To see if the tree is on a strip of city property, go to city hall and look at the city map. If it is, notify the city department in charge of tree maintenance. In some cities, this is the public works department; others have a tree service office. The city clerk can point you to the right office.

Even if the tree is on private property, the city may trim it back if it might interfere with city property—for example, by obstructing a sidewalk or blocking the view at an intersection.

The city might also order the owner to trim or even remove a tree that is in violation of a local ordinance. Local rules often govern the following issues:

Trees that are used as fences. When trees are planted close together and used as a barrier, they are natural fences and may be subject to local laws regulating fences. Fence laws can govern the height allowed and also the location of fences on property. (See Chapter 11.)

Trees that block a neighbor's view. In a few cities, if a tree is blocking a neighbor's view, the neighbor can follow a procedure outlined in a view ordinance to force the owner to trim it back. (See Chapter 8.)

Trees that are prohibited by law or exceed height limits. Some local ordinances have a list of undesirable trees that are not allowed in the area. If the tree is of a species that is prohibited, the neighbor can be ordered to remove it, or the city may remove it. And occasionally, cities restrict tree heights in certain areas—for example, near an airport.

Trees in a fire zone. Some cities require homeowners to remove trees and brush within a certain distance from dwellings.

Diseased or unsound trees. Many cities require owners to remove dead and hazardous trees. And a few cities consider any damaged or diseased tree their responsibility, rather than the owner's. A city crew will simply come in and take care of the problem. (See Chapter 5.)

You can find out about local laws by calling your building or planning commission or reading the ordinances yourself at the public library or on the Internet. (See Chapter 18.)

Utility Companies

Check for utility use around the tree. A utility company, such as the telephone or electric company, will trim a tree that might damage its equipment—for example, if limbs are growing into or hanging menacingly over their lines.

Homeowners' Associations

If you live in a subdivision or planned development, residents may be subject to the restrictions in a document called the covenants, conditions, and restrictions (CC&Rs). Each property owner's deed will refer to the CC&Rs and a copy can be obtained from the homeowners' association office. CC&Rs sometimes dictate the location, kind, and especially height of trees. For example, they may require keeping tree height to roof level or set an absolute height limit.

When an owner has a tree that is in violation of these regulations, a neighbor can notify the homeowners' association. It may formally direct the owner to trim the tree. Some homeowners' associations enforce deed restrictions by applying sanctions to a member in violation—for instance, removing swimming pool privileges or fining the person. Some will even sue a resident who doesn't cooperate. And one neighbor can sue the other for enforcement of deed covenants, although this is complicated and expensive and is appropriate only in extreme cases.

Mediation and the Magnolia

Here's one example of a case that should greatly encourage fighting neighbors to try mediation. One neighbor had a large magnolia tree that was being strangled by the other neighbor's even larger live oak tree. When the magnolia owner attempted to prune the oak branches over her own property, the owner of the live oak got a court order to prevent her action. Cutting the oak to the property line would have killed it, but the oak was killing the magnolia.

This dispute went on for several years; the neighbors finally did not even speak to each other. When the city planner suggested mediation, he was quite surprised to find both of these angry neighbors weary of the dispute and eager to work something out. With the aid of a tree expert, they sat down and reached an agreement in one morning that allowed very skillful pruning of the oak, saving both of their trees and restoring peace to the neighborhood.

Trimming a Neighbor's Tree: The Right of Self-Help

Property owners in every state have the right to cut off branches and roots that stray into their property. In most states, this is the only help provided by the law, even when damage from a tree is substantial.

This right to cut away at somebody else's property is not written down as a state statute or local ordinance. It is a common law right, created by court decisions. The reasoning behind the rule is that neighbors should sort out their own problems, along with a distaste for lawsuits between neighbors cluttering up the courts. Numerous judges also share the sentiment that a property owner should have the wit and responsibility to prevent harm to property when he can do so, that "his remedy is in his own hands."[1]

Generally, the neighbor who does the trimming must pay for it. In Hawaii, however, a neighbor who faces substantial damage from a tree may have the trimming done and then demand payment for it from the tree's owner.[2]

Limits on Self-Help

A neighbor who cuts back limbs or roots of a tree belonging to someone else must stay within certain guidelines. The neighbor:

- can trim only up to the boundary line
- needs permission to enter the owner's property, unless the limbs threaten to cause imminent and grave harm
- may not cut down the tree itself, and
- cannot injure the tree by the trimming.

It is especially important to take care not to damage the tree when cutting back roots. Neighbors who do not use reasonable care when trimming roots and damage the tree may end up in court owing monetary damages.

A permit may be necessary in some cities for any tree trimming or for pruning certain species of trees; check with the city clerk's office.

If a large tree is involved and the tree service must climb it or use ladders to reach some of the branches, permission of the owner must be obtained before the trimming.

It's wise to use a professional tree service whenever possible. Cutting branches and roots stresses a tree at the very least. If a neighbor doesn't have the necessary skills, especially when large branches are involved, the trimming could destroy the tree.

Splitting the Cost

When encroaching limbs are large and many, trimming them back can be a costly procedure. In states where self-help is the only legal remedy, going in with the owner to trim the entire tree is often by far the most satisfactory solution. It can't hurt to suggest it.

An owner who fears trimming will destroy the tree can hire a lawyer, go to court, and ask a judge for a court order preventing the trimming.

Pesky Roots

The risk of causing permanent damage to a tree has always been particularly great when roots, not branches, are removed. In the past, blocking tree roots was not only intimidating but tricky as well, because chemicals used to block invading roots often poisoned the tree itself.

Fortunately, a new method of stopping invasive roots is easier, less expensive, and unlikely to harm the tree itself. It consists of cutting the roots and installing a physical barrier (a synthetic shield) to prevent regrowth. A good tree service can provide further information.

Before You Cut

If you decide to trim encroaching branches or roots of a neighbor's tree, always warn the tree owner before you hack away at the tree. If you want to do a major pruning, the owner may well want to take responsibility for the work to ensure the health and symmetry of the tree. An effective approach might be to offer to share the cost of trimming the whole tree.

Another practical reason to give the neighbor notice is to prevent a breach of the peace. Tree owners can be extremely protective; the last thing you want to do is create a screaming disturbance that lands you and the neighbor on the evening news.

If the Owner Is Uncooperative

If a tree owner objects to your trimming plans, you should sit down and describe the situation and your intentions in writing. A sample letter is below.

Sample Letter: Tree Trimming

801 Shady Street
Greenacres, CA 96678

Oct. 17, 20xx

Dear Edith,

As I told you yesterday, I am concerned about the encroachment of your elm tree over my property. The leaves this fall are so numerous that I have paid someone $80 so far to remove them from my yard. This will have to be done again at least twice within the next few weeks. I am also alarmed by the new crack in my patio and wish to avoid more serious harm from the roots. The branches and roots have become a nuisance to me.

I have engaged Loving Care Tree Service to trim back the limbs over my property and to cut and block the roots near the patio. They have assured me that the health of the tree will not be endangered and that the trimming will be done with skill and care. It is my legal right to take this action, and I hope that you find this arrangement satisfactory.

Sincerely yours,

John

John

Hopefully, this will end Edith's objection. She's worried about the tree, and John has given her reassurance. Paying a professional service is probably worth the money to maintain a good relationship. John has also made it clear that he means business and gives his reasons. Edith may seek a legal opinion and that will be the end of her objection.

But suppose Edith doesn't bother to learn the law. Instead, she calls John and tells him that she will meet him outside with a shotgun if he so much as touches one twig. Does John wait until she is not at home and then sneak the tree service in? This does happen, but it's a poor choice. Angry neighbors seek revenge, and problems with Edith would escalate.

A better approach is to send another letter, explaining the law in more detail. Unfortunately, because the right to lop off branches and roots is a common law right, there is no specific statute or ordinance waiting in the library to be photocopied and mailed to Edith. John could do a little legal research and present her with a court opinion on the subject. (If you need to do this, read Chapter 18.) Under these volatile circumstances, however, it may be easier to pay a visit to a lawyer. Often a letter on a legal letterhead will get prompt attention and cooperation, and can be money well spent.

If the dispute is still not resolved, any good neighbor relationship has probably vanished. John may choose to proceed to trim at his personal peril. But he can also contemplate remedies other than self-help.

One good alternative for neighbors who can't agree on tree trimming may be mediation—that is, meeting with a neutral third party who can help you resolve the problems without resorting to a courtroom. Whether you are dealing with a protective owner who won't allow trimming or one who won't accept responsibility, mediation can help you resolve your dispute without resorting to a lawsuit.

The underlying problem with encroaching branches and invading roots is usually expensive. Pruning a large tree can run anywhere from $300 to over $1,000. In mediation, a compromise is possible that considers who is willing and able to pay what. You may also work out a prevention program that could later save time, money, and relationships. Chapter 19 explains how the mediation process works.

When a Neighbor Can Sue

In most situations, a neighbor who is bothered or worried by encroaching branches or roots of a healthy tree won't be able to successfully sue the tree owner. Instead, the neighbor can go ahead and trim the tree. In some states, however, neighbors may sue under certain conditions, including:

- If the tree encroaches onto the neighbor's property, the neighbor may sue to make the owner cut the branches, even if no damage has been done yet.
- If the invading roots or branches cause serious harm to the neighbor's property or threaten to do so, the neighbor may sue. "Serious harm" generally means structural damage to property, for example damaged roofs or walls, crushed pipes, clogged sewers, or cracked foundations.
- If a tree encroaches on neighboring property, the neighbor may sue if the tree was planted, not "wild."
- A neighbor may sue only if the tree is "noxious," in other words if it both causes actual damage and is inherently dangerous or poisonous.

In many other states, the law is unclear. In these states, a case might be successful if the tree:

- does substantial damage to the neighbor's property, or
- seriously interferes with the neighbor's ability to use and enjoy his or her property.

See Chapter 18 on Legal Research to learn how to find your state's rules on suing neighbors when their trees' branches or roots invade your property.

The Healthy Tree Itself

A neighbor who sues over the roots or branches of a neighbor's tree can ask only that the offending branches and roots be removed. A court won't order a healthy tree removed if the problem can be solved by less drastic measures. A Minnesota court, for example, did order a tree cut down, but only because to have trimmed it would have killed it, and the tree was creating major problems for the neighbor.[3]

Generally, however, a court will order a whole tree removed only if it is rotten, dangerously unsound, or causing grave harm. (See Chapter 5.)

Going to Court

For a court order making the owner cut back the tree, the neighbor will probably have to use regular trial court (not small claims court), which probably entails hiring a lawyer.

A neighbor who is suing only for compensation should bring suit in small claims court if the amount requested is within the state's small claims limit. Most states limit small claims to $2,500 to $15,000 and may also limit the types of claims allowed. (Chapter 20 lists each state's limit.)

Encroaching trees can cause a lot of harm, especially when concrete foundations are involved. But even if a claim is over the small claims court limit, you may want to stick with small claims court and just ask for the limit to avoid spending the additional time and shelling out money on attorneys' fees.

Notifying the Owner

Notifying the tree owner of the law actually avoids the courtroom in most cases. Just talking to the owner and asking that the owner please cut back the tree can be very effective, once the owner understands who is responsible.

If the owner won't cooperate, the neighbor should write a letter. This letter is called a demand letter. Many small claims court judges require proof of the demand before a lawsuit. A sample letter is below.

Sample Letter: Tree Trimming

2345 Shady Avenue
Oakton, CA 95544

July 7, 20xx

Dear Mike,

   As I pointed out to you two weeks ago, the limbs
of your oak tree are pressing against my garage, and
the roots are buckling part of my driveway. I have
obtained the enclosed estimate of $500 to repair the
broken concrete.

   According to the law, these branches and roots
are a nuisance to me, and you are responsible for my
damages and for cutting back the tree.

   Please have this tree cut back immediately before
it causes further damage, and contact me about the
repair bill. Otherwise, I will be forced to take
legal action.

Sincerely yours,

Robin

Robin

Keep a copy of the letter and give the neighbor time to respond.
Before you head to court, make one last attempt to avoid the bitterness
of a lawsuit by suggesting mediation to the neighbor. (See Chapter 19.)

What the Neighbor Must Prove

A neighbor who files a nuisance lawsuit against a tree owner must prove
all the following things to the court:
   • The tree belongs to the person being sued.
   • The branches or roots are over or under the neighbor's property.
   • The neighbor notified the tree owner in writing.
   • The tree adversely affects the neighbor, and what the damage is.

Figuring Damages

A neighbor who has suffered harm because of an encroaching tree is entitled to compensation (damages) for all repair costs, including money spent to fix or clean up the property. A court in Hawaii awarded a neighbor the cost of having the tree trimmed, and other courts might do the same, especially if the trimming prevents further harm. The court will want to see proof in the form of receipts of amounts spent due to the tree and written estimates for work yet to be done.

If the property is seriously damaged and can't be fixed, the neighbor is entitled to the difference in the property value caused by the damage. A real estate appraiser can estimate the amount.

For more on how to use small claims court, see Chapter 20. ●

Endnotes

1 *Michelson v. Nutting*, 275 Mass. 232, 175 N.E. 490 (1931); *Alvarez v. Katz*, 199 Vt. 510, 124 A. 3d 839 (2015).

2 *Whitesell v. Houlton*, 2 Haw. App. 365, 632 P.2d 1077 (1981).

3 *Holmberg v. Bergin*, 285 Minn. 250, 172 N.W.2d 739 (1969).

Unsound Limbs and Trees

The tree will wither long before it falls.

—**Byron**

The flip side of the years of shelter provided by trees is that they grow old, become diseased, and die. What was a source of great enjoyment can seemingly overnight become an unwelcome object of peril—especially when it hangs menacingly over the property of the next-door neighbor.

Even a cordial relationship between neighbors may be strained by the prospect of a large expense, and trimming or removing large trees is not a nickel-and-dime matter.

Smart tree owners keep an eye on the health of their trees. They may be liable for injury or property damage caused by an unsound tree, even if they wouldn't be liable for the problems caused by a healthy tree in similar circumstances.

Happily, there are ways to prevent harm from unsound trees, so neighbors don't end up in nasty court battles. This chapter explains them.

Preventing Damage

If you own large and older trees, it is probably wise to invest in an annual inspection by a tree expert. If you are a fearful neighbor, you could do the same thing. Getting an expert's opinion could reduce uncertainty and possibly avoid a disaster. Court decisions abound with the testimony of tree experts—sadly, most of them are called in only after the damage is done.

Getting Help From the City Government

City governments often step in to take care of, or make the owners take care of, dangerous or unsound trees. If you are imperiled by someone else's tree, contact your local city or county government. Someone at city hall or a county courthouse can direct you to the appropriate office. (You may also get help from utility companies or homeowners' associations; see Chapter 4.)

Trees on Private Property

In many cities and towns, after the appropriate city office is notified of a dangerous or diseased tree it will demand that the owner eliminate the problem. In some cities, if the owner doesn't respond within a brief time—48 hours, for instance—the city will step in and remove the hazard. It then bills the owner for the cost. Some place a lien (legal claim) on the property if the owner doesn't pay.

In the aftermath of a series of deadly fires in California, many cities are adopting strict new fire safety regulations for property owners. These new regulations prohibit dead or dying trees on private property. If you live in any area where fire is a potential hazard, check your current city or county regulations at city hall, the public library, the county law library, or on the Internet. (See Chapter 18.)

A few cities remove hazardous trees, even on private property, at their own expense when asked. They have the equipment and consider eliminating the danger a city responsibility.

Some cities have a general ordinance that prohibits maintaining any dangerous object or condition on private property. A menacing dead tree would violate such a law, and the city could issue a fine and demand that the owner comply with the ordinance.

Unfortunately, most cities do not have ordinances that cover dangerous trees on private property. If the tree menacing your property was damaged by a storm or another natural event, your city may take emergency action to protect you. We have all watched on television, for example, as crews work to clear dangerous situations after a disaster. But if a tree has simply grown old and died, you may not receive any help.

Trees That Threaten Public Property

If a dangerous tree is located on city property, the city is responsible for removing it. And when a large private tree threatens to fall, city streets or sidewalks—and people using them—may be in the path of potential destruction. The city, in protecting its own interests, can protect you as well.

Sometimes it is unclear where city property begins and private property ends, especially in border areas near the streets. Many people live under the impression that their lots extend all the way to the curb. This is often not the case. The city may be responsible for a wide strip across what appears to be a private yard. To find out who owns the property a tree is located on, go to city hall and look at the official city maps.

Trimming a Neighbor's Tree: The Right of Self-Help

A property owner always has the right to cut down dangerous limbs of a neighbor's tree that hang over the first owner's property. This is the right of self-help, of cutting off the offending branches up to the boundary line.

How a neighbor can legally exercise the right of self-help is explained in Chapter 4. The main points to remember are that a neighbor:

- may not go onto the neighbor's property when trimming, unless it's necessary to avert imminent danger
- may trim only up to the boundary line
- may not cut down the tree, and
- may not destroy the tree itself.

When the branches are dead and dangerous, the owner would probably welcome having the neighbor trim the tree. Often it's the easiest, most expedient avenue a neighbor can take, especially if immediate action is necessary to avoid harm from branches.

One note of caution if you're considering trimming a neighbor's unsound tree: Although you probably have the legal right to go onto your neighbor's property to trim a tree so you can prevent serious damage to your property, we do not recommend any such deliberate trespass. You would be liable for any harm done, and if the danger is not as serious as you think it is, you could be arrested for trespass or sued. There is almost always another way to deal with the problem.

Ask the Owner to Trim the Tree

If you're worried about the danger posed by a neighbor's unsound tree, and you can't fix the problem by trimming the branches yourself, ask the tree owner to remedy the situation. It may help to explain the owner's legal liability—that if warned of the danger from the tree and does nothing, the owner will probably be liable for any damage that results. (See "After Damage From an Unsound Tree," below.) Prevention is likely to be much less expensive.

Talking to the owner is also important because if you later decide to sue to try to force the neighbor to remove the dangerous trees or limbs, you'll need to show that the owner refused your requests to solve the problem.

Get an Expert Opinion

The most effective way to notify a tree owner that a tree is unsound and threatening you is to put it in writing, accompanied by an expert opinion on the tree's condition. Sometimes an expert will come out and give an opinion for free. (See "Finding an Expert" in Chapter 3.)

Write a Letter

Once you find an expert who confirms your fears, enclose the opinion when you write to the owner. A sample letter is below.

Sample Letter: Dangerous Tree

> June 14, 20xx
>
> Dear Fritz,
>
>   As I mentioned to you last week, several limbs of your oak tree that hang over my back yard are dead and in danger of falling. I enclose the opinion of a registered forester that confirms this dangerous situation. The dead limbs create a hazard and are a nuisance to me; I am afraid to go in my backyard.
>
>   Please eliminate this risk by having these limbs cut back immediately. If you do not have the limbs cut back and my property is damaged, you may be legally responsible for the damage. Thank you.
>
> Sincerely yours,
>
> *Monica*
>
> Monica

It's also a good idea to take photographs of the tree and keep copies of all correspondence with the neighbor.

Negotiation Procedures in Local Laws

Some cities have ordinances that set out a procedure to follow when a neighbor suspects that a tree is dangerous but the owner disagrees. Oakland, California, has adopted such a law, which helps neighbors negotiate and agree on a solution. If the owner refuses to have the tree removed or submit to arbitration, the law allows the neighbor to sue.

And if a court rules in favor of the threatened neighbor, the tree owner can be fined $1,000.[1]

Neighborhood Mediation Services

When neighbors can't agree on what to do about a tree that at least one of them thinks is dangerous, mediation can help them resolve the problems without going to court. Many communities have free or low-cost neighborhood mediation services.

The big problem with dead trees or limbs is usually the expense. Pruning or removing a large tree can run anywhere from $300 to more than $1,000. In mediation, a compromise could be reached that considers who is willing and able to pay what. (See Chapter 19.)

Suing to Prevent Damage

If a tree owner knows harm is likely from an unsound tree and does nothing, maintaining the tree may be considered an unreasonable use of property—which means it is, legally, a private nuisance.

That means a neighbor can sue the tree owner for interfering with the neighbor's use and enjoyment of property. The neighbor can ask the court to make the owner cut the limbs, remove the tree, or pay compensation. To succeed, the affected neighbor will need proof that the tree poses a real danger.

A neighbor who wants only monetary compensation for the nuisance can sue in small claims court, where lawyers are not necessary. A neighbor, for example, could ask for money to compensate for loss of enjoyment of property. If the neighbor can't use the back yard for fear of a dead tree, he or she could ask for a reasonable sum per day—as much as $50 a day in some circumstances.

However, a neighbor who wants an order requiring the tree owner to eliminate the problem may need to sue in regular (not small claims) court, which probably involves hiring a lawyer.

A few states do not allow lawsuits over trees to proceed in small claims court. For a discussion of small claims court, see Chapter 20.

Homeowners' Insurance

Most homeowners' insurance policies allow payment for damage done to your own property if a neighbor's tree falls. (The insurance company will compensate you and then probably turn around and sue the neighbor.) If the company won't pay, or won't pay enough, you can sue the tree owner. (See "After Damage From an Unsound Tree," below.)

Homeowners' policies also pay, under the liability section, for damage done to property of another by your tree, even if the damage is due to your carelessness.

The only time some policies won't pay is when damage is caused intentionally. So if you intentionally damage someone's property, don't expect your homeowners' insurance to pay for it. But if you are warned that your tree presents a danger but do nothing, and the tree does in fact cause damage, your insurance will pay, because you did not *act* to intentionally cause the harm.

Surprisingly, a tree owner's liability insurance can create a problem for a neighbor threatened by a dangerous tree: It can sometimes encourage the owner to act slowly or even ignore the neighbor. The problem arises when insurance pays only after the damage is done. This gives the owner a choice: Incur heavy out-of-pocket expense to prevent harm, or do nothing until the tree falls and insurance steps in.

Insurance companies, however, do not enjoy paying large sums of money when a claim could have been avoided. If the company knows about the situation, it may order the policyholder to eliminate the dangerous condition on the property or face cancellation of the policy. And once a company does cancel a person's insurance, it can be quite difficult to get a policy from anybody else. Threatening a tree owner with a lawsuit can sometimes be very helpful because the owner will probably inquire of the insurance company about what's covered. The company may then give the policyholder an ultimatum.

Some Thoughts About Insurance

Liability insurance may even pay for punitive damages—a sum above the cost of actual damage to the injured person, designed to punish the wrongdoer. Punitive damages are awarded when conduct has been outrageous or wanton. For instance, if a large dead tree—obvious to anyone—is threatening a neighbor's house, the neighbor begs the owner for help, and the owner refuses, the owner has shown reckless disregard for the neighbor's safety, and a court may award punitive damages if something happens.

There is much debate over whether or not liability insurance should cover punitive damages. If insurance companies refused to pay them, uncaring, reckless tree owners who know their inaction will cause grave harm would have strong motivation to act.

After Damage From an Unsound Tree

There is a strong trend across the country toward making tree owners legally responsible for damage caused by unsound trees, if the owner knew or should have known that the damage was likely.

The legal theory is that the owner, by not acting to prevent the harm, was "negligent." Negligence is conduct that is unreasonably careless under the circumstances. A failure to act can be negligent if a reasonable person would act under the circumstances. For example, if a reasonable person would remove a dead tree limb after learning it threatened a neighbor's home, then an owner who does nothing in the same circumstances may be negligent.

A Tree Owner's Dilemma

Several years ago, I had the privilege of living in a house sheltered by an enormous oak that grew on the property. The tree's limbs hung over our property and that of two neighbors.

One day in January, following a heavy rain, there was a thunderous crash. A 20-foot limb had fallen across the backyard, but caused no damage. There had been no warning, no sign of decay the previous summer. I called the local county agricultural extension service, whose expert took one look at the tree and refused to go in the yard. He predicted that many more limbs could come down, even though the tree itself was very much alive.

Because it was January (no foliage) and because the tree was water-soaked, a tree service couldn't go in and trim the tree. We would have to wait. Wait? I was terrified.

My state's law does not make tree owners liable for harm caused by a tree that is apparently healthy. But it was simply against my nature to deny responsibility for my tree (keep this in mind when you approach a tree owner). I told the neighbors of the danger and we all walked on tip-toes until the tree, or rather part of it, budded. Several limbs fell during this time, luckily with no damage.

When the tree service finally pruned the tree, I watched closely, pretending that I actually knew what the trimmers should and should not do, attempting in some way to be part of the decision-making process. Like most tree owners, I would have been most unhappy had the neighbors or a court been in charge of the work.

Liability in Urban and Residential Areas

In most states, landowners in urban and residential areas are legally liable for damage caused by an obviously unsound tree. That means that if a rotten limb or dead tree itself falls on a neighbor's property, and the owner knew or should have known of the danger, the neighbor can sue the tree owner for compensation for the damage.

When should a tree owner know a tree is endangering the neighbor? If the question goes to court, a judge will look at what should have been obvious to the owner: lack of foliage, for example, which signals a dead limb or tree, or a tree that is leaning precariously to one side.

The owner is not expected to be a tree expert. A city slicker could look elm disease in the face and not recognize a problem. And if a rotten tree falls but there was no outward or obvious sign of decay, the tree owner may not be liable, even if severe damage results.[2] A landowner who has a degree in forestry, however, could be alerted to danger from a casual observation of the property. A landowner with such special knowledge would be held to a higher degree of responsibility.

The Changing Responsibilities of Tree Owners

Until recently, if a neighbor was damaged by a naturally growing tree (not planted by the owner), the owner was not required to pay. No one was responsible, the theory went, for consequences of nature. Courts felt that imposing a duty to inspect property for dangerous natural objects would have placed an unacceptable burden on the landowner.

Even in horse-and-buggy days, however, some judges ruled that a property owner who actually knew of a dangerous condition had a duty to alleviate the danger. For example, in 1896, a neighbor asked a tree owner on three separate occasions to remove a 75-foot pine tree that was obviously decayed. When a heavy gale deposited the tree on the neighbor's house, the New York judge declared that the landowner had been negligent (unreasonably careless) by failing to do something to avoid the harm.[3]

The New York ruling was far from an overnight success. Other courts remained for many years unwilling to make landowners responsible for preventing tree damage to neighbors. In the 1970s and 1980s, however, one court after another declared that urban landowners were liable for harm from dead or rotten trees. Owners were liable if they knew or should have known of potential harm, whether the tree was one the owner planted or had just grown naturally on the land.

Because each situation is loaded with variable facts that could present problems in court, if you have questions about liability when an owner "should have known" a tree posed a danger, consult a local lawyer.

Liability in Rural Areas

In all states, the rule is that in a rural area, a tree owner is liable for harm caused by the tree only if the owner actually knew of the danger and failed to prevent the damage. Even when there is obvious decay, an owner who is unaware of it is not liable. Rural owners are not expected to routinely inspect acres of trees for potential danger.[4]

If you live in a rural area and believe a neighbor's tree is endangering you or your property, notify the neighbor in writing. An expert opinion delivered to the owner is the best possible notice to be sure the owner realizes the danger. (See "Finding an Expert" in Chapter 3 to learn where to find a tree expert.)

Going to Court

Often, claims against tree owners end up in small claims court, where neither side needs a lawyer. Most states limit small claims cases to $2,500 to $15,000 and a few do not allow lawsuits over trees. (Chapter 20 lists each state's limit.) If you're suing a neighbor, you may want to reduce a larger claim to the allowed limit to avoid higher legal fees and the delay of going to regular trial court.

Writing a Demand Letter

Before a neighbor can sue, he or she must demand compensation from the tree owner. Because nobody wants to go to court, just telling the owner about the problem and what the law is usually results in a solution.

A sample letter is shown below.

Sample Demand Letter Before Lawsuit

                                    1602 Oak Street
                                    Oakton, CA 95544

                                    May 2, 20xx

Dear Steve,

   As I pointed out to you two weeks ago, several
dead limbs from your oak tree have fallen against
my garage, damaging the roof. I have obtained the
enclosed estimate of $500 to repair the damage.

   According to the law, you are responsible for my
damages. Please contact me about the repair bill.
Otherwise, I will be forced to take legal action.

Sincerely yours,

Yvonne

Yvonne

Keep a copy of the letter to show the judge; it explains your case in a nutshell.

You may still avoid a lawsuit if you're willing to be flexible—for example, accepting several smaller payments instead of a lump sum. Before you head to court, make one last attempt to suggest mediation to the neighbor. (Mediation is discussed in "Ask the Owner to Trim the Tree," above.)

What the Neighbor Must Prove

Someone who files a lawsuit against a tree owner for damage to property must prove to the court all of these elements:

- The tree that caused the damage belongs to the person being sued.
- The tree owner knew the tree posed a danger (or, in an urban area, should have known) but didn't take reasonable steps to prevent it.
- The tree (or its branches) damaged the neighbor's property.
- The damage cost money to repair.

How Much the Neighbor Is Entitled To

The neighbor is entitled to compensation for all repair costs, including money spent to fix or clean up the property. The court will want to see proof (receipts) of amounts spent due to the tree and written estimates for work yet to be done.

If the property can't be fixed, the neighbor is entitled to the difference in the property value caused by the damage. A real estate appraiser can estimate the amount.

Insurance Proceeds

Some insurance companies demand reimbursement for what they have paid if the insured person is also paid by someone else. If your company has paid you, ask whether you are required to pay the money back if you sue successfully. If you get to keep it, subtract what they paid you from your total. The resulting figure is the amount of your actual damage that you can sue for.

A neighbor who was physically injured is entitled to be reimbursed for all medical bills and money lost from missing work. If the incident turned the neighbor into a complete emotional wreck, resulting in loss of sleep, lost work, or physical illness, the injured person can request money for mental anguish. How much? Try figuring it on a daily basis. Someone in terrible shape for ten days might ask for $50 a day—that's $500.

If the tree owner showed reckless disregard for the neighbor's safety, the neighbor can also ask the court to make the owner pay punitive damages. This is an extra amount designed to punish a person for extremely careless behavior. For example, punitive damages might be awarded if an owner knew the tree would fall, could have easily chopped it down or pruned the dangerous branches, but refused to act even after the danger was pointed out. (Small claims courts in some states, however, don't have the authority to award punitive damages.) ●

Endnotes

1 Oakland, Cal., Mun. Code § 12.40.040–12.40.080.

2 For example, see *Ivanic v. Olmstead*, 66 N.Y.2d 349, 497 N.Y.S.2d 326, 488 N.E.2d 72 (1985); *Meyers v. Delaney*, 529 N.W.2d 288 (Iowa 1995); *Lewis v. Krussel*, 101 Wash. App. 178, 2 P.3d 486 (2000).

3 *Gibson v. Denton*, 4 App. Div. 198, 38 N.Y.S. 554 (1896).

4 *Israel v. Carolina Bar B. Que, Inc.*, 292 S.C. 282 (Ct. App. 1987).

Boundary Trees

A tree may grow a thousand feet tall, but its leaves will return to its roots.

—Proverb

When a tree stands on or near a boundary line, sometimes we are not really sure who is supposed to take care of it or who owns it. When the tree is a bother, we want it to be our neighbor's; if it is loaded with fruit, we would just as well it belong to us.

The laws concerning boundary trees are not the same as the general laws on trees because they are based on co-ownership. Co-owners have different legal responsibilities and different legal remedies if a tree is damaged.

Rows of boundary trees that have grown close together and spread to form a barrier can be considered fences. When they are, they are subject to state and local fence regulations. (See Chapter 11.)

Ownership

The Basic Rule: Location of the Trunk

The location of a tree's trunk usually determines who owns the tree. If a tree's trunk is entirely on one person's property, that person owns the tree, even if the roots spread under a neighbor's land or the branches hang over it. When a tree trunk straddles a boundary line, the common rule is that it belongs to all the owners of the properties.

A few states have written this definition of ownership into their state statutes. In California, trees whose trunks are partly on the land of two or more persons are called "line trees"[1] and are commonly owned by all such neighbors. Other states have no statutes, but the common law— rules of law developed by the courts—usually says that a tree whose trunk straddles a boundary belongs to both property owners.[2]

Sometimes, however, neighbors don't know exactly where the boundary between their properties is, so they don't know whether a tree truly sits on the line. When the boundary line can't be found from deed descriptions or property records, neighbors may agree on where they believe the boundary is. Any tree whose trunk straddles that agreed-upon line is a boundary tree, co-owned by both neighbors. In fact, in this situation, neighbors often choose a tree or another landmark to mark the boundary line.

This agreement doesn't have to be explicit between the neighbors; it can be implied when both neighbors act as if the tree marks the boundary between their properties. Even mowing the grass on each side up to the tree can reflect a neighbor agreement about the location of the boundary line. Such agreements can sometimes create uncertainty. If you're concerned about a tree that may sit on an agreed boundary line, see Chapter 9.

Researching State Tree Ownership Laws

In states without statutes, to determine the exact law on boundary tree ownership, you will have to do a little research on court decisions in your state. Chapter 18 will show you how to get started.

Exception to the Rule: Conduct of the Neighbors

If a tree trunk is located on two properties, there is a strong legal presumption of joint ownership. But if the boundary line is in dispute at all, a court presented with the question of who owns a tree might look at the conduct of the property owners. In two court decisions, one from Nebraska[3] and the other from Colorado,[4] the judges suggested that for any tree to be a boundary tree, the neighbors must either jointly plant it, jointly tend it, or treat it as the boundary between their properties.

EXAMPLE: In the Nebraska case, a man sued for an order to prevent his neighbor from cutting a large cottonwood. The neighbor who wanted to remove the tree claimed it was all his; other argued that it was a boundary tree. The boundary line was unclear. These neighbors had jointly tended the cottonwood for years. It had become diseased and together they had treated it, cabled it, even strengthened it with concrete. The court declared that because the boundary was unclear, their conduct indicated that they both owned the tree. The judge ordered the ax-happy neighbor not to harm it.

Because there is so little written law on this subject, it's difficult to predict what another court might do in a similar situation. It is doubtful that a judge would allow the presumption of common ownership to be overcome unless there were other circumstances present—for example, when the boundary line has been in dispute, or when the trunk has grown into the boundary line (see below).

When the Trunk Grows Into the Boundary

A tree that starts life wholly on one person's property may, as the trunk grows, spread into the adjoining yard. Does the neighbor become a co-owner? It depends on what state you're in and how the neighbors treat the tree.

In all states, when the trunk grows into the boundary *and* both neighbors treat the tree as a boundary tree, it is one. In some states (for example, California, Louisiana, North Dakota, and Oklahoma), trees growing into the line become common property no matter how the property owners act. Once the trunk starts to straddle the line, the originally treeless neighbor automatically becomes an owner. Courts in some other states, however, including Colorado and New Mexico, require the neighbors to agree that a tree that has grown into a boundary line is a boundary tree, or to act as if it were—for example, sharing the cost of maintenance. Otherwise, if the original owner remains in total charge, the tree still belongs to that owner.[5]

Let's look at two examples with opposite results.

EXAMPLE 1: Fred plants a small eucalyptus tree on his property near the boundary line. His next-door neighbor Henry thinks Fred is making a big mistake and refers to the tree as Fred's Folly. During the next 15 years, Henry ignores the tree except for periodic complaints about how dirty and ugly it is. Finally, the roots begin to buckle any concrete within their reach, including Henry's patio and Fred's driveway, and the tree becomes a real nightmare to both of them. By now the trunk is huge and firmly straddles the line. They live in California, where the location of the trunk determines the ownership. When they decide to have it removed, who is legally responsible for paying for it? Both of them, half and half. Fred's Folly has become the Co-Owners' Common Concern.

EXAMPLE 2: Ken has an oak tree whose trunk has slowly grown into the property of his neighbor, Suzy. Suzy enjoys the tree but has never acted as an owner—she's never paid for a trimming, for example. One day Ken gets very tired of the leaves and debris and chops the tree down. They live in Colorado, where a tree growing into the boundary line must be affirmatively treated as a boundary tree for both neighbors to become owners. Suzy sues Ken for cutting down a tree that also belonged to her, and she loses. The tree was never treated as a boundary tree, and it still belonged to Ken.[6]

Who Owns How Much of a Boundary Tree?

Usually, ownership of a tree on a boundary line is shared equally by each co-owner. But how about arguing that if the trunk is mostly on one property, that neighbor owns a proportionately larger share? You could, although the only law supporting that theory is a suggestion to that effect in a court case from 1895.[7]

Nevertheless, if each owner maintains the tree roughly according to the percentage that the trunk occupies, and perhaps also reaps proportionate rewards, this would seem fair. In case of a dispute, say over a large tree service bill, or even over who gets how much fruit, a small claims court might allow proportionate ownership and responsibility.

Co-Owners' Responsibilities

When a tree is owned in common, both owners are responsible for it. Each owner usually maintains the portion on that owner's property, but when the tree as a whole needs attention, both owners are obligated to pay for the work. And if the tree harms someone else, both owners are liable—for instance, if the tree fell on a third property, both would be responsible for the damage.

Maintenance and Care

Most neighbors have no problem with sharing responsibility for a boundary tree's care and maintenance. In fact, they may never think about it. They go about year after year cleaning up whatever debris falls on their own properties, and trim any limbs on their sides that may bother them.

If the tree demands the attention of both owners—for instance, if it grows higher than a legal limit, becomes diseased, or poses a problem to passersby or other neighbors—the co-owners may need to cooperate. Both owners are legally responsible for the cost of necessary maintenance.

But for one owner to demand contribution, the tree as a whole must need work. A co-owner who can solve the problem without help, on his or her own property, shouldn't expect the neighbor to share the cost. For example, if one limb of a boundary tree is dropping sap on your car and you can easily lop it off, don't ask the neighbor to pay for trimming the whole tree. You always have the right to cut limbs of any tree over your own property as long as you don't harm the tree. (See Chapter 4.)

Getting a Co-Owner to Cooperate

One owner may refuse to do a fair share or may disagree about what care is needed. In this situation, the more conscientious owner can have essential maintenance done and then demand half the cost from the neighbor. If the neighbor won't pay, the other can sue for reimbursement. If you co-own a boundary tree with an uncooperative neighbor, or you and the neighbor disagree about how much work the tree needs, here are some guidelines for working out the disagreement. If all your attempts fail, you can try taking the neighbor to small claims court.

Be Sure You Know Who's Responsible for the Tree

If it's not a boundary tree, the neighbor isn't responsible for its care or maintenance, so be sure that both you and your neighbor co-own the tree before demanding contribution from the neighbor. (See "Ownership," above.)

Be Sure the Problem Requires Joint Contribution

If you determine that a particular tree is a boundary tree, the next question is whether the problem that bothers you is one your neighbor is legally obligated to help put right. These problems usually fall into the following categories:

- legal necessities, such as conformity with a height limit in a local ordinance or mandatory spraying for insects
- care essential for the health of the tree, for instance, treatment if it becomes diseased, or
- avoidance of serious damage, such as from falling limbs when danger is predictable.

Many other types of problems don't require contribution. Overhanging branches that are cluttering one yard with debris shouldn't be the other owner's responsibility. Even aggressive roots that threaten one driveway are usually considered that owner's problem if it's possible for that owner to remedy the situation.

Document the Problem and Obtain Cost Estimates

Take photographs and obtain a written expert opinion if necessary. Get several estimates from tree services so you know you won't be overcharged.

EXAMPLE: The mighty oak belonging to neighbors Kelly and Arthur has become top-heavy. Arthur, fearing that it may be dangerous, contacts a tree expert with a degree in forestry for an opinion. The expert confirms that the danger is real and suggests having a number of heavy limbs removed to greatly reduce the danger and save the tree. Arthur knows that Kelly will be reluctant to help with the cost, so he gets this opinion in writing and obtains estimates for the work from three different tree services. He now has written proof of the necessity for the work and of what a reasonable charge is for the job.

Ask the Other Owner to Contribute

If a friendly conversation with the co-owner doesn't solve the problem, you should always follow up in writing. Sometimes people respond better to a written request—they take it more seriously than an over-the-fence chat. And later you may need to document your requests for a judge.

You should keep copies of these requests. Here are examples of the sort of letter you should write.

Sample Letter: First Request

March 1, 20xx

Dear Kelly,

The oak tree growing on the boundary of our properties has become top-heavy, which is not only dangerous, but also unhealthy for the tree. John Edison of Edison Tree Service (a licensed arborist) confirms that several large limbs are unsound. In his opinion, removing the limbs should save the tree and prevent any damage they could cause if they fell. I am enclosing Edison's opinion and three cost estimates to have the necessary work done.

Since this tree straddles our boundary line, we both own it and are mutually responsible for this expense. Please contact me so that we may agree on the details of the work. Thank you.

Sincerely yours,

Arthur

Arthur

Sample Letter: Second Request

March 25, 20xx

Dear Kelly,

   Having received no response from you concerning our dangerous boundary tree, I have arranged to have the necessary work performed on April 20.

   Enclosed is the estimate from Edison Tree Service for pruning and treating our tree. As you can see, the tree is extensively damaged and in need of professional care for its survival.

   The total bill for the work will be $500, which means your half is $250. Please send me this amount by April 20.

Sincerely yours,

Arthur

Arthur

Between Letter #1 and Letter #2, if your neighbor has told you to go jump in a lake, or what you can do with the precious tree, don't waste time and effort with anger. Just include a line about this being a shared legal responsibility. At the end of the letter add "or I will take this matter to small claims court." Keep your cool. All the name-calling in the world doesn't change the fact that you and your neighbor are jointly obliged.

And remember, even if your neighbor really is a hopeless idiot, it makes sense to save your sarcasm and write a polite businesslike letter. Demand letters can be presented to a small claims judge and are an excellent way to outline the facts of your case if you end up going to court.

Suggest Mediation

If you still receive no response, try contacting a mediator to try to resolve the problem. Mediation involves meeting with a neutral third party (mediator) whose job it is to help the disputants come up with their own solution. Unlike a lawsuit, mediation lets the owners themselves keep control of decisions about their properties and provides a framework for future discussions if other problems arise. It also has the advantages of being inexpensive and, if it works, avoiding the long-term hostility a lawsuit breeds. (For more on mediation, see Chapter 19.)

Go to Small Claims Court

If nothing works out with the neighbor, you can file a lawsuit against the neighbor for the money owed to you. In most cases, small claims court is the best place to sue—amounts are almost never enough to justify hiring a lawyer and going to regular trial court. The amount that you ask for must be within the small claims court limit, which is usually $2,500 to $15,000. Also note that a few states' small claims courts will not hear boundary tree disputes.

When you go to court you must show all of the following:
- The tree belongs to both you and your neighbor.
- The work done was necessary.
- The amount charged was reasonable.
- You asked the neighbor for his or her share.

Chapter 20 discusses how to prepare and present a claim in small claims court and lists each state's small claims court monetary and subject matter limits.

Damage to or Removal of a Boundary Tree

One owner of a healthy boundary tree may not remove the tree or harm it without the permission of the other owner.

Co-Owners' Rights

Except in rare circumstances—usually necessity for building purposes (see below)—a co-owner may not harm or remove a healthy boundary tree without the other owner's permission. Owners can trim away at their own side, but neither may damage the tree. If your neighbor's property has the major part of the trunk and the neighbor cuts away at it, damaging the remainder, you are still entitled to compensation for your loss, no matter how small.

If, however, a boundary tree is dead or diseased beyond repair, a co-owner may remove it without the other's permission. The other co-owner can't complain because there really was no loss. In fact, a co-owner may be under a legal duty to remove a dead or diseased tree if it presents an obvious danger to people or property. (See Chapter 5 for a discussion of tree owners' liability for unsound limbs and trees.)

If you and a neighbor share a row of boundary trees, each tree is common property, and you can't harm any of them without permission. This may seem like common sense, but apparently it wasn't to one fellow who went along his boundary and cut down every other tree for firewood. He evidently thought that if he and his neighbor owned 20 trees together, then ten could be considered his. Not surprisingly, he found himself in court, with the judge ruling against him.[8]

Boundary Trees as Official Boundary Markers

If a boundary tree is officially used as a marker to describe property in a deed or a survey, it is protected under state law. Almost every state has a statute providing for a hefty fine or jail for someone who removes such a tree. These statutes are easy to look up in the law library. See Chapter 18.

The only time a co-owner can remove a healthy boundary tree over the neighbor's objections is if destruction of the tree is absolutely necessary for the reasonable use of one neighbor's property. This would be the case if one owner had to remove a tree entirely, excavate roots, or remove a large portion of a boundary tree in order to build a house, driveway, or business building close to the line. If the builder exercises all possible care to protect the tree—cutting as little as necessary— but the tree still dies, under these circumstances, he or she normally won't be liable.[9] When one co-owner protested in court, however, the judge refused to let a co-owner remove a tree without the other owner's permission, even though one owner needed the space to build a house.[10]

Few uses of land, however, justify destroying a tree that belongs, in part, to someone else. Thus, a neighbor who wants to build a 20-foot deck will likely find a judge unsympathetic—17 feet ought to be big enough if it would spare the tree. And someone who wants to kill a boundary tree because its roots interfere with a proposed tennis court will likely learn that the judge considers tennis less necessary than he or she does.

Note to Louisiana Readers

As is often the case, the law in Louisiana is slightly different from the rest of the country. Your state statute, Number 687 of the Civil Code, provides relief for one owner if the tree poses a real problem. If a boundary tree "interferes with the enjoyment" of one of the properties, that owner can demand removal of the tree, but must bear the expense of removal.

You can find out how the courts in Louisiana define interference with enjoyment of property by looking at court cases listed under the nuisance heading in an annotated version of the Louisiana statutes. (See Chapter 18.)

Even the cultivation of crops does not usually justify destruction of a boundary tree when one of the owners is benefiting from the tree. A good example of this is when a row of boundary trees is used as a windbreak. If you drive down a country highway, you will notice these strands of windbreak trees. Sometimes they stand to the side of a residence; often they form a line to protect growing crops from the elements. The owner who is downwind relies on the trees and their loss can be disastrous. The upwind owner has a different problem as the roots invade crops, or the foliage blocks the sun.

If the upwind owner threatens or begins to remove the trees, the other owner may go to court. In most cases, a judge will order the neighbor to leave the windbreak standing.[11]

You Want to Remove a Boundary Tree

If you want to remove a boundary tree and your neighbor is reluctant to allow it, try a little negotiation. Perhaps the co-owner would agree to several smaller replacement trees, or a tree in a different place, or be more cooperative if you agree to fix the broken sidewalk in front of your house that has bothered him or her for years. You could also offer to pay for the co-owners' loss of the tree, as well as paying for the entire cost of removal.

Once you reach an agreement with a co-owner allowing removal, it would be wise to get it in writing before you act. If it's practicable, have all owners, including spouses, sign the agreement. Also, be aware that some cities require a permit to remove any tree at all—even your own.

Never cut a tree if there is any doubt of the ownership. The city may own the strip of land between the sidewalk and the street, for example. If you want to remove a tree from city land, you'll need the city's permission.

Preventing a Co-Owner From Removing a Boundary Tree

As a practical matter, what should you do if your neighbor is grumbling about the tree on your boundary and wants to cut it down? If you value the tree and you have reason to believe the neighbor may cut it down when your back is turned, inform the neighbor that it's not okay to harm the tree without your permission. Here is a sample letter.

Sample Letter: Boundary Tree Removal

> 14 Shady Lane
> Pine Hill, CA 98876
>
> November 1, 20xx
>
> Dear Wayne,
>
> After our talk about the amount of leaves this year from the oak on our boundary, I realize that you're tired of the work the tree requires and may even be thinking of cutting down the tree. But please remember that the trunk of the tree straddles the boundary line and the tree belongs to both of us. According to the law, neither of us has the right to harm it in any way without the other's permission.
>
> At this time of year, the tree does require a lot of work by both of us. But because it shades my roof and keeps my house cool, it is also of enormous benefit to me during the summer and I do not want to lose it. Perhaps, instead of talking about removal, we can get together and figure out a pruning schedule that would reduce the debris that falls on your yard and enhance the tree.
>
> Sincerely yours,
>
> *David*
>
> David

Some people wouldn't be this diplomatic, but it will probably pay off in the long run. At least you are trying to keep lines of communication open. However, if you are sure that a polite approach won't work, add that you will file a lawsuit if the neighbor cuts the tree.

Should you suspect that despite your letter, the neighbor plans to kill your favorite boundary tree, see an attorney. The lawyer will probably first write a letter and try to get assurances that no action is planned by the neighbor.

If there is a good reason to think your neighbor may soon act illegally, the lawyer can ask the court for an emergency order prohibiting the cutting. You will have to swear in a statement under penalty of perjury that harm is likely. If the judge issues the order, it is only temporary until a full hearing is held on whether a permanent order is needed. The whole process will be expensive and time-consuming, but may be necessary if all else has failed.

When a Co-Owner Damages or Removes a Boundary Tree

If one co-owner harms a boundary tree, the other can sue for the value of the tree, and for a court order making the offender stop the harmful activity. But there are lots of less drastic steps to take first.

Contact Your Insurance Agency

Many homeowners' insurance policies will reimburse a policyholder whose tree is destroyed. Some have a dollar limit on tree claims—$500 a tree is common. Sometimes the policy of the person who caused the damage will pay the neighbor for the entire loss, especially if no harm to the neighbor was intended. Always check with your insurance agent before you do anything else. The company may handle the whole situation for you.

Most trees are worth more than $500; if your loss is larger than what the company will pay, you can still sue the neighbor for the extra amount to compensate you for your actual loss. If you do, find out from your insurance company whether you will have to give back what the company paid you. Some companies require reimbursement if you collect from someone else; otherwise, you would be paid twice. But sometimes, a company will issue a waiver that frees you from reimbursement obligations; always ask for one.

Calculate Your Loss and Demand Compensation

If your insurance won't pay—or won't pay enough—you can seek compensation for your actual loss from the neighbor. Anyone who ever cuts down a tree belonging to someone else is in legal trouble, and boundary trees can provide an expensive lesson about this rule. You should be entitled to the amount it would cost to replace the tree. If the tree cannot be replaced, the basis for the amount of compensation is the diminished value of your property as a whole.[12]

For a full discussion on how to calculate your loss in dollar terms, see Chapter 3. Note, however, that the stiff penalties that often apply when a neighbor destroys someone else's trees do not appear to apply when one co-owner damages a boundary tree.

Sample Letter Demanding Compensation

> 568 Shady Lane
> Forest City, CA 98878
>
> November 1, 20xx
>
> Mr. Howard Henson
> 570 Shady Lane
> Forest City, CA 98878
>
> Dear Mr. Henson:
>
> Last Tuesday, October 28, 20xx, you removed the large oak that was a boundary tree between our properties. You had no right to do this as the tree straddled our property line and so was owned by us in common.
>
> The tree's appearance greatly enhanced the value of my property, and it also sheltered my house from the sun in the summer. I have enclosed an estimate of my loss of $3,500. Please submit this amount to me immediately, or if your insurance company will handle it directly, please have the insurance adjuster contact me.
>
> Sincerely yours,
>
> *Carolyn Smith*
>
> Carolyn Smith

After putting a dollar figure on your actual losses, make a written demand to your neighbor for that amount. A sample letter is shown above.

You may well hear from the neighbor or the neighbor's insurance company. The neighbor may have been mistaken about who owned the tree, and a homeowners' policy may cover your damages.[13]

Suggest Mediation

Before you file a lawsuit against the neighbor, try to arrange mediation. You and the neighbor can sit down together with a neutral third party (mediator) and work out an agreement between you. An acceptable payment plan, a replacement tree, or a compromise is far better than a lawsuit between next-door neighbors. (See Chapter 19 on how mediation works.)

The Case of the Disappearing Damage

A lawsuit over boundary trees in Connecticut gives a great example of why judges are always complaining about neighbor disputes clogging up their courts unnecessarily. The trees at issue were actually a fence, a privet hedge, 12 feet high. One neighbor cut the whole thing down to five feet, and the other neighbor sued for harming the joint property. By the time the case came before a court, the hedge had not only grown back, but was healthier than ever from the pruning. The judge wearily lectured the neighbors on invading each other's rights, and noted that the damage had disappeared.[14]

Sue in Small Claims Court

If all else fails, go ahead and sue for the money owed you. The loss of a large tree can easily be equal to the small claims court limit in property devaluation alone. Unless your loss greatly exceeds your state's small claims court limit or unless your state's small claims court does not hear suits for tree loss, you're probably better off voluntarily scaling your claim back to that amount rather than paying an attorney to take the action to formal trial court.

If there is a serious dispute over the location of the boundary, you may need to get a survey done before you go to court. This can cost between several hundred and several thousand dollars. (See Chapter 9 on what is involved in a survey.) If the neighbor is claiming the land that the tree stands on, you need to see a lawyer. The legal issues can be very complex and may require not only regular court but also an experienced property lawyer.

In small claims court, you will need to prove the following:

- The tree belonged to both of you (see "Ownership," above).
- The neighbor removed it without your permission.
- You suffered losses in the amount you're asking for.

Have copies of all documents ready to show the judge. This includes the letter to the neighbor requesting payment and written receipts or estimates showing all your losses.

For pointers on preparing and presenting a small claims court case, see Chapter 20. ●

Endnotes

1 Cal. Civ. Code § 834.

2 *Happy Bunch, LLC v. Corandview North LLC,* 142 Wash. App 81, 173 P.3d 959 (2007).

3 *Weisel v. Hobbs,* 138 Neb. 656, 294 N.W. 448 (1948).

4 *Rhodig v. Keck,* 161 Colo. 337, 421 P.2d 729 (1966); see also *Love v. Kloskey,* 417 P.3d. 862 (2016)

5 For example, in New Mexico, the court ruled in *Garcia v. Sanchez,* 108 N.M. 388, 772 P.2d 1311 (1989), that either an oral or written agreement was necessary to establish common ownership when a tree's trunk grows into the boundary line.

6 See *Rhodig,* 161 Colo. at 337.

7 *Robinson v. Clapp,* 65 Conn. 365, 32 A. 939, *aff'd,* 67 Conn. 538, 35 A. 504 (1895).

8 *Scarborough v. Woodill,* 7 Cal. App. 39, 93 P. 383 (1907).

9 In *Higdon v. Henderson,* 304 P.2d. 1001 (Okla. 1956), one owner was allowed to remove a boundary tree to build a residence.

10 *Robinson,* 65 Conn. at 365.

11 For example, see *Musch v. Burkhart,* 83 Iowa 301, 48 N.W. 1025 (1891); *Anderson v. Weiland,* 12 Cal. App. 2d 730, 55 P.2d 1242 (1936).

12 For example, see *Cathcart v. Malone,* 33 Tenn. App. 93, 229 S.W.2d 157 (1950).

13 The insurance company was forced to pay in the case of *York Indus. Center, Inc. v. Michigan Mut. Liab. Co.,* 271 N.C. 158, 155 S.E.2d 501 (1963); see also *Westfield Ins. Co. v. Davis,* 232 F. Supp. 3d 918 (2017).

14 *Cooke v. McShane,* 108 Conn. 97, 142 A. 460 (1928).

Fruit and Nuts: Who Owns What?

Where the apple reddens
Never pry—
Lest we lose our Eden,
Eve and I.

—Robert Browning

In this scenario, your neighbor's tree branches are intruding over the property line into your yard. But you don't mind a bit. They are hanging heavy, loaded with ripe, succulent peaches. Whose peaches are they?

Who Owns the Tree?

The location of a tree's trunk determines who owns the tree. If the trunk stands next door, the tree, branches, leaves, and peaches belong to your neighbor. You may not legally help yourself to the fruit. If you do, you are, in theory, converting someone else's property to your own use, and your neighbor could sue you.

Most people don't actually run to the courthouse over a few pieces of fruit. When there is almost no value attached to the items, there simply are no lawsuits. Nevertheless, this doesn't change the principle of ownership—the fruit still belongs to your neighbor.

There is a certain logic to this rule—given that a tree owner is sometimes liable for damage to a neighbor caused by overhanging branches, it makes sense that if those same branches are full of fruit, they also belong to the owner of the tree.

Rights of the Fruit Tree Owner

This rule of ownership may seem pretty nit-picking when we are talking about one peach, plum, or walnut. But think for a moment about living next door to an orchard, with thousands of peaches involved rather than two or three. The owner of the orchard is not in the business of giving truckloads of fruit to an adjoining landowner. The owner of the lone fruit tree has the same legal rights as the orchard owner.

Given that the tree owner owns the fruit that hangs over a neighbor's property, a practical question instantly arises: Can the owner go get it? It is easy to picture a situation in which the grower claims the fruit and wants to collect it, but the neighbor orders the owner not to set foot on the adjoining property.

The law in the United States is very unclear on the question. People don't take a lawsuit over a few apples all the way to a court in which written opinions are given, and the legislatures have not considered this issue worthy of attention, so there aren't any specific laws on this issue.

Some legal scholars say that an owner has the right to enter another's land and retrieve possessions under certain circumstances.[1] An example would be when a boat breaks loose from a dock in a storm and lands on somebody else's beach. But these occasions involve the unexpected loss of valuable property, not the desire to collect a few peaches.

A court faced with a dispute over access to fruit would probably weigh the conflicting legal rights of the people involved. You have a right to keep intruders off your property and to have them arrested for trespass if you forbid them from coming on your yard. This right will be protected by the law unless there is a good reason for an exception. When compared to the right to possess a few pieces of fruit, a strong argument could be made that the neighbor's right to keep people out outweighs that of the owner of the tree who demands entry.

What about just leaning over the fence and picking what belongs to you? People do this all the time with no complaint from their neighbors. But should you be the unfortunate one who lives next to a truly nasty neighbor, even this could put you in danger of trespassing.

There is another factor to consider here besides legal rights. The ripening of fruit is a predictable event. A tree owner not only knows it will happen, but probably can be fairly certain when it will happen. An owner who wants the fruit should have the wit to make an arrangement in advance.

> ## Arguments That Won't Work
>
> When fruit tree owners have sued neighbors for stealing fruit, the neighbors have used several unsuccessful arguments to try to establish rights to the forbidden fruit. For example, one man who took 20 bushels of pears claimed that he was a part owner because the roots of the tree extended into his property and were nourished by his soil. The court disagreed, informing him that the location of the trunk alone established ownership.[2]
>
> Another case came before a court after the attempted picking of a handful of cherries resulted in a physical fight and injury. The cherry collector insisted that she possessed everything above as well as below her land. "Not so," said the judge. She could use the space over her land, but she couldn't have the cherries.[3] Although these cases are quite old, they are still cited and followed by contemporary courts.

The Right to Trim the Neighbor's Fruit Tree

A landowner has the right to trim overhanging branches of a neighbor's tree up to the property line within certain guidelines. (See Chapter 4.) Does this mean that someone can get around the fruit-picking prohibition by finding a legal reason to cut off a fruit-laden branch? It's not so easy.

When overhanging branches, fruit and all, are creating problems on someone's property, that person is allowed to eliminate the problem— that is, to cut back the branch. This is not the same thing as taking the branches and fruit. Or more directly, a neighbor gets to remedy the annoyance; the tree's owner gets to make the pie.

Extending this logic, a tree owner probably also has the right to request possession of limbs that have been legally removed from his or her tree. Because the limbs are often worthless, however, there is almost no law on the subject. One Louisiana case does discuss the value of the wood itself and gives a guideline. In that instance, 800 pounds of oak limbs had been legally cut by the neighbor over his property because the limbs were an annoyance to him. The oak had value as firewood. The court did inquire whether the tree owner wanted access to the wood.[4]

The safest rule to follow is very simple: Anything growing from a tree or a bush, whether it is fruit, nuts, vegetables, or flowers, even if it extends into another person's yard, belongs to the owner of the tree's or bush's trunk. If you cut branches that the neighbor may want, ask the neighbor. If you suspect a misunderstanding may arise, put it all in writing. And of course it is always a wise idea to notify the owner any time you are planning to prune a tree that doesn't belong to you. (See Chapter 5.)

Just in case this whole concept of ownership appears blatantly unfair to anyone, let's take an example that would seem absurdly picky in any other legal area but is all too ordinary when it comes to neighbor spats.

> EXAMPLE: Oscar and his neighbor, Mildred, both grow kumquats as a serious hobby. The annual local kumquat festival approaches, complete with prize money of several hundred dollars. Oscar is deeply disappointed with his own puny fruit, and Mildred is unexpectedly called out of town. There on Mildred's tree, growing over Oscar's property, hangs the most splendid kumquat he has ever seen. He plucks it, enters it in the show and wins first place. Mildred returns the next day, sues Oscar and recovers the prize money. Oscar is stripped of his award and banned from the kumquat festival for life.

Fruit That Has Fallen

But what about the apple that has fallen to the ground? Who does that belong to? Common sense and common practice would seem to favor a neighbor's claim to fruit and nuts that fall on the neighbor's land.

In the autumn, when the tree next door drops its leaves into your yard, the leaves usually become your problem. Can you imagine a tree owner rushing over and saying "Oh, I'm so sorry. Those are my leaves; let me rake them up for you." If the same tree also deposits apples or pecans in your yard, you may have a right to them. But there is precious little, if anything, written on the subject. One state, Mississippi, has statutes that address the matter of fallen pecans, a major business in the state.[5] The statutes make it a misdemeanor to gather someone's pecans when they have fallen onto public property during harvest season. One can be fined up to $100 and jailed for up to 30 days. Only after the harvest season are the pecans considered abandoned by the owner and available to anyone. These statutes talk only about public property. Silence about private property lets us assume that the pecans falling on your own yard are your pecans.

If one looks at what is called "finder's law," the finder of a lost object is under an obligation to its true owner. But the apple in question is not really lost, so this doesn't seem to fit the situation. If an object is abandoned by its owner, it belongs to whomever picks it up. But determining whether something really was abandoned means struggling with questions of the owner's intent and how long to leave it, while the apple is rotting on the ground.

In the frustrating attempt to answer this overwhelmingly important question, we finally took an informal poll of several lawyers.

The question posed was "Would you take the fruit and eat it if it fell on your property?" Some of the answers:

"Of course, it's on my property."

"Of course not, it doesn't belong to me."

"Only at night."

"No; if the tree isn't mine, neither is the fruit."

"If the neighbor isn't home."

You get the general idea; nobody really knows. We asked the lawyers who assumed the fruit was theirs what they would do if the neighbor's coconut fell and cracked them on the head. Suddenly the tree owner still owned the coconut and was liable for every injury they could dream up.

We did find it most interesting when we took the survey that not a single lawyer suggested a very simple answer: Why not ask the neighbor's permission?

And now for our view. Practically speaking, we believe it's safe to pick up and eat small quantities of fruit that a neighbor's tree or bush has shed on your land. In the rare situation where your neighbor becomes upset, the fact is that fruit that has fallen to the ground has little or no monetary value. So even if a small claims judge ruled that it was your neighbor's fruit and not yours, you would have to pay the neighbor only a nominal amount to compensate for the loss.

Avoiding Problems

Fruit trees along the borders of property create a potential for friendly and comfortable neighbor relationships. Whether you are the owner of the tree or you're the neighbor, consider this example.

> **EXAMPLE:** Eliot and Kathe moved into a new house. The yard next door boasted lovely fruit trees, some of them hanging over the fence with fruit exactly at picking height. Art, the next door neighbor, stepped over to introduce himself and to welcome them. They walked together along the division fence and Art asked permission to enter the yard once a year and trim his trees. At the same time, he suggested that they help themselves to any fruit hanging over their property or on their ground. Within five minutes the foundation of a cordial and responsible good neighbor relationship was in place.

We are not all as lucky as Art's neighbors. Sometimes we are too timid, don't have time, never meet the neighbors, or find ourselves dealing with an absent landlord. Under these circumstances, perhaps the easiest solution is to simply follow a rule of custom. A tree owner who says nothing about the fruit year after year probably does not consider it private property or doesn't want it. On the other hand, a tree owner who races over to grab it puts the neighbor on notice that the fruit isn't for sharing.

Either way, a little courtesy and common sense can actually avoid any problems, and in this case, could result in freshly baked apple pie for everybody involved. ●

Endnotes

1 *Restatement (Second) of Torts* § 198 (2019 update).
2 *Lyman v. Hale*, 11 Conn. 177 (1836).
3 *Hoffman v. Armstrong*, 48 N.Y. 201 (1872).
4 *Beals v. Griswold*, 468 So. 2d 641 (La. 1985).
5 Miss. Code Ann. § 69-33-3 to § 69-33-9.

Obstruction of View

For purple mountain majesties above the fruited plain.

—Katherine Lee Bates

From the plains, seas, and sparkling city lights, to the purple majesty of mountains, Americans want to look at this beautiful country. The privilege of sitting in one's own residence and gazing out over desirable scenery is a highly prized commodity. And especially in and near our cities, it can be a very expensive one.

In many areas, especially where there are oceans, bays, lakes, or mountains, buyers and sellers put a price tag on views. If you pick up a newspaper and read the classified ads for houses for sale, you will find such terminology as "view," "partial view," and the ultimate, "panoramic view." Houses that are quite similar in size, construction, and other amenities can be priced many thousands of dollars apart depending upon what the occupant sees from the breakfast table or living room. Potential buyers, sometimes overwhelmed by the stunning landscape, commit their life savings to properties, assuming that the view is permanent. Sometimes it is not.

Suppose a neighbor builds on the property down the hill. A second-story addition can suddenly stand in place of city lights, the Hudson River, or San Francisco Bay. Similarly, apartment buildings can spring up, ten stories high, to block the mighty Mississippi or a panorama of the Blue Ridge mountains.

And it's not just new construction that can cause a problem. As nature runs its usual course, the sapling on the property several blocks away may slowly become a huge and untamed tree, at first an annoyance, and finally a maddeningly unwelcome obstruction to the precious view.

Whether near the lakes of Washington state or the hills of Tennessee, when a view is threatened, the property owner often looks to the law for help. But help will be forthcoming only if:

- a local law protects views
- the obstruction violates private subdivision covenants, or
- the obstruction violates some other specific law.

The Basic Rule: No Right to a View

In our country, there is no right to light, air, or view, unless it has been granted in writing by a law (usually local) or subdivision rule. The exception to this general rule is that someone may not deliberately and maliciously block another's view. If a structure has no reasonable use to the owner and serves a purely malicious function, the affected neighbor can sue and ask a court to order it removed.

Almost any structure, however, is useful to the builder, whether it's a high-rise office building, a fence, or a tool shed. It's uncommon that a structure is built maliciously solely to annoy or inconvenience a neighbor. (Spite fences are an exception; see Chapter 12.) Because trees are considered to have reasonable use to the owner, they may legally block another's view unless a specific local law or subdivision rule is violated.

This legal rule that a property owner has no right to light, air, or view has been favored in this country because it encourages building and expansion. But the consequences can be harsh in individual cases. A typical court case from the late 19th century, before widespread access to electricity, involved a photographer. When a bank was built only 18 inches from his windows, he lost not only air and view, but the light necessary for his livelihood.[1] He had no legal recourse because the building that blocked the light had a reasonable purpose.

View Ordinances

Despite the general common law rule that a property owner has no legal right to a view, a few cities have adopted view ordinances that specifically protect an owner from having a view obstructed by growing trees. Not surprisingly, these ordinances are most common in cities that overlook the ocean or other desirable vistas.

Even if your city has a view ordinance, however, don't expect the city to step in and solve the problem of a lost view for you. The ordinances simply allow someone who has lost a view because of a growing tree to sue the tree owner for a court order requiring restoration of the view. And a neighbor who wants to sue must first approach the tree owner and request that the offending tree be cut back.

Solar Energy Access

A person who is using solar collectors to provide residential energy can sometimes purchase a right to sunlight from a neighbor. The neighbor agrees never to block access to the sun for the collectors. (See "Easements," in Chapter 10.) Today, more states are recognizing rights to solar access, including California, Oregon, Alaska, and Utah.

Berkeley, California, has a local ordinance that provides protection for solar access from a neighbor's growing trees. The same law protects views and sunlight.[3] (See "View Ordinances," above.)

The Wisconsin Supreme Court wrote at length about possible rights to sunlight for any user of solar energy. In this case, the owner of a home that used solar energy sued a neighbor who had built a house that blocked sunlight. The argument was that blocking sunlight might be an unreasonable use of property that the solar user could complain about in court. The neighbor who later built his residence evidently had plenty of room to build without obstructing the neighbor's sun. This court ruled that the solar user had a right to sue the neighbor, even when there was no local ordinance.[4]

Is the homeowner who lost sunlight necessary to operate solar collectors more harmed than the poor photographer mentioned above? Hardly. But society is shifting its priorities, and the law is beginning to reflect the changes.

You can find out whether you have a view ordinance addressing trees by calling your city clerk or checking your local ordinance in the public library or on the Internet. (See Chapter 18.) Local view ordinances don't cover buildings or other structures that block neighbors' views. If you're concerned about a construction project that threatens to ruin your view, see "Subdivision Rules That Protect Views" and "Other Laws That May Protect Views," below.

What the Ordinances Provide

The view that is protected under a view ordinance is usually the view that you had when you bought the property or moved in. Sometimes the ordinance specifies the date at which the view became protected. If you complain, you must have proof, such as photographs or reliable testimony from others, that your view has become blocked by a tree that has grown into it.

Just because there is a view ordinance doesn't mean you can force an uncooperative neighbor to cut down a tree. A judge presented with such a lawsuit will consider more than just the lost view. The health of the tree is also important, as are the tree's benefits to the owner. Some ordinances list the remedies available in an order of preference to try to preserve the tree. Thinning is preferred by most experts, and you may find yourself with a filtered view. In some cities, windowing—cutting out part of a tree to allow a view through it—may be suggested. If the tree can bear it, topping may be ordered. In the extreme case of court-ordered removal of a tree, the judge may also order the complaining neighbor to buy small replacement trees for the owner.

The complaining person usually bears the cost of trimming, unless the tree was planted after the law became effective or the owner refuses to cooperate. Then, depending on the ordinance, costs may be divided. If the complaining neighbor wins in court, some towns place all costs of restoring the view on the tree owner.

When Property Is Sold

When property protected by a view ordinance changes hands, usually the buyer only gets a right to any view on the date of purchase. If the seller has allowed the view already in existence to become diminished by neighboring trees, a wise buyer will negotiate to have the seller claim and restore any lost view before purchasing the property.

While some view ordinances are fairly tough, others contain extensive limitations which, in effect, take most of the teeth out of them. Some examples:

- Some cities protect certain kinds of trees from view ordinance lawsuits, especially if they are native species. In Oakland, California, the list includes redwoods, California live oaks, box elders, bigleaf maples, and others.[5] If a protected tree is blocking the view, a neighbor has no case.

- An offending tree on city property may be exempt from a view ordinance. But even though you can't sue the city, there may be a complaint procedure. In Oakland, California, for example, you can complain in writing to the city, and a city office will make a decision. Sometimes a hearing will be held where any citizen can argue to protect the tree. If you disagree with the decision, you may be able to appeal it to a higher level within the city, such as the city council, and the decision made at that level is final.

View ordinances are usually long and complicated. If you hope to use one, the first step is to get a copy of it. (See Chapter 18.) Be prepared to spend plenty of time figuring out exactly what the language means. Some even lecture us extensively about not just the glory of nature, but also the responsibility of neighbor cooperation. Once you wade through the discourse on how we should all behave, you'll find a step-by-step guide for the owner who wishes to regain a lost view.

How to Proceed

Once you've spent some time reading a local view ordinance, you'll see that it is designed to keep people out of court. These ordinances encourage efforts at solving view problems informally and sometimes penalize tree owners who don't cooperate. Before you can sue a neighbor for a lost view, you must take specific steps, which will be set out in your local view ordinance, to work things out. These steps usually include:

- **Notifying the tree owner of the problem.** This will often include documenting how big the tree was when you moved in (or when the ordinance was adopted).

- **If you and the neighbor can't agree, suggesting the use of a mediator—** someone to help you work out a solution yourselves without going to court. (See Chapter 19.)
- **If mediation fails, agreeing to abide by the decision of an arbitrator** after a hearing at which you and the neighbor make your arguments and present evidence. In some towns, the arbitrator may be any person the people involved agree on; others require a licensed arbitrator. There may be a fee for arbitration, but nothing like the cost of a lawsuit.
- **In a few cities, appearing before the city tree commission,** which holds formal hearings on view claims and issues orders for any trimmings. If the owner does not comply with the city's order, the neighbor can sue the tree owner.
- **Documenting refusals of the tree owner to cooperate with you or a lack of response.** Most towns require proof that you sent the neighbor letters by certified mail before you can file a lawsuit.
- **Filing an official complaint with the city,** furnishing proof of the view loss and the previous steps taken. In some cities, you fill out a form at city hall between the unsuccessful mediation attempts and arbitration. In others, you just give the city a copy of the actual lawsuit papers when you file the suit with the court.

If none of this solves the problem, you can sue the neighbor and ask for a court order making the neighbor trim the tree. If you win the lawsuit, the neighbor may also have to pay a fine (as much as $1,000) to the city for not cooperating under the ordinance.

If your view does become obstructed by a neighbor's tree, and the situation fits the ordinance, try to keep the whole situation a private one between you and the neighbor. It will avoid costs of arbitrators and attorneys and keep the city out of your business.

Go down and introduce yourself to the neighbor with the tree. Invite the neighbor over to your house for a cup of tea; you want to demonstrate, from your property, how the tree obstructs your view. The neighbor may not even know there is a problem. When you offer to pay for having the tree trimmed, you may find the neighbor is delighted.

Have a copy of the ordinance in your back pocket in case you need it; you may want to go over the provisions together. If the neighbor is uncooperative, leave the ordinance, and give the neighbor a little time to digest it. Try again in about a week. If you still get nowhere, then it's time for the written requests that most ordinances require. Below is a sample letter to a neighbor.

Sample Written Request to Restore View

2411 Skyline Avenue
Ocean View, CA 97765

June 25, 20xx

Ms. Doris Dawson
2411 Hill Avenue
Ocean View, CA 97765

Dear Ms. Dawson:

As you know, I live one block directly east of your property. This year, your pine trees have grown so large that they obstruct my view of the ocean.

Having them trimmed by a skilled professional would be good for the health of the trees and would restore my view. Our local view ordinance provides that I have a right to the view that I had as of June 11, 20xx. I have enclosed a picture of the view from my property that is dated about that time.

Under that ordinance, I am responsible for paying to have the trimming done, and I will be happy to do so.

May we arrange to consult with a licensed tree service of your choice, and at a time that will be convenient for you? Please contact me at 555-6888. Thank you for your cooperation.

Sincerely yours,

Juan Cuevez

Juan Cuevez

Keep a copy of all correspondence. If you get no response to a letter, send another copy to the neighbor by certified mail. Include a copy of the ordinance. All correspondence from then on should be registered or certified so you will have proof of your efforts if you must later file a complaint or lawsuit. If the neighbor still doesn't respond, write again, suggesting mediation, and then again, to suggest arbitration.

Carefully follow each step of the ordinance, but keep the letters pleasant. You want the neighbor to cooperate, and you probably will get that result before a dispute reaches the lawsuit stage. It is to your advantage to stay on the best terms possible because this problem is going to happen again; you will likely be dealing with the same neighbor over it for many years.

If all efforts fail, you are entitled to sue for a court order forcing the neighbor to allow the trimming. Remember to file a complaint with the city as well as with the court. You must use regular court, not small claims court, which means you will probably need to hire a lawyer. This will be expensive and time-consuming, but if you have proof of your lost view (photographs or the testimony of neighbors) and have carefully followed the required steps, you are likely to regain at least a portion of the view.

Subdivision Rules That Protect Views

If you live in a subdivision or planned unit development, another method to protect a view may be found in a property deed. Often, the deeds to subdivision lots contain restrictions on the use the owner may make of the property. Called "restrictive deed covenants" in legalese, these written regulations can protect views.

Usually, the same set of restrictions binds all the lots in a subdivision. The deed itself may contain the regulations if there are very few, but usually it refers to a separate document called the covenants, conditions, and restrictions, or CC&Rs. The CC&Rs regulate most matters that could be a concern to a neighbor—for instance, what can be built on the property and what activities are allowed. If your neighbor is bound by a deed covenant that forbids blocking the view of others in the subdivision, you may be able to force the neighbor to comply with the terms of the deed—and get your view back.

Typical Subdivision Rules

You'll have to read your CC&Rs carefully to determine whether a neighbor who is obstructing your view with a tree or a new garage is violating them. First, look for rules specifically about views. For example, a rule may state: "Nor shall any tree be planted that may in the future obstruct the view from any other lot." That means, according to a California court, that tree height is limited to roof level.[6]

Look at other sections, too. A rule may simply limit tree height to 12 or 15 feet. Most CC&Rs also restrict the height of buildings and fences, and require structures to be placed ("set back") a certain distance from the property boundaries.

Finding Out Who Is Subject to a Deed Covenant

Sometimes, even within the same neighborhood, not all owners are subject to the same deed restrictions. Someone who bought property before the restrictive covenants became part of the deeds, for example, is unaffected by them. And subdivisions have boundaries that may be visible only on paper. If you happen to live at the edge of the protected group, the people across the street or down the hill may not be under any restriction at all.

The easiest way to find out whether you and the neighbor have the same restrictions in your deeds is to ask the subdivision homeowners' association. It should have a list of all members of the protected property group. If you have an active association, it may also have a formal dispute resolution mechanism to help solve the problem. (See "Help From Homeowners' Associations," below.)

But what if there is no association or list of who is subject to the restrictions? Property deeds are part of the public record, and all deeds are on record at the county land records office, which is usually in the courthouse. You can go there and try to look up a neighbor's deed yourself. This may be possible if you have a helpful clerk who is not too busy to show you how to look up a deed.

Unfortunately, especially if you don't know the person's name, finding a deed can be time-consuming. If you have the address of the property, a clerk in the local tax assessor's office may help find the neighbor's name.

Some post offices and public libraries provide cross-referenced name and address listings, which can give you the person's name if you have the address. You might need the assistance of an attorney or a paralegal trained in title searches.

Help From Homeowners' Associations

Many homeowners' associations in subdivisions and planned unit developments will assist when one member of the group violates the restrictions and creates problems for another. A committee or designated person may visit the one causing the problem and apply pressure to conform. Sanctions are often used, such as removing the privilege of using a swimming pool or another common area.

Some associations have the power to bring a lawsuit to enforce the restrictions in the deed. When this is the case and your neighbor violates the covenants, the association itself can sue and solve the problem for you. That's an expensive and time-consuming undertaking, however. The association may not want to sue except for serious violations of the rules.

If you and your neighbor can't work something out, and you believe there is a violation of your subdivision rules, contact the board of directors of your homeowners' association. You may need to file a written complaint or appear at a meeting of the board.

Proceeding on Your Own

Some homeowners' groups have no real power to pressure anyone and no will to sue. They may be sympathetic to your plight but, for any number of reasons, unwilling or unable to help you. And some subdivisions with deed restrictions have no active association at all. In either of these cases, you are on your own.

If the other neighbor is also under the tree height restrictions, it is time for a talk, even if you don't know the neighbor. Go over and ask the neighbor to please trim the trees to the limit allowed. Explain the problem with your view—for example, try inviting him over to see his trees from your perspective. Most people just need to be reminded and do not violate the restrictions intentionally.

If this particular neighbor is not like most folks, and refuses your request, now you need to do some thinking. Even paying part of the trimming cost would be a lot cheaper than a lawsuit; you might want to make an offer to share the cost. If the neighbor is unsympathetic or drags his or her feet, put your request in writing. Some people respond better to a written request because they realize you are serious about the matter. Below is a sample letter.

Sample Letter Offering to Share Cost of Pruning

1632 Lakeview Drive
Hilldale, CA 94567

May 15, 20xx

Mr. Marvin Mott
1627 Lakeview Drive
Hilldale, CA 94567

Dear Mr. Mott:

As you know, I am the owner of a house several houses up the hill from yours. This spring, your acacia trees have become so large that my view of the lake is obstructed. In our house deed restrictions, we are obligated to keep our trees trimmed to a height of twelve feet. Would you please have yours pruned so that my view will be restored?

Because I would benefit from the pruning, I am willing to share the cost of having this done. Please contact me so that we can work out a satisfactory arrangement. Thank you for your cooperation.

Sincerely yours,

Lillie Lewis

Lillie Lewis

Give the owner time to respond before you follow up. If you run into a really stubborn neighbor, suggest sitting down with a trained, neutral mediator to work out a solution. (See Chapter 19.)

Suppose that nothing you suggest works out. Or suppose your view is being blocked by a three-story addition going up in violation of the deeds. In either case, consult an attorney, who may be able to obtain prompt action with one stiff letter. If not, your only legal alternative is a lawsuit in regular (not small claims) court. You'll probably need to hire a lawyer to handle the lawsuit.

If you decide to take the neighbor to court, be aware that the enforcement of restrictive deed covenants can be a legal jungle. Covenants concerning trees and views are usually legal and enforceable. But be prepared for a lengthy and expensive process.

Other Laws That May Protect Views

If a neighbor is blocking your view or planning to, you might find help from local laws that do not directly address views—such as a law that restricts the height of fences or buildings or limits the square footage of a structure. In most places, local ordinances regulate trees, structures, and fences, including trees that serve as fences.

If you do some research and determine the neighbor is in violation of a law, all that may be necessary is to talk to the neighbor or write a letter. It's possible the neighbor could be unaware of the ordinance.

If you get no response, you can contact your local planning, zoning, or building department, or the office of the city attorney; they should take it from there. The local government can cite a person for a violation, issue a fine, and may even sue for conformity to the law.

For details on the laws on fences and trees, see Chapters 11 and 6.

Below are some of the kinds of laws to look for.

Fence Height Limits

Local laws almost always limit artificial (constructed) fence heights. Commonly, they restrict fences in residential backyards to six feet and in front yards to three or four feet. They also restrict where you can build a fence—for instance, not too close to the street. Most of these types of regulations are found in the zoning laws.

But an artificial fence is not usually the culprit when a neighbor's view is blocked. The important application of fence laws in view cases usually occurs when the fence is a naturally growing one, such as a hedge. When bushes or trees are used as fences, height restrictions in fence laws may apply to them. Even if a tree owner claims that the trees are only for shade or greenery, if they are planted in a row and grow together to form a barrier, they are usually considered a fence and subject to the laws that govern fences. In these situations, a neighbor's view problem can be solved by the city when it enforces the fence ordinance.

A lawsuit in the town of Clyde Hill, Washington, provides a good example of how a local ordinance can be applied. The local law prohibited naturally grown fences above eight feet tall. A man who had 13 Douglas fir trees along his border was found to be in violation of the ordinance and ordered to cut them, even though he claimed the trees were not a fence but only lovely landscaping.[7] We aren't told whether a view was involved, but can almost assume that it was; why else would someone want to cut back Douglas firs?

Remember that the violation occurred only because the trees were a fence, not because a neighbor's view was blocked. If your view is obstructed by a lone tree in someone's backyard, fence regulations won't apply.

Utility Companies

Any time trees are growing into wires or becoming a menace to them, the affected utility company will promptly cut them back when the situation is brought to its attention.

A few states, such as Illinois, explicitly require natural growth to be cut back to a designated height when used as a division fence.[8] A state statute such as this one can be welcome relief to a person who has lost a view. Often the tree owner is unaware of the restriction, and pointing out the statute will result in prompt trimming. When only a state law is involved, you must sue the neighbor directly if you want to force compliance. To find out if your state has a law that specifically restricts natural fences, you may need to go to the law library. (See Chapter 18.)

For more on fence regulations, see Chapter 11.

Laws That Regulate Trees

If your view is obstructed by a tree and the tree is not part of a fence, you may find help from local laws that regulate trees in general. Certain kinds of trees may be prohibited—for example, trees that cause allergies or tend to harm other plant growth. Height and location restrictions may apply—for instance, it may be too close to the street (especially an intersection) or electric wires or even an airport. If the tree looks sick or dangerous, specific laws could affect it, including nuisance laws. (See Chapter 5.)

The city may remove such offending trees itself or require the property owner to do so. In the case of a dangerous tree, the city sometimes removes it and bills the owner.

> EXAMPLE: Roger notices one day that his neighbor's tree that blocks his view appears to be diseased and dying. He checks his local laws and discovers that there is not only an ordinance against objects on property that create a hazard, but that the city itself will remove a diseased tree under some circumstances. He simply reports the situation (in his town to the Department of Public Works) and looks up the next week to find the tree gone.

Zoning Laws

Just about all cities have local zoning regulations that control the size, location, and uses of buildings. Zoning laws divide cities into different areas according to use, from single-family residential all the way to industrial. In a single-family area, height restrictions usually limit buildings to 30 or 35 feet. When multifamily units or commercial uses are allowed, the height limit goes up.

Another common restriction deals with "setbacks." The setback is the distance that must be left between the street and a structure or between the side and back of structures and the boundary lines.

A third important zoning regulation limits how much of a lot can be occupied by a structure. For instance, many suburban cities limit a dwelling to 40% to 60% of the property.

These regulations can have a direct impact on property with a view. A next-door neighbor who suddenly throws up a 50-foot addition, blocking your view, may be violating the zoning laws. Sometimes a neighbor adds an extension toward the boundary or street in violation of the setback rules. In other situations, someone may attempt to tack on a view-blocking addition that would be fine except that a city ordinance restricts structures to covering no more than 60% of a lot, and the offending neighbor is already at or near that limit.

Occasionally, an unusual law may help you—for instance, the three-story colonial mansion going up to block your view may be located in a district that limits house designs to Southwestern ranch styles. Even in towns that require building permits before a structure goes up, some people ignore the laws or are unaware of them.

Almost every neighborhood has at least one house that doesn't completely conform to current zoning laws. The builder may have ignored the law and nobody complained. Or the house may have been built before the laws were passed. If the structure violates a restriction by just an inch or so, the builder may have substantially complied with the law and so have been left alone by zoning officials.

Sometimes a city allows a "variance," which is an exemption from the zoning regulations for a particular property if there is a good reason. Be aware of this exception and always on the lookout for a "variance requested" sign on property that could affect your view. If the neighbors will be harmed by a variance, they can complain to the city; if enough of them do so, it will probably be denied.

Using the Local Laws

When you have a view obstruction problem, you need to know exactly what your local laws say to see if something may help you. If your question is specific, such as a maximum fence height, try calling the city's planning or zoning department first. If you need to search a little to find a law that fits, the best thing to do is to use the Internet or make a trip to the public library or city hall to look at the ordinances. Be prepared to spend a little time; the indexing in some local ordinances is badly done.

You may have to sit down and read all of the ordinances under zoning, subdivisions, and miscellaneous—practically the entire code. If you live in a small town or city, this can actually be fun. Most people never open the pages of their local ordinances. In many towns, you'll discover that almost anything causing someone to complain is against the law. If you want to check your state laws, you will probably need to go to a law library or use the Internet. (See Chapter 18.)

If you find a law that you think may help you, tell the neighbor about it. Give a copy of the law to the neighbor and then wait a reasonable time for a response. If you must complain to the city, you can usually find out from the city clerk's office where to complain and what the procedure is. In some towns, a phone call to the appropriate office will be enough. In others, you may have to go down to city hall and give someone the information or fill out a form.

Don't go in and simply tell a clerk that someone a block away from your house is obstructing or threatening to obstruct your view. Bring a copy of the law that is being violated with you and be sure you can document that a violation is taking place or imminently threatened. Have the address and be specific as to the details.

Ask which office will handle the matter, what the city will do, and how long you must wait before you can expect action. If nothing happens within a week, call or go down there again. Especially in large cities, city offices can be terribly busy, understaffed, and backlogged. Be persistent, so your situation will not end up at the bottom of the list.

Views That Are Not Legally Protected

Now let's address the problems most of us face when a tree grows into our view. We own a house that isn't in a planned community, the neighbor's deed doesn't restrict tree height, and there are no local zoning, tree, or view laws to assist us. What can we do? The only avenue available may be diplomacy. To regain the view, you will have to convince your neighbor to cooperate.

The first step is to take a good look at the tree that is blocking the view. From the street you should be able to ascertain the property on which the tree is growing, the address, maybe even the name of the occupant on the mailbox.

You may gain a different perspective at the tree's own level. What is only a pain in the neck to you may be a highly valued asset to the owner. If it has a treehouse for the children or provides needed shelter to the property, you need to know this at the start. The owner may be resistant to you and extremely protective of the tree.

Next, review the material discussed in this chapter and consider whether the tree violates any local ordinances or interferes with utility easements. If it's on city property, too close to a street, or soon to interfere with power or phone lines, you may have an obvious remedy.

If the tree is on a protected species list, find out what action the city will allow and what kind of permit is needed.

Answer these questions before you approach the owner:

- Does the tree affect the view of other neighbors? If it does, you could get them to approach the tree owner with you, and trimming costs could be divided among you.
- Which part of the tree is causing view problems for you— one limb, the top, one side of it?
- What is the least destructive action that could be taken to restore your view? Maybe the owner will agree to a limited and careful pruning.
- How much will the trimming cost? Be ready to pay for it. Remember that every day you wait and grumble is a day for the tree to grow and for the job to become more expensive. The loss of your personal enjoyment is probably worth more than the trimming cost, not to mention the devaluation of your property (which can be thousands of dollars).

Now, if you know the neighbor, go have a talk. Even if you don't know the neighbor, you may want to start with an in-person visit. Be sure to put your money offer up front, so the neighbor won't think you are just criticizing the tree. Invite the neighbor over to see the situation from your property so the problem will be clear.

Give the neighbor a chance to voice any neighborhood concerns, even if they are unrelated to the tree. For example, if the neighbor is concerned about safety, noise, parking, or anything else, perhaps you could do something to help. Your own offers to aid a neighbor could result in cooperation that will help you with your needs, too.

If you would feel more comfortable keeping a distance, write a letter to the tree owner, instead. A sample letter is shown below.

Sample Letter: Offer to Pay for Tree Trimming

46 Hilltop Drive
Oceanscape, CA 98876

June 15, 20xx

Mr. Nathan Norris
44 Pine Lane
Oceanscape, CA 98876

Dear Mr. Norris:

I am writing to offer to have your pine trees trimmed at my expense. The trees are obstructing my view, and because I would benefit from the pruning, I am willing to bear the cost. A skillful trimming would enhance the health and beauty of the trees and would restore my view.

I suggest employing a professional service of your choice to perform the work at your convenience. The responsibility for clearing any debris will also be mine.

If you are interested in pursuing this, I would be most appreciative. Please contact me at 555-4454 so that we may discuss arrangements. Thank you.

Sincerely yours,

Dennis Duke

Dennis Duke

Will it work? In some circumstances, it will. Given the chance, and if approached properly, people are usually basically cooperative. They also like to be needed and to feel important. What do you have to lose?

If you run into a stone wall in your efforts, at least keep an eye on the house in case it changes hands. You may have lost your view for the time being, but be alert to the possibility of dealing with a new owner.

Breaking the Law Is Never the Answer

Never make the mistake one California fellow made when he sneaked a service in to cut his neighbor's trees. After proceeding to top 14 redwoods and one bay tree, he was sued by the owner and ordered to pay triple damages, based on the loss of the trees to the value of the property itself.[9] He was very lucky not to have been jailed and fined. If you even think of doing such a thing, first read about the penalties you'll face. (See Chapter 3.)

Avoiding View Problems

Before you part with your life savings to purchase the perfect view, you can take steps to find out the chances that the view will be permanent. Ask whether the property is protected by a view ordinance. If so, negotiate with the seller to be sure the view you buy is the one the seller is entitled to (see "View Ordinances," above).

Check with the seller or real estate agent to see whether the property deed incorporates restrictions on your use of the property. If it does, ask to see a copy of the restrictions. Also find out about the homeowners' association—whether it's active and enforces the restrictions.

You also need to know what the zoning is, not only for your own property, but for any property that might affect you. This means finding out where the zoning changes, and checking all property between you and the view. Can the neighbor down the hill add a second-story addition? What's the height limit anywhere within the view? This kind of caution may sound a bit extreme, but it can pay off.

EXAMPLE: Jack and Margaret, after saving for many years, purchase their dream house. It comes with a view of the ocean that adds $50,000 to the price. They know that their property is zoned single-family residential and think that the view is forever. Ten blocks away, however, the zoning allows ten-story condominium buildings. A few years later, up goes a five-building, ten-story complex, replacing their view with stone and glass. Jack and Margaret simply hadn't anticipated this problem, and they are out of luck. It happens all the time.

Buying a View

One reader of this book inquired into the possibility of purchasing view rights over a neighbor's property from the neighbor. The homeowner seeking to protect a view may ask the other homeowner/neighbor to grant an easement for the view, which requires an express (written) agreement between the two. For a sum of money, the neighbor would agree never to block the other neighbor's view.

This would appear to be a binding contract between these two neighbors. But the question arises of whether new owners would be bound by this agreement. California has passed a law supporting purchases of solar access protection, but not view protection.

We make no recommendation on this subject but will certainly keep an eye on the law.

Before you buy, go to city hall or the planning department and look at the zoning map. See if you can get a copy of the zoning regulations; if not, proceed to the public library.

You need to go to the library anyway because you want to sit down and study other city laws as well. Look up all the topics in the list below.

Trees

- view laws
- protected and prohibited species.

Structures (Zoning Laws)

- maximum heights
- setback rules
- percentage allowance—percentage of structure to lot
- style requirements
- permit requirements

Fences

- height limits
- setback rules
- natural fences (trees, shrubs)

If you find that the zoning law prohibits people downhill from you from erecting a structure that will block your view, but there is no view ordinance, you can make one further effort to ensure your view. Look very closely from the property to see just which trees might later become an obstruction to your view. Then go introduce yourself to the neighbor and explain your concerns. A neighbor who also has a view will probably understand your concern and admire your precautions. If you find an unfriendly and uncooperative neighbor, you stand warned.

Remember, even if the neighbors are reassuring and you feel quite comfortable, property changes hands. New owners may not be as receptive to your needs. A certain amount of risk may be unavoidable when investing in a view. ●

Endnotes

1 *Lindsay v. First Nat. Bank of Asheville,* 115 N.C. 553, 20 S.E. 621 (1894).

2 Cal. Civ. Code § 801.54; ORS § 105.885; AK § 34.15.145; and Utah § 57-13-1 and following.

3 Berkeley, Cal., Mun. Code § 12.45.

4 *Prah v. Maretti,* 108 Wis. 2d 223, 321 N.W.2d 182 (1982).

5 Oakland, Cal., Mun. Code § 15.52.030.

6 *Ezer v. Fuchsloch,* 99 Cal. App. 3d 849, 160 Cal. Rptr. 486 (1979).

7 *Clyde Hill v. Roisen,* 48 Wash. App. 769, 740 P.2d 378 (1987).

8 765 Ill. Comp. Stat. Ann. 130/3.

9 *Roche v. Casissa,* 154 Cal. App. 2d 785, 316 P.2d 776 (1957).

Boundary Lines

Oh, give me land,
lots of land
under starry skies above.
Don't fence me in.

—**Cole Porter**

Most of us don't know where our exact property boundaries are located, and many of us don't care. Unless we have the property surveyed, the only way we may be able to go outside and physically touch the limit of what is ours is when permanent markers are described in a deed, such as a tree or stone monument. And even when a permanent marker can be located, the boundary may not run in a straight line.

Settling Uncertain Boundary Lines

If you or your neighbor want to fence the property or build a structure close to the line, you need to know where the boundary line actually runs. If you can't figure it out from the property descriptions in your deed or subdivision map, or you and the neighbor think it is in different places, you have several choices.

Setting the Boundary With a Quitclaim Deed

To establish a clear boundary, adjoining property owners can decide where they want it to be and then make it so by signing deeds that describe the boundary agreed on. If you have a mortgage on the property, consult a local attorney for help in drawing up the deeds. Whoever holds the mortgage may need to be notified and permission obtained before you transfer even a tiny piece of the land. Some mortgage companies will not be concerned or want to be involved. But others put a clause in the mortgage that allows the company to demand full and immediate payment of the entire loan if the borrower transfers any interest whatsoever in the property.

Even if you have no mortgage, you might want to get an attorney to draw up the property descriptions in the deed, or just to look over your work if you draw up your own deed (perhaps, if you live in California, using *Deeds for California Real Estate*, by Mary Randolph (Nolo)). It may be worth spending the money for this small service to avoid any possibility of later confusion.

Each neighbor should sign a quitclaim deed, transferring to the other neighbor any right they have to the property that falls on the other side of the line they have agreed on. Once the deeds are recorded (put on file) in the county land records office (usually in the courthouse), there will never again be a question about the boundary. All future buyers will be able to find the deed and know what belongs to whom, when they buy the property.

> **EXAMPLE:** Janet and Rod, next-door neighbors, aren't sure where the boundary line is between their properties. Rod wants to enclose his yard with a fence, but doesn't want to pay for an expensive survey of the property to find the exact boundary. He and Janet agree that the fence will mark the boundary. Then they each draw up a quitclaim deed. Rod signs a deed giving any rights to the property on the other side of the fence to Janet, and she signs a comparable deed.
>
> In the deed Rod signs, he describes and gives up any interest in Janet's property. Janet makes out a deed quitclaiming any interest in Rod's property. Each property is identified exactly as it is in the deed already on record, with the addition of the description of the fence. Then they both put the deeds on file (record them) at the county land records office.

Sample Deed

Recording requested by

Rodney E. Rivera
245 Poplar Street
Sunset, CA 98876

and when recorded mail
this deed and tax statements to:

same as above

QUITCLAIM DEED

For a valuable consideration, receipt of which is hereby acknowledged,

Rodney E. Rivera
hereby quitclaim(s) to
Janet S. Johnson

the following real property in the City of Sunset ,
County of Lake California:

Any interest in Lot 4 of the Lake Park Tract, filed June 3,
1926, in Book 32 of Maps, at page 67, in the Office of the
County Recorder of Lake County, California, and bounded on
the north by a wooden fence, erected in April of 20xx.

Date: April 10, 20xx   *Rodney E. Rivera*

State of California

County of Lake   } ss

On April 10, 20xx , Rodney E. Rivera ,
known to me or proved by satisfactory evidence to be the person(s)
whose name(s) is/are subscribed above, personally acknowledged that
 he executed this deed.

Sarah Currington   [Notary Seal]
Signature of Notary

Setting Boundaries by Owners' Agreements

When a boundary line cannot be located because deeds or maps are ambiguous, the two adjoining neighbors may simply agree where the boundary line is. Once this agreement is made and certain conditions (discussed below) are met, the line is the permanent legal boundary. It is binding not only on those neighbors but also on later buyers.[1] Unlike a quitclaim deed, the agreement does not change the ownership of land. Instead, it interprets ambiguous property descriptions in the deeds.

If both neighbors genuinely agree, this approach is highly recommended. It is easy, inexpensive, and fixes a certain boundary line. Done properly, it will end confusion for the neighbors and for later buyers.

The purpose of this rule, according to one judge, is "to prevent strife and disputes concerning boundaries."[2] This may ring with truth for two neighbors who come to a solution, write it down, and record it (file a copy) in the public land records. However, if the agreement isn't written down and filed in the land records office, it can wreak havoc when property changes hands or one of the neighbors dies.

Requirements for an Agreed Boundary

For neighbors to agree on a permanently binding boundary between their properties, four conditions must be met:
- There must be genuine uncertainty as to where the true boundary line runs on the ground.
- Both landowners must agree on the new line.
- The owners must then act as if the new boundary line really is the boundary (lawyers often call this "acting in reliance on the agreement").
- The agreed boundary must be identifiable on the ground.

Only after all these requirements are satisfied does the agreed boundary become the legal line. Some courts can be extremely strict when looking to see if a boundary agreement meets these criteria. If one of the requirements is absent and the line is ever challenged in court, the agreement will be ruled void and the boundary line will be as uncertain as it ever was. We discuss each of these requirements below.

Original uncertainty. For an agreed boundary line to become the fixed legal boundary, the two owners must not only agree, but agree because they really can't locate the line. This doesn't mean that the neighbors must call in a surveyor to try to find the boundary. It is enough if they cannot reasonably locate the line from their deed descriptions, from a previous survey recorded in the land records, or from markers on the ground.

Usually, what happens is that someone wants to put up a fence, or maybe both neighbors want to put one up together. When they attempt to find the boundary, they discover that the property descriptions in their deeds conflict or perhaps make no sense at all. Not wanting hard feelings or lawsuits, they simply agree on a line convenient to both of them. Many are the neighbors who have done this and proceeded to live happily side by side for many years.

But if someone challenges the boundary line in court—perhaps the next buyer of one of the properties, who is unhappy with or confused by the agreed boundary—and the real boundary line could have easily been found, the general rule is that the owners' agreement doesn't count. A judge may make an exception to this requirement only if the owners had relied for many years on the agreement and great harm would result by not recognizing the agreed line.[3]

> **EXAMPLE:** A California case illustrates the kind of legal microscope a court will often use when determining whether or not the requirement of uncertainty has been met. The new owner of a piece of property assumed that an 80-year-old fence was the boundary and proceeded to make major changes on the land. The next-door neighbor claimed that he was trespassing and sued him. Because the fence was so old, former owners from years before were brought in to testify as to whether or not it had been an agreed boundary. They gave conflicting stories; some had assumed the fence was the boundary, others had not. As it turned out, arguments about whether or not the fence was the agreed boundary made no difference whatsoever, because there were some old boundary markers on the property that could have been found by any of the owners if anyone had searched. In short, there was never real uncertainty. The new owner's mistake and his trespass on his neighbor's land cost him dearly: He was ordered to pay the neighbor $26,000.[4]

Agreement by the owners. A neighbors' agreement about an uncertain boundary doesn't have to be in writing to be legal. But obviously, a written agreement avoids confusion and disputes later.

Sometimes, if a line has been treated as the boundary by both owners for many years, an initial agreement between them will be inferred by a court that is deciding on the validity of an alleged boundary agreement. A court might make this inference when all of the other conditions of an agreed boundary have been met.

Mediating an Agreement

If you and your neighbor can't seem to agree on where you think the boundary line should run, you may be able to get some help from a trained mediator. A mediator helps people iron out difficulties and reach an agreement that is satisfactory to everyone involved. Mediation of disputes between neighbors is often free or very inexpensive. See Chapter 19.

Acting in reliance on a boundary. Once adjoining landowners agree that a particular line marks an uncertain boundary, for that line to become the legal boundary they must then act as if it is the boundary. They can do this by simply going about their business, treating the line as the partition between their properties for whatever time period is required by state law. The time required ranges from five years to 20 years. If you need to know what your state's required time period is, you must find a state court opinion dealing with an agreed boundary in your state. (See Chapter 18.)

If, however, great harm would be caused were the agreed boundary not considered the legal one, the agreed boundary can become the legal one before the required time period has elapsed. Courts will rule this way when one or both of the neighbors does a substantial act relying on the validity of the agreed line, such as building a house close to it, and the other neighbor does not disagree.

EXAMPLE: Two people purchase lots in a subdivision. The boundary line between their properties is unclear, both from the subdivision map and their deed descriptions. One wants to fence his lot, and they agree on a boundary. These two fellows are friendly neighbors; one even gives the other the lumber for the fence. A lovely split rail fence is built, along with a comfortable house. Both properties are then sold. The new owner of the fenced house comes home from shopping one day and discovers a crew tearing down his fence. The other owner has had a new survey done which shows the boundary line running squarely through the shopper's bedroom.

This actually happened in California, and the owner of the fence sued the other owner. When the lawsuit came before the court, the ruling was: The legal boundary line was the one agreed upon by the previous owners, even though the state had a five-year period for an agreed boundary to become fixed, and five years had not passed since the agreement. The court based its ruling on the fact that the housebuilder had relied on the agreed boundary to build a house. Making him tear the house down, the court decided, would be too severe and unfair. The man who tore down the fence was ordered to pay the neighbor not only the replacement value, but also $500 in extra damages for the malicious behavior he showed in ripping down his neighbor's fence.[5]

Identifying the agreed boundary. When two owners settle confusion by agreeing on a boundary line, the line should be physically obvious in some way. Often, a fence or a natural boundary marks the line. It could be a tree, road, creek, driveway, even the edge of a house. If not, something needs to be constructed, or stakes or some other markers put in the ground, so that the owners can point to the line.

The reason to have a visible line is to alert a new buyer as to where the line is, to prevent trouble in the future. Anyone who purchases property is expected to make a visual inspection of the site. If someone else's driveway is two feet from the house he's buying, he is expected to notice it. This is the time to inquire about it and to call in a surveyor if necessary—not after buying the property and settling in.

Putting Boundary Agreements in Writing

An informal, unwritten boundary agreement can be a ticking time bomb, ready to go off when the property is sold. To avoid an explosion, if you make an agreement about a land boundary, put it in writing.

A sample agreement is shown below.

If you and your neighbor make such a written agreement, use the exact property descriptions that are in your deeds. Be sure that all owners sign the agreement. Have it notarized and make copies to keep with your deeds.

Sample Boundary Agreement

REAL PROPERTY BOUNDARY AGREEMENT BETWEEN
ALVIN AND ELOISE LEWIS AND WARREN OLSEN.

Alvin and Eloise Lewis, owners of real property in the City of Sunset, County of Woodland, State of California, described as:

Lot 20, Subdivision Map of Lots 1, 2, 3, and 4, Ridge Park, Sunset, filed January 12, 1892, map book 11, page 32,

and

Warren Olsen, owner of real property in the City of Sunset, County of Woodland, State of California, described as:

Lot 19, Subdivision Map of Lots 1, 2, 3, and 4, Ridge Park, Sunset, filed January 12, 1892, map book 11, page 32, agree as follows:

1. Because of ambiguities in the property descriptions in our deeds and the subdivision maps, we are uncertain as to where the true boundary line between our properties is located.

2. The location of the split rail fence standing on this date between our properties is the true boundary line.

_____   _____
Alvin Lewis   Date

_____   _____
Warren Olsen   Date

_____   _____
Eloise Lewis   Date

NOTARIZATION

State of California   )
County of _____   )

[Notary's Statement]

                          _____
                          Notary Public for
(Notary Seal)   the State of _____
                          My commission expires: _____,_____

File the Agreement With the Records Office

Once you have a signed, notarized agreement, take it to the local property records office (often in the county courthouse) and ask the clerk to record it. When you record a document, it becomes part of a public record, so other people can find it. You will have to pay a small fee, probably just a few dollars per page of the document.

The clerk may be a little surprised at your request, because not a lot of boundary agreements are recorded. In a very few states—Kentucky is one—there is a procedure in the state statutes for setting an agreed boundary, putting the agreement in writing, and recording it at the courthouse.[6]

If there is no standard procedure in your state, ask to put a copy on file with the land descriptions of each property. In some states, the clerk may be able to make a note in the margin of your deed that refers to the agreement. At least get it filed under both names on the agreement, so that it will be part of the public record.

Calling in a Surveyor

If you are willing to spend several hundred dollars or more to find out exactly where your boundary is, call a licensed surveyor. The surveyor will survey the entire property and give you a copy of the survey, showing the boundary lines of your property. In addition, the surveyor will place official markers on the boundary lines, which will remain to mark the boundaries.

Dealing With the Surveyor

When the surveyor comes out, do everybody a favor and stay out of the way. Find out what the surveyor will need from you, such as a copy of your deed or any other records, and have everything ready. Then let the professionals do their job. You and the neighbor standing there explaining who built what and what belongs to whom is nothing but a waste of time and money.

Be aware that you and the neighbor could be in for further conflict when the boundary is found. The line may run several feet away from what you expected—maybe even through one of the houses. When this happens, one neighbor may have to pay the other for property that was being occupied by mistake. This can get complicated, especially if the new survey conflicts with one in the past or the descriptions in the deeds, and you may need a lawyer.

In a new subdivision that still has markers from a city survey, the cost of a survey can run around $500. When streets have been renovated and the surveyor has to bring lines in from far away, the cost goes up accordingly. Be prepared to spend several hundred dollars to more than $1,000 dollars if you live in an area where no survey has been done for a long time or if the maps are unreliable and conflicting. Sometimes, the surveyor really can't know just what will be involved until the job begins. If you and your neighbor share the cost and have both properties done at the same time by the same surveyor, you should be able to save some money.

If you are in the midst of a heated dispute with your neighbor and hire a surveyor on your own, the neighbor will probably have to allow the surveyor onto the property. It is against state law in many states to interfere with a surveyor or to refuse a right of entry. However, to avoid confrontations, it is best to notify the neighbor when the surveyor is coming, if practicable. If the neighbor indicates that there will be trouble, have a lawyer write a letter outlining the law and asking for entry to the property for the survey. If necessary, the lawyer can get a court order to allow the survey.

Laws Protecting Boundary Markers

Permanent boundary monuments or survey markers are protected by state law. A marker may be a naturally occurring landmark, such as a tree. Or, a surveyor may place iron stakes or small brass caps in the ground to officially mark the property line. In Massachusetts, anyone removing such a marker can be jailed for six months or fined $200 or both.[7] In the District of Columbia, the penalty is stiffer, and includes a fine of up to $1,000 and/or 180 days in jail.[8] The laws are similarly serious in other states.

Once you have a survey done, ask whether the survey company will record it for you in the local public land records. If not, take a copy to the courthouse and ask that it be recorded; there will be a small fee. (See "File the Agreement With the Records Office," above.)

Letting a Court Decide on the Boundary

When a boundary line is not clear and the neighbors can't agree, a few states have statutory procedures allowing one neighbor to ask a state court (regular court, not small claims court) to settle the line. This will probably involve a new court-ordered survey and will be expensive. In other states, you can hire a lawyer and file a suit to "quiet title" (decide who owns what). Again, the judge may order a survey done, and the whole thing will take a lot of time and money.

When a Neighbor Doesn't Honor the Boundary

Most neighbors get along for years with no serious questions concerning their boundary lines. But one day you may look out your window to discover a frightening scene. There stands the next-door neighbor on what you think is your property, putting up a fence or taking yours down. Or perhaps the neighbor is sitting atop a backhoe, digging up your property for a new garage. What you have long assumed was the boundary line has been crossed.

Act Promptly

If a neighbor starts to build on what you think is your property, do something immediately. If the neighbor's encroachment is minor, for instance a small fence in the wrong place, you may think you shouldn't worry. You are wrong. When you go to sell your house, the title company may refuse to issue insurance because the neighbor is on your land.

It is important to act promptly because if you don't, you could lose part of your property. A person who uses another's land can gain a legal right to do so and, in some circumstances, gain title to (ownership of) the property. (See Chapter 10.)

Also, if you don't get the construction stopped, even if you later sue for trespass and win, all you may be able to collect is a money award, not an order to remove the neighbor's addition. Judges do not like to order property destroyed. Only if the neighbor intentionally trespassed can you even hope for an order of removal of a substantial structure.

Talk to the Neighbor

Any time a neighbor starts to build on what you think is your property, step over for a chat and find out what is going on. Most likely, a mistake has been made. There may be a conflicting description in the neighbor's deed or just a wrong assumption about the line. You may even discover that neither one of you is really sure where the boundary is. You may want to make your own agreement about a boundary or hire a surveyor to find the existing one. (See "Settling Uncertain Boundary Lines," above.)

If your neighbor is hostile and insists on proceeding, let the neighbor know that you will sue if necessary to stop the construction. If you are already certain about the boundary and have proof, such as a survey, you can threaten to call the police and have the neighbor arrested for trespassing.

A Little Common Sense

If you are having no trouble with your property and your neighbors, yet you feel inclined to go rushing out to determine your exact boundaries just to know where they are, please ask yourself a question. Have you been satisfied in the past with the amount of space that you occupy? If the answer is yes, then consider the time, money, and hostility that might be involved if you pursue the subject.

When a problem exists on your border, keep the lines of communication open with the neighbor if possible. Learn the law and try to work out an agreement between yourselves. Boundary lines simply don't matter that much to us most of the time; relationships with our neighbors matter a great deal.

Hire a Lawyer If Necessary

Perhaps a firm and threatening letter on legal stationery will at least stop the building. If a letter and a threatened lawsuit don't make the neighbor stop, waste no time in having a lawyer get a judge's order to temporarily stop the neighbor until a civil lawsuit for trespass (being on your property without authorization) can come before the judge.

If the neighbor is actually claiming part of your land, for example under a conflicting survey or because he or she has been using it (see Chapter 10), you'll need an attorney to file a lawsuit to have the neighbor or his or her property removed. Or the attorney can file a suit to "quiet title"—to let the court decide who owns what. ●

Endnotes

1   For example, see *Needham v. Collamer*, 94 Cal. App. 2d 609, 211 P.2d 308 (1949).

2   *Young v. Blakeman*, 153 Cal. 477, 95 P. 888 (1908).

3   For example, see *Minson Co. v. Aviation Finance*, 38 Cal. App. 3d 489, 113 Cal. Rptr. 223 (1974). See also *Ernie v. Trinity Lutheran Church,* 51 Cal. 2d 702, 336 P.2d 525 (1959), where the property in dispute was a strip less than a foot wide; *Bryant v. Blevins*, 9 Cal. 4th 47, 884 p. 2d 1034 (1994).

4   *Armitage v. Decker*, 218 Cal. App. 3d 887, 267 Cal. Rptr. 399 (1990).

5   *McCormick v. Appleton*, 225 Cal. App. 2d 591, 37 Cal. Rptr. 544 (1964).

6   Ky. Rev. Stat. Ann. § 73.190. The procedure in Kentucky is quite elaborate and involves having a new survey done.

7   Mass. Gen. Laws ch. 266, § 94 and following.

8   D.C. Code Ann. § 22-3309.

Using Another's Land:
Trespass and Easements

Man, like a tree in the cleft of a rock, gradually shapes his roots to his surroundings, and when the roots have grown to a certain size, can't be displaced without cutting at his life.

—Justice Oliver Wendell Holmes

People have the right to keep unwanted intruders off their property. They do this all the time, sometimes with fences or with signs, sometimes just by asking trespassers to please stay away. In cases of serious, repeated annoyance or threatened harm, landowners can call the police, who will usually warn the person to stay away and, if necessary, make an arrest. Trespass is a minor criminal offense, and someone convicted of criminal trespass can be fined and jailed.

Another kind of trespass is more permanent: using another's property as an owner would use it. If someone drives across a neighbor's land every day, it is a trespass unless the owner has granted permission or the driver has a legal right, called an easement, to use that part of the neighbor's property. A neighbor who puts up a fence two feet over the boundary line is trespassing, as is the one whose garage has been on the neighbor's property for several years.

These trespassers can also be asked to leave or warned away. But there's a chance that any of them may have, or could gain, a legal claim to the property.

Trespassers Who Become Owners

Many landowners are surprised to learn that under certain circumstances, a trespasser can come onto land, occupy it, and gain legal ownership of it. The trespasser may acquire a few feet of property or whole acres in this way. If someone is using your property, even a small strip on the edge, you should be alert to the risk.

The legal doctrine that allows trespassers to become owners is called "adverse possession." Another legal doctrine—called "prescriptive easement"—gives a trespasser the legal right to use part of someone's land for a particular purpose but does not make the trespasser the legal owner of that piece of land. (See "Easements," below.)

Although the term "adverse possession" sounds nasty (and the results can be), the trespasser is not necessarily an intentional evildoer—far from it. The trespasser may simply have made a mistake—relying on a faulty property description in a deed, for example. In rural areas, the person who moves in and occupies several acres may believe he owns it, having purchased it from a scoundrel who sold someone else part of the Brooklyn Bridge. Questions about ownership often wind up in court after an absent owner of rural property discovers that someone is living on his or her land or a title insurance company refuses to issue insurance when a piece of urban property is sold because the neighbor's garage is found to be standing squarely on the property. If the people involved can't work something out, the property owner may sue the trespasser, or the trespasser may bring a lawsuit to "quiet title"—a request for the court to settle who owns what. (For information on how next-door neighbors can work out boundary agreements themselves, see Chapter 9.)

Requirements for Obtaining Land by Adverse Possession

A trespasser obtains legal ownership of property if his or her occupation of the property is:

- hostile
- actual
- open and notorious
- exclusive, and
- continuous for a period of years set by state statute.

(We explain each of these terms below.) Some states also require the trespasser to have paid the local property taxes on the land. The time required, which varies from state to state, is usually 20 years. It can be as short as five years when the trespasser pays the property taxes. (See Chapter 18 for more information on how to research your state's laws on adverse possession.)

Hostile Claim

The word "hostile" does not mean that the trespasser barricades himself on the land with a shotgun. Most courts follow one of two legal definitions of hostile.

Awareness of trespassing. One definition is called the "Maine rule" and requires that the person be aware that the use of the property is trespassing.[1] For example, in Arkansas, a state that follows this rule, two men gained ownership of a portion of a neighboring drainage ditch that they paved and used for years. They knew the ditch was not theirs, so their use was "hostile" under Arkansas law.[2]

Simple occupation. The other popular definition, the "Connecticut rule," defines "hostile" simply as occupation of the land.[3] The trespasser doesn't have to know that the land belongs to someone else. The Connecticut rule, kinder to the innocent trespasser, is followed by most states today.[4]

> EXAMPLE: Jesse isn't sure where his property line is but he thinks an old fence marks the boundary. When he builds his new garage, he builds up to the fence line, which is actually ten feet over on his neighbor's property. Under the Connecticut rule, Jesse's intention doesn't matter, and his occupation is hostile even though he thinks he is on his own land.

Good-faith mistake. A few states follow a third rule, which is directly opposite of the old Maine rule of requiring intentional trespass. The trespasser must be completely innocent and must have made a good-faith mistake, such as relying on an invalid or incorrect deed. For example, in Iowa, which follows this good-faith rule, a woman attempted to claim a strip of her neighbor's land by adverse possession. The court denied her claim because she knew it was not her property, even though she had treated the property as her own for 30 years.[5]

Actual Possession

The trespasser must actually be in possession of the property and treat it as if he or she were an owner. This means there must be a physical presence on the land. It's not enough for someone just to make a claim, orally or in writing, of ownership.

Open and Notorious Possession

The words "open and notorious" simply mean that it must be obvious to anyone, including an owner who investigates, that a trespasser is on the land. Actual (physical) possession is usually open and notorious. Someone out in the field harvesting crops is obvious, as is a person pruning the rose garden that she planted on a strip of the neighbor's back yard. Similarly, a neighbor who puts a fence up slightly on the next-door property is obvious. So is the one who just poured a concrete driveway two feet over the boundary line.

The point of this requirement is that the owner knows someone is occupying the land and thus has a chance to do something about it. According to the theory of adverse possession, an owner who allows someone to trespass for years without giving permission, complaining, or taking action loses rights to the land.

Exclusive and Continuous Possession

The trespasser must possess the land exclusively and without interruption for the time period set forth in the state's statute.

A trespasser must occupy the land continuously for the full time period. A trespasser can't give up the use of the property and then return to it and count as possession the time that it was abandoned—that wouldn't be continuous possession for the whole time.

"Exclusive" means that the person trespassing must be the only one occupying the property—the trespasser can't share possession with strangers or the owner. (By contrast, a trespasser can gain the right to use a certain part of another's property, a prescriptive easement, even if possession or use is shared with others. See "Easements," below.)

If one person uses the property for a while and leaves, and another shows up for a while, the times can't be combined—the possession hasn't been exclusive by one person.

If, however, the trespasser actually sells or gives the property to someone else, the recipient becomes the adverse possessor and the years that the first trespasser spent occupying the land count for the new one's claim. This is called "tacking." When one trespasser passes the land to the next, then that person's claim is tacked on to the previous one.

> **EXAMPLE:** Joe occupied part of a neighbor's land for ten years. He then sold his land (including the part that was not legally his) to Adam, who stayed for ten years. If his state's adverse possession statute requires 20 years of occupancy, Adam has met the 20-year requirement through tacking. On the other hand, if Joe stopped trespassing before Adam bought the property and started his own period of trespassing, the ten years of Joe's trespass don't count for Adam.

Payment of Property Taxes

Some states require the trespasser to have paid the taxes on the property for the statutory time period. If all the other requirements are met except the tax payment, a court will usually grant a prescriptive easement to use the property to the trespasser, instead of ownership through adverse possession. (See "Easements," below.)

What Can the Owner Do?

Landowners who don't keep tabs on their properties can lose them. Nobody should allow the boundaries to be redrawn by inattention and inaction—in a city, a loss of even 20 feet could be devastating to a property investment.

If you become seriously concerned that someone has a possible claim to your land, check the local property tax records to see if anyone has made tax payments for the property. Paying taxes always bolsters an adverse possession claim, even when it is not required for a successful claim.

There are several steps an owner can take to prevent a trespasser from gaining a legal claim to the ownership.

Post Signs and Block Entry

Some people put up "Posted" or "No Trespassing" signs to keep people off their properties. Signs can alert a trespasser that the land belongs to someone else but they are not protection against adverse possession unless state law requires the trespasser to believe that he or she is on his or her own land to make a claim (see "Hostile Claim," above). Signs are never a substitute for periodic inspection of the property. It is easy to imagine someone tacking up a few signs and returning 25 years later— or never, a new buyer returning instead. By that time, the signs are long gone and a neighbor may have shifted over onto the land.

Signs that don't tell trespassers to stay off but instead grant permission to use the property may actually protect an owner if a neighbor later attempts to claim a permanent right to use part of the property. A grant of permission may be revoked, but a failure to either grant permission or stop the neighbor using your property may have serious negative consequences. (See "Easements Acquired by Use of Property," below.)

Locked gates at entry points to the property when the land is enclosed, or across an access that is being used, will stop most trespassers. But you should routinely check to be sure someone is not ignoring them, or worse, removing them.

Give Written Permission

One effective way to thwart a possible claim is by giving permission to use your land. If Norma is out planting a garden in your backyard, treating it as her own land, step over and say, "Hello, you are on my property by a few feet, but that's okay." You don't have to throw her off your property; simply claim it. Then put the permission in writing and obtain an acknowledgment from Norma. The chain has been broken. She can tend that garden for 40 years and still never acquire a legal claim to your property if she has your permission. The use is no longer hostile under the law.

An example of written permission is shown below.

Sample Agreement Granting Permission to Use Property

I, Frank Feldman, owner of the property located at 356 Hill Drive, Sunset, California, give my permission to Norma Neal to plant and tend a garden located on a five-foot strip of my property bordering the west side of the property line. I reserve the right to revoke this permission at any time.

Frank Feldman   *April 1, 20XX*
Frank Feldman   Date

I, Norma Neal, acknowledge that my use of this strip of land belonging to Frank Feldman is by permission only, and that the permission may be revoked at any time.

Norma Neal   *April 1, 20XX*
Norma Neal   Date

This type of agreement can be used to grant permission for parking, using a shortcut across property, or even growing crops. It not only can defeat adverse possession claims but also a claim to an easement (a use permit) across your property. (See "Easements," below.) When you use such a written permission, be absolutely sure that the portion of your land being used is described in enough detail so that it is easily identifiable.

If your neighbor is upset or insulted by the idea of a written permission, show the neighbor this book. Explain that while you have no objection to the use of your land, you must protect your interest for later years.

If the neighbor refuses to acknowledge the permissive use, you are then on the alert that there's a possible claim adverse to your interest, and you should take steps to prevent further use of your property.

Offer to Rent the Property to the Trespasser

If someone wants to remain on your property, you can always offer to rent it to them. In fact, the presentation of a rental agreement can be very effective in getting some trespassers to immediately leave on their own.

Call the Police

If someone refuses to acknowledge a permission and ignores your requests to stay off your property, you can call the police or notify the sheriff and have the person removed or arrested.

When the trespasser is a next-door neighbor, you may understandably be reluctant to bring in the police. But sometimes it is necessary to protect your property.

Hire a Lawyer

Any time it appears that a trespasser may be entertaining the idea of claiming your property under an adverse possession theory, see a lawyer. You may need to file a lawsuit to eject the trespasser from the land. Or you may want to ask a court to order a structure removed or a person to stay away. You must act before the trespasser has been on your land long enough, under your state's law, to make a successful adverse possession claim. (See "Time Required for Adverse Possession," above.)

Easements

An easement is a legal right to use someone else's land for a particular purpose. For example, the municipal water company may have an easement to run water pipes under your property. Your name is on the deed (you're the title holder) and you still own the property, but the water company has the right to use a part of it for its pipes. Easements are sometimes in writing and referred to in property deeds or title papers prepared by a title insurance company or attorney.

Easements are part and parcel of the land they affect. They don't change when the property changes hands. Subsequent owners are obliged to let whoever owns the easement use the property.

The owner of the property may not interfere with the purpose of a legal easement. If, for example, the electric company has wires strung across its right of way, you cannot take them down or block their path. A property owner who interferes with an easement can be liable to the easement owner for damage and be subject to a court action ordering him or her to stop.

The easement holder has responsibilities, too. For example, the city of New York was found liable for damage caused to privately owned water pipes that were located on city property under the terms of an easement. The damage was caused by oak trees that the city had planted. When the pipes broke and the property owner sued, the court said the city should have known that roots from oak trees would cause damage and held it liable.[6]

Utility Easements

Probably the most common kind of easement is the one that has been given in writing to a utility company or a city. Utility easements are sometimes described in a property deed or certificate of title as "those certain utility easements as set out and shown on the map and plat of record in such-and-such a book on page something-or-other."

The existence of these easements doesn't have much day-to-day effect. You can plant on the property, live on it, even build on it, as long as you don't interfere with the utility's use of the easement.

When an easement is underground—for instance, a water pipe easement (and increasingly, electric and phone line easements)—you may still use the land above it. But again, you may not interfere with the purpose of the underground easement.

> **EXAMPLE:** A man in Los Angeles found himself having to spend an extra $32,000 when he erected a heavy building over a sewer. The weight of the building interfered with the sewer pipes and had to be redesigned so that it straddled the easement.[7]

Utility companies rarely bother property owners. If an occasional nightmare comes along, such as the property dug up for underground repair, the work is usually done with care. And if a utility company comes in and harms your property unnecessarily, you may be able to sue the company if it won't pay for the damage.

The existence of utility easements across your property (and your neighbor's) can sometimes even be an advantage. For example, when trees are encroaching on power lines or are diseased, the utility company or city is usually quite helpful with trimming and removing dangerous branches. (See Chapter 4.)

If you want to know where these easements are located on your property, call the utility company. Or you can go to the county land records office or city hall and ask a clerk to show you a map of the easement locations. A survey of the property will also show the location of utility easements.

Other Written Easements

In addition to utility easements, property may be subject to another kind of written easement, an easement that an owner sells to someone else to use as a path or driveway or for sewer or solar access, for example. Private easements across another's property are not uncommon but they are easily overlooked. If you see an easement mentioned in your deed or title certificate and assume it is a utility company easement, you could be wrong.

Especially in hillside communities, where the fall angle (degree of slant or fall) can be essential for water pipes, private sewer easements are often sold when the uphill house is being built, so the pipe from the house to the street can slant properly—sometimes right under your property.

If your title contains private easements, you should get copies of the actual easement documents. You need to know where the easements are and what uses they allow. If you are unaware of the terms of a private easement, you could unknowingly interfere with the easement rights and be liable for damage.

If a solar access easement has been sold to a neighbor, you may find that you are severely limited in what you can build or grow on your property, because you can't block sunlight to the neighbor's solar collectors.

Any private easement referred to in your property papers should have a reference number, such as a book and page number. Your county clerk can help you locate it in the public records and obtain a copy to keep with your deed.

Watch Out for Private Easements

The time to find out exactly what easements a property is subject to is before you buy. When some very good friends of ours bought a house, the title papers referred to what they thought were the usual utility easements. But years later, when the neighbor's sewer pipe backed up, it was discovered that the pipe causing the problem ran directly across our friends' property, about eight feet from their front door.

Our friends took their documents to the courthouse, where a clerk helped them look up their easements. There in the land records was a private easement, exactly where the pipe ran. The original owner (four owners back) had sold the easement to a previous owner of the neighboring house. None of the current owners had known of it.

The plumbers found, after digging up both yards and the driveway with a backhoe, that the neighbor's pipe was substandard and had been crushed by roots from a large tree belonging to our friends. Luckily, the neighbor's liability insurance paid for replacing the pipe, the yard, and the driveway. If the pipe had not been substandard and our friends' tree had been the sole cause of the damage, they might have been liable for the whole mess because they had interfered with the easement.

Easements by Necessity

Even if it isn't written down, a legal easement usually exists if it's absolutely necessary to cross someone's land for a legitimate purpose. The law grants people a right of access to their homes, for example. So if the only access to a piece of land is by crossing through a neighbor's property, the law recognizes an easement allowing access over the neighbor's land. This is called an "easement by necessity." When land is subject to such an easement, the landowner may not interfere with the neighbor's legal right.

It's easy for a dispute to arise between neighbors when someone buys property without knowing about this kind of easement across it. For example, a new owner may discover that the neighbor is using what the owner believed was a private drive for access to her own property. The new buyer puts up a locked gate and soon finds himself in court. If you find yourself in such a dispute, either as the neighbor with the private drive or the one who needs it, and you can't work out some sort of agreement, see a local property lawyer.

In fact, if you become embroiled in any escalating easement problem that appears to be headed for the courthouse, consult a local attorney who has experience with real estate problems. The doctrines of unwritten easements that are created by people's actions and certain circumstances can be very complicated. The laws vary from state to state, and you may need more tailor-made advice than can be given in this book.

Easements Acquired by Use of Property

Someone can acquire an easement over another's land for a particular purpose by using the land hostilely, openly, and continuously for a set period of time. These terms are explained in "Requirements for Obtaining Land by Adverse Possession," above. The length of use required varies from state to state and is often the same—ten or 20 years—as that for adverse possession (acquiring ownership of land by occupying it). An easement acquired in this way is called a "prescriptive easement."

Comparing Prescriptive Easements and Adverse Possession

Depending on the circumstances and on state law, someone who uses another's property may eventually gain ownership of the property (by adverse possession) or gain the right to use part of the property for a particular purpose (prescriptive easement).

To gain ownership of someone else's land, a trespasser must occupy it hostilely, openly, exclusively, and continuously for a certain period of time set by state law. Some states require that the trespasser also pay the property taxes on the land during the period.

The requirements are much the same for a prescriptive easement: The trespasser must use (as opposed to occupy) the land hostilely, openly, exclusively, and continuously for the required period of time. For instance, if the trespasser abandons the use for several years and then goes back to it, the element of continuity is missing, and no easement is created. If a prescriptive easement is challenged in court and one of the elements is missing, there is no easement.

But there are also important differences. First, payment of property taxes is never necessary for a successful prescriptive easement claim. In states that require a trespasser to pay property taxes to obtain ownership, courts will grant the trespasser a prescriptive easement, but not ownership, when all requirements have been met except paying the taxes.

Also, to acquire a prescriptive easement a trespasser does not need to be the only one using the land. A trespasser can gain the easement when others are also using the property—even the owner. It follows that more than one person can acquire a prescriptive easement in the same portion of land.

EXAMPLE: One of the most common ways in which several neighbors gain a prescriptive easement is by using a driveway or road on another's land for many years without being challenged by the owner. This was the result in a Washington state case when neighbors treated a driveway as their own for 40 years, finally expanding it into a road. When the owner tried to reclaim the area, the court ruled in favor of the neighbors—they had established a legal right to the road by prescriptive easement.[8]

Courts sometimes appear more willing to grant a prescriptive easement than actual ownership (through adverse possession) to a trespasser. The results are far less drastic for the owner. The easement does not take away the ownership of the property; it only requires the owner to allow the particular use of the property by somebody else.

On the flip side, courts also do not like wasting property. When an easement results in the nonuse of the land by either the easement owner or the actual owner, the court will interfere.

EXAMPLE: Two neighbors in Maryland built fences that blocked access to 20 feet of easement property. The court ordered the two fences removed to allow the easement owners the right to use the easement for the purpose intended, which was access to land. The court's order also gave the other property owner the right to use the property as long as he did not interfere with the easement.[9]

Researching Prescriptive Easements

To understand how the courts in your state have interpreted different requirements, check your state's court decisions on prescriptive easements. (See Chapter 18.)

Establishing a Prescriptive Easement

Typically, a prescriptive easement is created when someone uses land for access, such as a driveway or beach path or shortcut. But many times, a neighbor has simply begun using a part of the adjoining property. The neighbor may have farmed it or even have built on it. After the time requirement is met, the trespasser gains a legal right to use the property in the same manner as it has been used for the statutory period.

Public Easements

When the trespassing is done by the public, a public right to use property can be created. It is often called an "implied dedication" instead of a prescriptive easement. A public dedication is often created if an owner allows the city or county to make improvements or maintain a portion of the owner's land.[10] For example, the owner of beachfront property may let the county pave a private drive, which is used by many people for access to the beach. The public would then gain a right to use the drive.

When disputes over prescriptive easements find their way into court, judges vary on what kind of use of property justifies creation of an easement. Some courts find that simply using a strip of land regularly for a shortcut is enough for a prescriptive easement. But some are very reluctant to grant rights on someone else's land unless the use is substantial.

Blocking Acquisition of a Prescriptive Easement

Methods of removing intruders from property are discussed in "Trespassers Who Become Owners," above. If you don't mind someone's using part of your property but don't want the person to gain the legal right to do so, the simplest way to prevent a prescriptive easement is to grant permission to use the property.

Permission of the owner to use property cancels a trespasser's claim to a prescriptive easement. If your neighbor is parking his car on a small strip of your property and you give him permission to do so, he is no longer a trespasser, and he can't try to claim an easement by prescription. Giving permission to a current user also prevents neighbors who move in later from claiming they have inherited a prescriptive easement.

Sometimes, your permission can even be implied. For example, if you allow a neighbor to use your property because you are on friendly terms, your implied permission is called "neighborly accommodation." This implied consent based on a friendly relationship is only between you and that neighbor—not anyone else, including later owners.

EXAMPLE 1: A new owner of property in Washington, D.C., went to court and tried to claim an easement across a neighbor's yard because the neighbor had allowed the former owner to cross the property. The court ruled that he had no right to use the property because the friendship between the previous owner and the neighbor created a limited implied permission.[11]

EXAMPLE 2: A court in Ohio found an implied permission from neighborly accommodation when the neighbor had used a private road for access for over 40 years. When the property was sold, the new owner had no right to the road.[12]

Relying on implied permission, or even oral permission, however, is not a wise idea for protection in the future. You could still end up in court having to let a judge interpret your intentions.

The safest way to protect your property interest when you do give someone permission is to put the terms in writing. An agreement similar to the one an owner may use to prevent adverse possession can be used for easements. (See "Agreement Granting Permission to Use Property," above.) If several neighbors use a strip of your property, you should draw up a permission agreement for each one to sign.

When the public is using a section of your property, you can post signs granting permission. In some states, such as California, posting these signs at every entrance and at certain intervals protects the owner from claims of a prescriptive easement.[13]

Depending on posted signs alone for protection, however, is always risky. If possible, take a further step: Put your permission for the public in writing, take it down to the courthouse, and record it (file a copy) in the county land records. California has statutes providing for this procedure;[14] check at your local courthouse to see whether or not it's allowed in your area. Recording the permission makes it part of the public record and available for anyone to check. ●

Endnotes

1 The name of this rule was established in the case of *Preble v. Maine Cent. R.R.*, 85 Me. 260, 27 A. 149 (1893). But that case was overruled in 2006, and the Maine rule is no longer the rule in Maine. *Dombkowski v. Ferland*, 893 A.2d 599 (2006).

2 *Anderson v. Holliday,* 65 Ark. App. 165, 986 S.W.2d 116 (1999).

3 *French v. Pierce*, 8 Conn. 439 (1831).

4 Helmholz, *Adverse Possession and Subjective Intent*, 61 Wash. U.L.Q. 331, at 339 (1983).

5 *Carpenter v. Ruperto*, 315 N.W.2d 782 (Iowa 1982).

6 *Norwood v. City of New York*, 95 Misc. 2d 55, 406 N.Y.S.2d 256 (1978).

7 *McCann v. City of Los Angeles*, 79 Cal. App. 3d 112, 144 Cal.Rptr. 696 (1978).

8 *Curtis v. Zuch,* 829 P.2d 187 (Wash. App. 1992); but see *Williams Place LLC., v. State ex. Rel. Dept. of Transp.*, 384 P.3d. 797 (2015).

9 *Miller v. Kirkpatrick,* 377 Md. 335, 833 A.2d 536 (Md. 2003).

10 For examples of the public gaining a right to use private property, see *County of Los Angeles v. Berk*, 26 Cal. 3d 201, 161 Cal.Rptr. 742, 605 P.2d 381 (1980), *cert. denied*, 101 S.Ct. 111, 449 U.S. 836, 66 L.Ed.2d 43 (1980); *Brumbaugh v. Imperial County*, 134 Cal. App. 3d 556, 184 Cal.Rptr. 11 (1982).

11 *Chaconas v. Meyers*, 465 A. 2d 379 (D.C. App. 1983); see also *Mavromoustakos v. Padussis*, 112 Md. App. 59 (1996).

12 *McCune v. Brandon,* 621 N.E.2d 434 (Ohio App. 1993).

13 Cal. Civ. Code § 1008.

14 Cal. Civ. Code § 813.

Fences

Good fences make good neighbors.

—Robert Frost

I n the United States, no law requires us to place fences on or around our lands; the right to "let the land lie" is an old one. But most people do choose to enclose their properties for various reasons.

Look about you, wherever you live, at the neat wooden fence, the enduring stone wall, the practical chain link, the ornate wrought iron, the traditional white picket fence complete with climbing roses. They are often fascinating reflections of the personalities of the residents. In rural areas, one finds practical fences over farmland and imaginative, expressive ones along houses.

Rural Areas: Fencing Livestock In or Out

Almost all states have fence statutes designed to protect livestock and also to protect people and property from the damage that livestock can do. These laws take two forms, called open range and closed range. States choose one pattern or the other, although some states also allow counties to make their own choices.

Open Range

In an open-range area, animals are allowed to wander, and it is the responsibility of neighbors to protect their properties by erecting fences to keep them out. Someone who doesn't put up a fence cannot, legally, blame a neighbor whose animals damage the unfenced property.

A landowner can protect him- or herself from straying livestock by building a fence that meets construction standards set out in state or local laws. Then, if the neighbor's cows, for example, break a farmer's fence and harm the crops, the farmer can sue the cattle's owner if the farmer's fence was built according to those standards. State fence laws often describe in detail what is required for such a "lawful fence." These regulations can get pretty specific, demanding certain types of wire, certain heights, even certain placement of posts.

Sometimes in open-range areas, however, custom is more powerful than a state statute. It is not uncommon for a livestock owner to assume responsibility for damage done by the owner's animals, regardless of the law.[1]

In the 19th century, most states chose open-range laws.

Researching Fence Laws

In any rural area, if you are concerned about liability for damage from livestock, you need to know exactly what your state or county fence law says. State laws are easy to find; look under "fences" in the index to the state statutes, which are available on the Internet or at a county law library (in or near the courthouse). You can also find the local ordinances on fences at one of these libraries or at the public library. (See Chapter 18.)

Closed Range

In closed-range areas, it is the responsibility of the animal owner to keep livestock enclosed or be liable for damage they do.

In some closed-range states, an animal's owner is liable for damage it causes, no matter what type of fencing the owner erects.

In other states, if the fence is lawful—that is, it meets the requirements set out in the statute or local ordinance—the owner is protected from liability if the animals break out. Missouri, for instance, a closed-range state, sets out detailed descriptions of what is required to create a proper fence to hold animals.[2] Closed-range statutes often refer to lawful fences as "livestock tight."

A livestock owner who has a lawful fence may, however, have to pay for damages if the fence is obviously inadequate for what it's being used for. An example would be an owner who acquires a large, raging bull with a penchant for breaking down and destroying everything in its path. If the owner realizes (or ought to realize) that a standard fence is not sufficient, the owner is expected to take reasonable steps to prevent damage to neighbors.

Urban Fences

Most of us don't have the pleasure of country living, so state fence laws don't affect us directly. Exceptions are boundary fences—see "Property Line (Boundary) Fences," below—or spite fences erected to annoy the neighbors, both of which are often regulated by state law (see Chapter 12). Urban fences, by contrast, are governed by local law and increasingly by rules of subdivisions or planned unit developments.

Local Laws

City and county fence ordinances in most urban and suburban areas can be amazingly strict and detailed. Most regulate height and location, and some also control the material used and even the appearance of a fence. Many cities require a building permit to construct a fence at all.

These fence regulations apply to all types of fences—any structure used as an enclosure, barrier, or partition. Usually, they include hedges and trees.

In reality, however, local fence laws are usually loosely enforced, if at all. Cities are not in the business of sending around fence inspection teams, and most localities contain lots of fence violations that no one has complained about. As long as nobody else minds and no one complains, a nonconforming fence may stand forever.

Also, what may have started out perfectly legal may later violate the law. For example, a nice little hedge fence may grow into a 15-foot natural wall. If both neighbors like it, nothing is ever said, and there it stands.

Before you complain about a neighbor's recently erected monstrosity (or one that is going up before your eyes), read your local fence ordinances carefully to see whether the neighbor is breaking the law. It's a wise idea to do the same thing if you are unsure of whether your own plans for a new fence comply with local law. Laws that affect fences may be found in the zoning ordinances, building codes, or under miscellaneous rules. (See Chapter 18 for more on looking up your local laws.)

Below are some of the types of restrictions found in the local laws.

Maximum Heights

Almost all towns place height restrictions on fences. In residential areas, local rules commonly restrict artificial (constructed) backyard fences to a height of six feet. In front yards, the limit is often four feet. Maximums vary, but front-yard height limits, especially, are usually low. Some people use creative methods to try to get around height limits. One homeowner was cited for building a back fence around his pool that exceeded the six-foot height limit in his city. His solution? Pile topsoil around the base of the fence, cover it with a layer of sod, and call it the ground—thereby "lowering" the height of the fence to comply with the city limit.

General fence height restrictions may apply to natural fences—fences of bushes or trees—whether or not they are specifically mentioned, if they meet the ordinance's general definition of a fence. Whether trees and bushes are considered fences depends on the location of the trunks, the language of the ordinance, and whether or not they are actually used as a fence. When natural fences are singled out in the laws, the height restrictions commonly range from five to eight feet.[3]

> **EXAMPLE:** A fellow in Washington state had 13 Douglas fir trees on the border of his property. He called them "yard landscaping." His neighbor complained, probably because of a blocked view, and the town sued the owner of the trees to comply with its fence ordinance. The court called the trees a fence, which under the local town ordinance was restricted to eight feet. The particular regulation in this case contained the language "naturally grown or constructed," so it applied to the Douglas firs. The man had to cut them.[4]

Setback Requirements

Most local fence laws contain what is called a setback rule, requiring fences to be set back a certain distance from the street or sidewalk, sometimes with special rules for corner properties. This is to provide the city room to maintain its own property, and also to promote public safety. If the location of the fence poses a danger—creates a blind driveway or diminishes visibility at an intersection, for example—it can not only interfere with the use of someone else's property but also can be a hazard to the general public.

Prohibited Materials

As long as a fence is made of materials that pose no threat of harm to neighbors or those passing by, the materials used probably don't violate any law. Occasionally, however, a town planning board approves only certain types of new fences—such as board fences—in an attempt to create a harmonious architectural look. Subdivisions also often restrict the kinds of fences allowed. (See "Subdivision Rules," below.)

Some towns prohibit the use of certain materials—for example, electrically charged or barbed-wire fences. And even without such a specific law, if a fence is made of unsound material or so poorly constructed that it is an eyesore or a danger, it may be prohibited by another law, such as a blighted property ordinance. (See "Appearance," below.)

There is a dreadful case from Texas that is an argument for the prohibition of barbed wire in a residential neighborhood. In this instance, the developer of a subdivision used barbed wire to fence off the remaining unimproved land from the property already sold. The result was a barbed-wire fence at the back of a yard occupied by a family with children.

After four children were injured on separate occasions and the developer ignored the complaints, the homeowner ripped down the fence. The developer sued him for willful trespass and the removal of the fence. The court found itself having to award punitive damages to the developer because the barbed wire was a legal fence.[5] Punitive damages are an extra sum of money, sometimes quite high, that the wrongdoer must pay as punishment.

We probably all agree who the real wrongdoer was in this situation, but the homeowner was the one guilty of trespass and destruction of someone else's property. We can only hope that this community now has an ordinance against dangerous fences.

Appearance

Unlike subdivision restrictions (see "Subdivision Rules," below), local laws usually do not dictate what a fence must look like. There are rare exceptions, such as in the city of Albany, California, where an ordinance requires all new structures to have colors that are "visually harmonious with the surrounding neighborhood."[6] (The ordinance doesn't say what colors are harmonious.)

But in most places, owners are free to choose how their fences look. Occasionally, an eccentric owner puts up such an ugly fence that the neighbors hope it's against the law because of its appearance. A hideous fence could reflect an intent to annoy a neighbor, and if it's useless to the owner, it may be an illegal spite fence. (See Chapter 12.) But unless it is a true spite fence or violates a height restriction or some other law, if you are the unfortunate neighbor who has to look at a fence painted like a psychedelic leopard, you probably can't do anything about it. You may not impose your own aesthetic values on someone else. Conformity with the community must be balanced with a person's freedom to use his or her property in a reasonable manner.

> EXAMPLE 1: In a California case, one neighbor was unhappy when another erected a plain board fence. He sued, accusing the builder of trying to annoy him by building an ugly fence. The judge refused to set up any aesthetic standards for fences and suggested that such action without a particular ordinance would be a luxury and indulgence not within the government's power.[7] Judging from the language of the decision, if the fence had been painted bright purple, it probably would have made no difference.

> EXAMPLE 2: The question of color did come up when a property owner, disgruntled after a nasty tree dispute, built a six-foot wooden fence between him and his neighbor. The side of the fence facing the neighbor boasted bright orange vinyl strips and orange construction material. When the neighbor sued, the judge left it standing, noting the courts' unwillingness to be arbiters of proper aesthetics and good taste. The fence-builder also erected a ten-foot bird house made out of a toilet seat. The judge let it stand as well, even though it could be "the ugliest bird house in Indiana or merely a toilet seat on a post."[8]

Disrepair

The appearance of a fence does matter in one particular situation—when it is not maintained and becomes a real eyesore. Some local ordinances don't allow what they call "blighted property" that decreases the value of surrounding property. A deteriorated fence falls into this category. A crumbling stone wall, a sagging chain link fence, or a broken or graffiti-covered board fence may all be blighted property, depending on the particular ordinance.

Dangerous Fences

A dilapidated fence can violate more than a blighted property law if it poses a risk of harm. There may be an ordinance prohibiting an owner from allowing a dangerous condition to exist on his or her property. If a fence has old rusty nails or sharp broken wires protruding into a neighbor's yard or public sidewalk, it may pose harm to others. And a fence can be dangerous if it is a retaining wall—if it becomes unsound, the property it holds back might slide into the neighbor's driveway.

What to Do

If your neighbor's fence does not comply with the law and it creates a problem for you, tell the neighbor as soon as possible. The neighbor probably doesn't know what the law is, and if the fence is still in the building stage it may be possible to make modifications at a low cost.

If the neighbor suggests that you mind your own business, then you can alert the city. All it takes in most circumstances is a phone call to the appropriate office—usually the planning or zoning department or the city attorney's office. The neighbor who is in violation of an ordinance will be given a written notification of violation and asked to conform. The city can impose a fine and even sue the person to force compliance (unless the fence is exempt from the law for one of the reasons discussed in "Exceptions to Local Laws," below).

A very slight violation will not usually be enough to trigger any help from the city or county authorities. When a fence doesn't quite comply with a local ordinance, the enforcement officials probably won't want to get involved. And if a neighbor or the city does sue, a court may look to see if there is "substantial compliance" with the ordinance. If part of a fence is a few inches too high, for example, but most of it fits the ordinance, the builder can be said to have substantially complied with the law. Courts are not usually willing to order a whole fence removed because of an insignificant violation.

If you are bothered by a neighbor's fence that seriously violates a law and the city or town won't help you, you can sue the neighbor. If it's money you're after, you can sue in small claims court to compensate for your loss of enjoyment of your property caused by the offending fence. Unfortunately, the fence will stay up, although if it is a constant annoyance to you, you can sue more than once. A few states' small claims courts do not hear cases involving fences. (See Chapter 20 for more on small claims court.)

If you want the fence removed, you probably must sue in regular trial court where, unlike small claims court, a judge can issue an order (usually called an injunction) to accomplish this. (Some small claims courts issue injunctions; see Chapter 20.) Taking this route will probably require hiring a lawyer. And be aware that the judge will look for the least drastic remedy—such as removal of a small portion of the fence.

The Importance of Complaining Promptly

Enforcing fence laws is never a high priority for city governments. So if you want the city's help, complain as soon as a disturbing fence goes up or you move into a new house next to an annoying violation. The city may enforce the law at any time, but if a complaining neighbor doesn't bother to speak up for a good long time, the situation will likely be on the bottom of the list of priorities.

And if you eventually bring a lawsuit, a judge will have little sympathy for someone who sat by and did nothing to protect his or her property while the offending fence was being built; you might even lose your case because of your delay.

Exceptions to Local Laws

There are a few situations in which a fence that appears to violate a local ordinance is perfectly legal.

Fences Built With Permits for Variances

Someone who needs to build a fence that violates a fence law—for instance, to screen a house from a noisy or unsightly neighboring use, such as a busy highway or a gas station—can apply to the city for a one-time exception to the fence law. The exception is called a variance. The ordinances explain how to apply for a variance, what kind of notice must be given to neighbors, when a hearing will be held, and who makes the final determination.

Once you make a variance application, the city usually posts a sign on the property to alert the neighbors that a variance has been requested. In some towns, the request is also published in the local newspaper. After a certain period of time, the city holds a hearing on the request. A neighbor who wishes to object can do so at the hearing. If the city decides that the variance is justified, it will grant it. Unless the variance is limited to a specific time period, it's permanent. So someone who moves in later can't complain about a fence that was already built with a variance.

Pointers to Follow When Seeking a Variance

- Be reasonable about your needs.
- Talk to the neighbors before you do anything else, to explain your problem and get them on your side. If you don't have support lined up before a notice is posted in your yard, someone may fear any change at all and try to organize objections.
- Work with the city zoning department staff so they understand the situation and are likely to recommend in your favor.

EXAMPLE: Stephanie runs a day care center in her home. The house is located near a busy street, and she fears for the children, who can easily scale her legal three-foot front fence. She applies to the city for a variance, a permit to allow a five-foot fence. The notice is posted, nobody objects, and the city planning commission grants the variance. Stephanie builds her five-foot fence, legally.

Fences Built Before the Law Was Passed

If a fence that is in violation of an ordinance existed before the law was passed, the city will probably allow it to remain. However, when the time comes to replace it, normally the new fence must conform to current regulations. If it doesn't, the city can step in and enforce the law, or a neighbor can sue for conformity.

This issue can arise when trees are used as a fence and are replaced with an artificial fence. For example, when one fellow in New York tried to replace a 12-foot natural fence with a six-foot board fence, he learned only after he had erected the fence that the local height limit was four feet. A neighbor sued, and the court ordered him to lower it.[9]

Subdivision Rules

House deeds in planned unit developments and subdivisions often restrict the owners' freedom to erect fences by dictating the materials to be used, maintenance, and maximum heights. This is done to ensure uniformity and adherence to design standards in the subdivision. People who buy property in the subdivision obligate themselves to abide by these restrictions.

If the restrictions are simple and very few in number, they may be in the deed itself—for instance, if the only restriction is that the property must be used for a single-family dwelling. However, when they are elaborate—and most are—the deed refers to a separate document usually called the covenants, conditions, and restrictions (CC&Rs). Fence regulations are usually found in these CC&Rs, a copy of which can be obtained from the homeowners' association.

If one member of the group does not follow the rules, a homeowners' association or an affected neighbor can sue to enforce the terms of the deed. Before the association brings a lawsuit, it usually tries a number of less drastic tactics to get the owner to come around. For example, it may revoke the recalcitrant owner's right to use common areas, such as swimming pools or tennis courts.

EXAMPLE: Rhonda buys a house in a planned subdivision. Her deed tells her that the use of her property is subject to the terms of the CC&Rs. In the CC&Rs are these restrictions: "Nor shall any backyard fence exceed six feet in height nor any fence in front of a house exceed four feet." Rhonda apparently thinks that nobody will care when she builds an eight-foot fence around her house to "ensure my privacy." The homeowners' association notifies her in writing that she is violating her deed restrictions. When she doesn't respond to repeated warnings, the association sues her for an order to remove four feet of the fence in front and two feet in back. If there were no association with enforcement powers, other homeowners, who are bound by the terms of the CC&Rs, could sue her directly for the same order.

Property Line (Boundary) Fences

A boundary fence is a fence that is located on the line between two properties and is used by both owners. It may also be called a division fence or a partition fence. A fence on a boundary line is subject to all the state and local laws that control fence height, materials, and so on. In addition, almost every state has a myriad of other laws specifically addressing boundary fences.

Who Owns What

Unless the property owners agree otherwise, fences on a boundary line are owned by both owners when both are using the fence. Neither may remove it without the other's permission. When either property is sold, the new owner purchases the shared ownership of the fence.

Co-Ownership Under the Law

Normally, the key to who owns a boundary fence, according to the law, is who uses the fence. A fence on the boundary, built and used by only one owner, belongs to the builder. It does not become a real boundary fence unless the other neighbor actually uses it as his or her own fence.

The concept of fence "use" is a unique jungle of definitions. Suffice it to say that a commonsense guess as to what the term means may well be wrong. Here is how "use" is legally interpreted in different states:

- A few states interpret use as occupancy. For example, Pennsylvania refers to using the land up to the fence[10]—such as planting crops or putting in a yard bordered by the fence.
- Other states, such as Tennessee, Utah, and Wisconsin, use the term "join" for use—a neighbor who hooks up another fence to the boundary fence is using the boundary fence.
- Most states interpret use more narrowly—a fence is used by a landowner only when the landowner's property is entirely enclosed, for example, by hooking up other fencing to the boundary fence.
- Some states do not define use at all.

> **EXAMPLE:** If Amy has neighbors' fences on two sides of her property but has nothing across the other two sides, under the enclosure rule followed by most states, she is not using the neighbors' fences and they are not boundary fences. If she fences the front and the back, and her property is then enclosed, the side fences become boundary fences.

A person who encloses property by using part of a neighbor's fence probably owes the neighbor some money. (See "Paying a Neighbor for the Fence," below.)

If you need to know whether or not a fence is a boundary fence, you should look up your state's fence law. There are not only variations among the states on what constitutes use of a fence but also ambiguities in other terms. If a statute refers only to "partition fences" and not boundary fences or division fences by name, it may be talking about a plain division fence, or it could mean a different legal animal—a fence erected as a result of a court order dividing one property into several parcels.

Appendix C lists the state boundary fence laws. You can look up the law at your local county law library or on the Internet. If the statutes themselves are unclear, you can try to find some judges' decisions on fence cases in your state. (See Chapter 18 to learn more about doing legal research.)

In states that have no statewide boundary fence statutes, local law may define boundary fences and create the joint ownership in the same ways that the statutes do. A few states exempt municipal areas from the state statute anyway and allow towns to regulate boundary fences as they choose. If there are local laws, they will probably be in the town's building code. You can check with city hall, at the public library, or on the Internet for your specific ordinance. The local ordinances will likely contain lots of fence regulations that apply to all fences, including boundary fences. However, special rules for these particular fences will refer by name to them as either boundary, partition, or division fences. (On how to find local ordinances, see Chapter 18.)

Regulations in the house deeds in subdivisions and planned unit developments may also specifically address boundary fences. These can be more explicit than the statutes, for instance, apportioning the building costs between owners. If you live in one of these restricted areas, check your CC&Rs.

Fences on Agreed Boundary Lines

Neighbors are often unsure of exactly where the boundary between their properties is, and surveys are expensive. Fortunately, you don't need to locate the precise boundary line to have a jointly-owned boundary fence.

If the deed, map, or plat of your property is confusing, and you are unable to determine the property line, you and your neighbor can simply agree that a fence—one you build or an existing one—marks the boundary. This is called an "agreed boundary." Certain requirements must be met: The line must be uncertain, both neighbors must agree that the fence is the line, and then both neighbors must treat the fence as the property boundary for a period of time. Once these requirements are fulfilled, the fence becomes the legal boundary line on the ground.

If you want to make such an agreement, it should be in writing and put on file (recorded) in the county land records office in case there is later any question about the boundary. (A sample agreement is in Chapter 9.)

Even without an explicit agreement, when two neighbors treat a fence as a boundary fence for a long period of time—for example, if both contribute to its maintenance for many years—it can become the legal boundary. (See Chapter 9 for a full discussion of agreed boundaries.)

A fence on an agreed boundary is subject to all the laws that affect any boundary fence. So when one of the properties is sold, the fence remains the boundary, and the new landowner buys mutual ownership of it along with the property.

You and your neighbor can also agree to co-own and maintain a fence that is not on the boundary line. (See "Sharing a Fence That Is Not on the Boundary," below.)

Fence Ownership Agreements Among Landowners

If neighbors don't want to share ownership of a boundary fence equally, as the law apportions it, they are free to make their own arrangements. For example, two property owners could agree that a boundary fence is to be the responsibility of only one of them or that its ownership is to be shared unequally.

In reality, the person who puts a fence up usually has a sense of ownership, takes care of it, and doesn't want the neighbors meddling with it. When purchasing property, it can be quite difficult to figure out who is responsible for what. In some areas, it is customary for the builder to have the unfinished side, the side with the stakes, facing in toward the builder's own property. In other areas, the smooth side faces in. Ask a real estate agent or the neighbors what the custom is in your area and whether there are any long-standing assumptions about fence ownership. Tradition and custom may be so strong that the law on the subject never comes up. If you try to rock the boat, you can find yourself an outcast in your own neighborhood.

Although it's unusual, neighbors can sometimes sign formal ownership agreements on boundary fences. In a few states—Vermont, for example —the statutes provide a procedure for placing written fence ownership agreements on public record (recording them). Once this is done, the agreement is not only binding on both owners but also on anyone who later buys the property.[11]

Most states don't have such a recording procedure, and any agreement you make is just between you and your neighbor. When your neighbor's property is sold, you will need an agreement with the new owner, or the statutes will dictate ownership of the fence between you and the new neighbor.

EXAMPLE: Jenny and Elmer are next-door neighbors who both plan to enclose their properties with fences. Jenny wants to simply unroll some chicken-wire and hold it up with a few posts. Elmer has grandiose plans to build a decorative wooden fence around his yard and wishes to maintain ownership of it. He also prefers that Jenny use this fence on her side and cringes at the thought of chicken-wire along his borders. Jenny and Elmer simply agree that the portion of wooden fence between their yards is Elmer's, even though Jenny uses it as a part of her enclosure. But the agreement is only between them. If one of them sells the property, the new owner will need a new agreement or they could assume, under state law, joint ownership of the elaborate wooden fence.

Paying a Neighbor for the Fence

If someone erects a fence on a boundary line, the fence remains that person's unless, or until, the neighbor uses the fence—which in most states means until the neighbor actually encloses her property. (See "Co-Ownership Under the Law," above.)

For example, if someone encloses her property using an existing fence on any side, most state fence laws require that she pay the other owner for the value of the fence. In other words, she must actually buy a share of the fence. Then she becomes a co-owner of the boundary fence. California describes this as a refund to the other owner of a just proportion of the value of the fence at that time. Many states set the required payment at one-half of the value of the existing fence to the other landowner.

Some boundary fence statutes appear to be intended only for farmers and ranchers. New York, for example, does not require landowners to pay anything to a neighbor for a boundary fence if the person enclosing has kept no livestock on the property for five years.[12] Minnesota provides town boards with the authority to exempt property when the land is less than 20 acres.[13]

In an urban setting, although the purposes of the statutes—such as retaining livestock—may not be applicable, the principle is the same. Many of us simply do not consider it fair to use someone else's property without compensation. In a suburb where backyards are neatly separated by fences, a new neighbor who encloses a yard using existing fences in compliance with local laws buys in to the fence.

> **EXAMPLE:** Claudia buys property that is unenclosed but bordered on either side with backyard fences erected by her neighbors. She builds a fence across the back and from her house to the sides, joining the other two. Her backyard is now enclosed, and she must compensate the neighbors who have given her the benefit of the fences already there. According to most state statutes, unless there is a different agreement, Claudia owes the respective neighbors one-half of the value of each of the portions of side fences she uses.

The state laws requiring a neighbor to pay for an existing fence are actually almost never enforced in urban areas because of tradition, implied agreements, and lack of awareness. But the statutes are there if someone wants to enforce them. In rural areas, where miles of fencing may be involved, laws are enforced more often.

If someone encloses his or her property by using a neighbor's fence, the statutes provide that the neighbor can demand a just proportion of the current value of the fence. The request for money must be a reasonable request. A fence owner should not expect to be paid a full 50% for an elaborate fence that the neighbor didn't choose. Sometimes the kind of fence that the owner can demand contribution for is set by statute—for example, wire fencing for rural land. Most likely, if a request is refused and the fence owner sues the neighbor for the money, the owner will receive a proportion of the value of the kind of fence most often used in the area.

Responsibility for Maintenance

Perhaps the most important aspect of boundary fences is that, unless agreed otherwise, both owners are mutually responsible for keeping a boundary fence in good repair.

State and Local Laws

State boundary fence statutes and most local ordinances place joint responsibility for maintenance on all co-owners of boundary fences, unless the owners work out their own agreement. For example, the Oklahoma statute says that adjoining owners are to equally maintain a boundary fence between them.[14] The requirements are pretty much the same across the country when there is a statute. If the fence needs fixing, the cost comes out of both pockets.

Some states impose special maintenance requirements on natural boundary fences—that is, those made of trees or hedges. For instance, Iowa demands that natural boundary fences be trimmed twice a year to a height of five feet unless a different agreement is made in writing between the neighbors and recorded (put on file) at the county land records office (usually at the courthouse).[15]

When There Is No Statute or Local Ordinance

In the few states that do not address fences in their laws, if there is also no local law on the subject, one neighbor can still ask the other to chip in for repair to a fence on the boundary that they both use. A neighbor who wants to pursue the matter all the way into a court could make two arguments to support mutual maintenance responsibilities. One is simply that the laws are so similar in all of the other states that they should be followed everywhere—a "law of the land" argument.

But secondly, and probably more important, is this: If two people use and benefit from the same fence, located on a property boundary, they should both be responsible for it. Unless they agree otherwise, the common use creates a mutual ownership. This is the logic behind the statutes—when you benefit from a fence, and it's on the boundary, you pay.

In states with no statutes, there may be some published court opinions on boundary fence responsibility. You can check in a law library or on the Internet for one that might help you understand your state's law. (See Chapter 18.)

Owners' Agreements

Even when two neighbors own a boundary fence together, one owner may want to be responsible for the fence's care. The neighbors may discuss this arrangement, or it may simply happen without anything ever being said. Especially if only one owner built the fence, that person may consider it solely owned and not want the neighbor bothering with it. Also, sometimes fences are used unequally; for instance, if a neighbor is using only a few feet of an extensive fence, the other may never expect payment for repair. And an owner who has children or a dog may be more interested in maintenance than the other.

These agreements are only between the current neighbors. Unless they are made part of the public land records (possible in very few states), when a new owner comes in, the old agreement is no longer in force.

Disputes Over Maintenance

Disputes usually occur when one neighbor thinks the fence needs repair or preventive maintenance, such as painting, and the other doesn't. A good general rule to follow is that the fence should be kept in such a condition that it enhances the value of both properties. If its appearance takes away from the property values, it needs repair. Following this rule will keep requests reasonable and objective.

If one owner refuses to cooperate in reasonable maintenance of a boundary fence, the other can fix the fence and demand reimbursement of the other's share. If the neighbor won't pay up, the neighbor who has fixed the fence can sue the other in small claims court under the state boundary fence statute unless the state does not allow fence cases in small claims court. (See Chapter 20.)

A few states have harsh penalties for refusing to chip in for maintenance after a reasonable request is made by the other owner. Connecticut, for example, allows one neighbor to go ahead and repair, and then sue the other owner for double the cost.[16]

Negotiating With the Neighbor

If you are faced with a recalcitrant neighbor, first try to work something out. The other owner may not really have noticed how bad the situation has become. If simply pointing out the problem doesn't work, write a letter like the one below.

Sample Letter: Repairing a Boundary Fence

4501 Cypress Road
Springdale, CA 92345

Aug. 15, 20xx

Dear Alice,

As I mentioned to you last week, the boundary fence between our properties is in terrible need of repair. Four of the main posts appear to be completely rotten at the bottom and several boards are broken. According to the state law that I have enclosed, we are mutually responsible for the maintenance of this fence.

I have obtained the enclosed estimate of $300 for having the necessary work done. Your share is $150. Please contact me so that we may proceed.

Sincerely yours,

Nelson

Nelson

If Nelson's request is ignored or refused, he should get out his camera and take some pictures of the fence that clearly show the state of disrepair. It would also be a good idea to get at least two estimates for the cost of the work, to be certain that the charge is reasonable. If Alice is determined to avoid her responsibility, Nelson can now fix the fence and demand her share of the cost. Afterwards, he should write another letter like the one below.

Sample Letter: Reimbursement for Fence Repair

4501 Cypress Road
Springdale, CA 92345

Aug. 30, 20xx

Dear Alice,

   I did not receive a reply from you to my letter dated _____, and so I have had the necessary repair work done on our boundary fence. Enclosed is the bill for $300. Please send your share of this amount, $150, to me promptly, or I will have to take the matter to small claims court.

Sincerely yours,

Nelson

Nelson

What Nelson has just written is called a demand letter. If he gets no response, he can sue Alice for the money and show this letter—along with all the written documents and pictures—to the judge.

Using Mediation

Before going to court, it's usually a good idea to seek help first from a mediator, an impartial third person who is trained to help you and your neighbor work out a solution yourselves. This is far less expensive and emotional than a court battle. Neighbors can often work out an agreement in mediation that both solves the current situation and heads off future trouble. (See Chapter 19 on how to use mediation.) If you and your neighbor don't work something out, with or without a mediator, a stranger (in other words, a judge) will end up telling you what you can and cannot do with your own property. Remember, the purpose of a fence is to prevent problems between neighbors, not create them.

Going to Local Authorities

Most boundary fence laws contain detailed methods of enforcement. Many statutes across the country—from Vermont to Indiana to Wisconsin—provide for "fence viewers" to come out and inspect the property and make recommendations as to who owes what. These viewers are usually ordinary citizens appointed by a constable, the sheriff, or another local official. The decision of the viewers is binding on the neighbors, although it can be appealed to a court.

Many people have never heard of fence viewers. Before you file a lawsuit against your neighbor, check with your local sheriff or constable or at city hall to see whether you can use this method in your area.

If you go to the office in charge of the fence viewers and make a complaint, the fence viewers will not only consider whether the fence needs repair at all but whether the amount sought by the neighbor is reasonable. If the viewers decide in favor of the one complaining, the uncooperative neighbor can be ordered to contribute a fair share of the cost of the maintenance, or risk a fine.

> **EXAMPLE:** The wooden boundary fence between Leslie's and Tony's houses has been sagging for a couple of years. Tony has propped up a few boards with stakes and considers the fence okay. Leslie wants to replace the sagging boards but Tony refuses to help. Leslie learns that her state statute has a fence viewer procedure, so she goes to city hall and fills out a complaint about the fence. The viewers come out, inspect the property, and issue a decision that the boards are rotten—and that Tony and Leslie are to split the cost of replacing them. Tony can either pay up or risk being sued by Leslie—and if he loses, he may have to pay an extra penalty. Even if he wants to go to the trouble of appealing to a judge, he will not likely win because the objective decision of the viewers is a very strong argument in Leslie's favor.

Disputes Over Boundaries

If you or your neighbor are putting up a fence, pay close attention to boundary lines. Don't make the mistake of putting up a fence on what you think is the boundary if it could be on the neighbor's property.

The neighbor can sue you for trespass and ask for money damages and removal of the fence. You might not even get to keep the fence materials. This is true even if you thought you were on your own land.[17]

If your neighbor starts to erect a fence on what you think is your property, do not stand by without objection. As soon as you see a fence being built, ask the neighbor to please stop until you can reach an agreement or have a survey done. (For more information on determining boundary lines, see Chapter 9.)

A talk with the neighbor or a letter may be all that is necessary, especially if a mistake is involved. However, these circumstances are serious; be ready to hire an attorney if you are ignored. If the fence is entirely on your property, you have the right to tear it down or take the neighbor to court to have it removed. If you do nothing, you could be giving away part of your property or the right to use it after a certain amount of time. (See the sections on adverse possession and prescriptive easements in Chapter 10.)

The Case of the Yo-Yo Fence

Two neighbors in Oregon disagreed on the location of the boundary line. One went ahead and put up a fence where he believed he was within his legal rights. He erected the fence in the daytime, and his neighbor took it down at night. The builder tried again and the same thing happened. This up-and-down scenario was completed six times before the neighbors went to court. The behavior of these neighbors is all the more amazing because this was no backyard dispute; 40 acres of land were involved— lots and lots of fencing.

The court found that the fence builder was within his rights and was on his own property. Every inch of fence that he erected was entirely proper, and his neighbor had no right whatsoever to take it down. The neighbor was found guilty of willful trespass and had to pay punitive damages (an extra fine to punish the wrongdoing) for the continuous destruction he had accomplished under the cover of darkness.[18]

Of course, don't go tearing down your neighbor's new fence unless you are absolutely certain of the true boundary and have already asked the neighbor to take it down. If you're faced with this type of situation, the cost of a survey may be well worth it.

Sharing a Fence That Is Not on the Boundary

If you want to use a fence slightly over on another's property, or if your neighbor wishes to share yours, be careful unless you want to make the fence the legal boundary. Write down your agreement, setting out your intentions in detail. Include the expenses and duties of each of you, and clearly state that use of the fence and land is by permission of the owner only and that the agreement conveys no right of land ownership or permanent right of use. You might want to check with a local land use lawyer to be sure that your agreement covers everything that is necessary.

This type of agreement binds only the signers, not future purchasers. Should you later sell the house, you can show the agreement to the prospective buyer (or the buyer's title insurance company), who may be confused when comparing the description of the property with the location of the fence.

Stating your intentions clearly in writing is important for another reason: This fence is not a real boundary fence. Unlike a real division fence, for which a new owner is responsible for a share of the maintenance and prohibited from removing the fence without permission of the other owner, this kind of fence won't involve future neighbors in the rights or responsibilities of co-ownership.

Of course, you or your neighbor can always sell a small strip of land along the fence to the other. This must be in writing and recorded (filed with the county property office) because it does change the boundary line and conveys the ownership of land. (See Chapter 9.) ●

Endnotes

1 Custom is one of the topics of a fascinating study of ranchers in Shasta County, California, described in Ellickson, *Of Coase and Cattle*, 38 Stan. Law Rev. 623 (1986). I recommend it not only to those interested in rural fence laws but to anyone who seeks to understand behavior between neighbors. It is available at larger law libraries.

2 Mo. Stat. Ann. § 272.220 and following.

3 For example, see *People v. Berlin*, 62 Misc. 2d 272, 307 N.Y.S.2d 96 (1970) (limit only six feet).

4 *Town of Clyde Hill v. Roisen,* 48 Wash. App. 769, 740 P.2d 378 (1987).

5 *Gardner v. Kerly*, 613 S.W.2d 795 (Tex. Civ. App. 1981).

6 Albany, Cal., Mun. Code § 20.100.50.

7 *Haehlen v. Wilson*, 11 Cal. App. 2d 437, 54 P.2d 62 (1936). This case, a spite fence case, was more complicated than just a question of the fence being ugly. However, appearance was an element of the neighbor's complaint and the court was forced to discuss it.

8 *Wernke v. Halas,* 600 N.E.2d 117 (Ind. App. 1992).

9 *Bornscheuer v. Corbett*, 175 N.Y.S.2d 913 (1958).

10 29 Pa. Cons. Stat. Ann. § 42.

11 Vt. Stat. Ann. tit. 24, § 3812. Also see R.I. Gen. Laws § 34-10-14; Wis. Stat. Ann. § 90.05.

12 N.Y. Town Law § 300.

13 Minn. Stat. Ann. § 344.011.

14 Okla. Stat. Ann. tit. 60, § 70.

15 Iowa Code Ann. § 359A.2.

16 Conn. Gen. Stat. Ann. § 47-51.

17 The rights of neighbors in this situation are discussed in a treatise called the *Restatement (Second) of Torts* § 164 (1977).

18 *Lemon v. Madden*, 216 Or. 539, 340 P.2d 977 (1959).

Spite Fences

Anybody can behave well when things are going smoothly.

—**George Bernard Shaw**

When next-door neighbors can't stand the sight of each other, or when small disagreements fester into open warfare, people no longer want to be neighbors. Because moving away is usually impractical, they sometimes choose the next-best thing. They build a high fence near the edge of their property, a fence that serves to put the neighbor out of sight and out of mind and, at the same time, has the added advantage of annoying and perhaps inconveniencing the neighbor. Such fences are aptly called "spite fences."

A fence builder who builds a fence to get back at a neighbor can easily go too far. The fence may be illegal under laws and regulations that limit fence height. And even if it isn't, if the fence meets the legal definition of a spite fence, the affected neighbor can sue the builder, have the fence removed or lowered, and receive money to compensate for his or her trouble.

General Restrictions on Fence Height

State and local laws regulate fences in general—their height, type, even their appearance. In addition, many subdivisions and planned communities have their own rules on fences. These laws and restrictions will take care of most fence complaints. (For more on fence height, see Chapter 11.)

The most useful rules, to someone annoyed by a neighbor's fence, are local ordinances that restrict fence height and sometimes dictate fence appearance within the city limits. For instance, if a neighbor's offending fence is unlawful under a local ordinance because it's too tall, you may get all the help you need from the city itself. Call the local zoning or planning office and ask what the rules say about fences. Or read your city's fence ordinances in the library or on the Internet. (See Chapter 18.)

Once you're clear on the law, tell the neighbor about it; delivering a copy of the ordinance is even better. If that doesn't produce results, notify the office of the city, county, or township attorney, depending on which ordinance is involved. An official will then warn the violator and demand conformity to the ordinance. If the neighbor doesn't conform, the city or county may impose a fine and even take the person to court.

Many subdivisions and planned unit developments have even stricter regulations on fence height and materials. These regulations are usually found in a document referred to in each property owner's deed called the covenants, conditions, and restrictions (CC&Rs). If someone violates a fence rule in the CC&Rs, pointing out the violation to the person may be all that is necessary. When a neighbor complains, the homeowners' association often takes action. It may begin by revoking privileges to use common areas, such as swimming pools. Some associations have the power to sue to enforce conformity to the regulations. One neighbor who is subject to the restrictions can also sue another directly to enforce the rules.

For more details on fence laws and regulations, see Chapter 11.

If a neighbor's fence isn't violating a local law or subdivision regulation, it may still be illegal under spite fence laws. For the most part, these laws trace their historical roots to a time when towns had not yet adopted local fence regulations. Even though spite fence law has been largely superseded in many communities by local or subdivision fence regulations, in some situations, the legal concept of the spite fence is still relevant. The rest of this chapter discusses these laws.

What Is a Spite Fence?

A spite fence is a fence that is erected to annoy or harm someone, and serves no reasonable purpose to the owner. Natural fences—trees and hedges—are not typically considered spite fences because they always serve some purpose to the owner.

If you are harmed or annoyed by a spite fence, you may be able to get relief under a state or local spite fence law, or if none exists, from a court under the common law theory of "private nuisance." If a court agrees with you that the fence is a spite fence, the judge can order its removal. It can also order the neighbor to compensate you for the interference with the use and enjoyment of your property. If your neighbor is in the process of building a spite fence, you can obtain a court order halting the work.

Spite Fence Laws

Several states have adopted laws defining spite fences. These laws create a presumption that a useless fence over a certain height, built to annoy a neighbor, is a nuisance to the neighbor. Under these laws, the neighbor has the right to sue the builder of such a fence on the legal ground that the fence is a nuisance.

Not all states have statutes on spite fences. Read Chapter 18 to learn how to research whether your state has a statute.

Spite Fence Statutes

In the states listed below, a fence over the designated height, built to annoy the adjoining neighbor, and with no reasonable use to the owner, is considered a spite fence and a private nuisance.

The definitions of spite fences in state statutes tend to be very similar. The differences are usually just the height that is allowed. California law, for example, states that a fence exceeding ten feet, built maliciously for the purpose of annoying an owner or occupant of adjoining property, is a private nuisance. Wisconsin and Massachusetts set the height at six feet. New Hampshire places the restriction at five feet.

A few states set no height limit and include all structures, not just fences. The Minnesota spite fence law says that a fence or any other structure, maliciously erected or maintained for purposes of annoying owners or occupants of adjoining property, is a private nuisance. In Connecticut, you can bring an action for the malicious erection of any structure that was intended to annoy or injure the use of your land.

Spite Fence Statutes	
State	**Statute**
California	Cal. Civ. Code § 841.4 (10 feet)
Connecticut	Conn. Gen. Stat. Ann. §§ 52-480, 52-570 (any height)
Indiana	Ind. Code § 32-26-10-1 (6 feet)
Maine	Me. Rev. Stat. tit. 17, § 2801 (6 feet)
Massachusetts	Mass. Gen. Laws Ann. ch. 49, § 21 (6 feet)
Minnesota	Minn. Stat. Ann. § 561.02 (any height)
New Hampshire	N.H. Rev. Stat. Ann. § 476:1 (5 feet)
New York	N.Y. Real Prop. Acts. Law § 843 (10 feet)
Pennsylvania	53 Pa. Const. Stat. § 15171 (4 feet)
Rhode Island	R.I. Gen. Laws § 34-10-20 (6 feet)
Vermont	Vt. Stat. Ann. tit. 24, § 3817 (any height)
Washington	Wash. Rev. Code Ann. § 7.40.030 (any height)
Wisconsin	Wis. Stat. Ann. § 844.10 (6 feet)

Spite fence laws can be very effective when a neighbor builds over the height limit. The neighbor may lower the fence as soon as he's told about the law or realizes he could be sued.

Even if your neighbor builds a spite fence that is under the height limit of your state spite fence law, you may still be able to sue the neighbor. Your options are discussed in the next section.

If No Spite Fence Law or Other Fence Law Applies

If a neighbor's offending fence doesn't violate any state statute, local fence law, or subdivision restriction, you can still sue the owner under the common law (written decisions in court cases). The legal theory is that the fence is a nuisance—an unreasonable interference with another's ability to enjoy property. Malicious creation and maintenance of a useless fence that harms a neighbor is considered an unreasonable use of property and a nuisance in every state.

You also may be able to successfully sue under the nuisance theory if your neighbor's fence doesn't quite fit the definition of a spite fence in your state's statute—for instance, if it's shorter than the limit in the statute. However, it's usually harder to convince a judge that a fence is a spite fence if a statute exists and the fence doesn't meet the description.

Under the common law, for a fence to be a spite fence and a nuisance to the neighbor, three conditions must exist:

- The fence builder's motive is malicious.
- The fence serves no reasonable purpose.
- The neighbor's use and enjoyment of property are harmed by the fence.

How to prove each of these elements if you sue is discussed in "Going to Court," below.

Negotiating With the Neighbor

It's really never too late to negotiate or mediate a solution with a neighbor, even when such a thing seems impossible. By the time a neighbor dispute reaches a spite fence stage, there is probably little or no communication. However, the real threat of a lawsuit may give even the most stubborn of neighbors second thoughts. The one building the spite fence may have no idea that it violates the law. It can't hurt to approach the neighbor to try to stay out of court.

Also consider mediation to resolve the problem. Mediation is a process in which a third party helps you work out your own solution. In a spite fence case, mediation may be a much more effective tool than an expensive and time-consuming lawsuit, not only to get rid of the fence, but to improve relations between neighbors.

Mediation may be especially appropriate in a spite fence case because the builder of the fence is almost certainly angry too. More is probably involved here than ten feet of wooden planks; there is likely to be a history of misunderstandings on both sides. If mediation is successful, you could gain an enormous amount of satisfaction from reaching your own solutions, saving everybody involved a lot of money, and helping to prevent future trouble. (Chapter 19 discusses the process of mediation at length.)

Going to Court

When all attempts at communication fail, you may choose to have your day in court and ask a judge for relief from a spite fence.

But before you go jumping into the legal system, do use a little common sense. How bad is the fence compared to a court battle? Are you really harmed, or just angry at your neighbor?

If you're determined to get the fence removed no matter what it takes, be aware that pursuing your goal could cost a small fortune if the neighbor is willing to fight.

Can Tenants Sue?

What if you're a tenant, not an owner, bothered by a neighbor's spite fence? The language of most spite fence laws uses the word "occupant" as the one who can be harmed, so tenants should be able to sue under these statutes. Similarly, in the absence of a statute, most courts will likely find that a tenant has the right ("standing" in legalese) to challenge a spite fence. Such court decisions are rare, but over a century ago, a court in Massachusetts stated that under its statute, either a tenant or an owner could bring a lawsuit.[1]

What the Court Can Do

A court can order the builder of a spite fence to stop construction, lower the fence, remove it, or pay the neighbor for the damage the fence has caused.

Depending on how much money you want to sue for, you may need to hire a lawyer and bring your lawsuit in regular trial court, not small claims court. And if you want the court to order the fence lowered or removed, you also may have to hire a lawyer and sue in regular trial court. Most small claims court judges do not have authority to order someone to take down a fence.

Halting the Work

Instead of wringing your hands while you watch a spite fence going up, you can try to stop the construction. Always remember to check subdivision regulations and local fence laws as well as spite fence laws. When a local ordinance is being violated, some city attorney offices might be willing to help by issuing a citation and a fine.

Once the fence is obviously above the height limit in the applicable law, you can get an emergency order from a judge requiring the neighbor to stop building, at least until the judge makes a formal ruling on the legality of the fence. You will have to go to regular court (not small claims) and probably hire a lawyer. That may be worth the money—once a fence is up, a judge may be reluctant to order the owner to destroy it, so it's better to try to nip things in the bud.

Getting the Fence Removed

You can ask a court to order the removal of a neighbor's spite fence, but be aware that a judge will not lightly order someone to remove or destroy property. The judge will look for the least drastic remedy—for example, ordering the top four feet of a 12-foot fence removed, instead of having the owner tear down the whole thing. If a fence has been placed right next to a house to block the windows, the judge would likely order it lowered below the windows. Or, there could be a court order to reduce a high fence to the height that is customary in the community.

To bring your case in front of a judge who has the authority to order the fence to come down or be lowered, you will probably have to use regular (not small claims) court.

Making the Fence Owner Compensate the Neighbor

Most neighbors upset by a spite fence don't particularly want money—they want the fence, or at least part of it, removed. But a court can also order the fence owner to compensate the neighbor, if the neighbor can prove he or she has been harmed. Even if your primary goal is to get your neighbor to tear down a monstrous spite fence, the threat of having to pay a substantial sum can be a powerful impetus for getting a spiteful neighbor to take the fence down or at least to lower it.

One situation in which compensation is definitely appropriate is when a spite fence makes life so uncomfortable that the injured neighbor gives up and moves out. Even after moving, however, the neighbor can still sue for the harm it caused.

> **EXAMPLE:** A neighbor dispute in the Los Angeles hills wound up in court after one family literally ran their neighbors off their property by making life so miserable that the beleaguered neighbors sold their house. Among the activities of the spiteful neighbors were hurling insults, "accidentally" flinging paint on the other house, and placing their garbage can under the neighbors' dining room window. Oh yes, they also built a spite fence. The relocated neighbor sued the spite fence's owner, demanding money for his aggravation. The fence was under the height specified in the California spite fence statute, but the court declared the fence a spite fence under the common law. The judge ruled that it had been built with no reasonable purpose for the owner and solely to annoy the neighbor—an unreasonable use of property and a private nuisance. The judge awarded damages for the whole mess and scolded the guilty neighbors for "delight in their display of malice and hatred for fellow man."[2]

If you sue for money alone, you can avoid lawyers and sue in small claims court if the amount is within the limit of your state's small claims law. Most states allow claims up to $2,500 to $15,000. Be aware that a few states' small claims courts will not hear spite fence cases. (Chapter 20 explains how to use small claims court and lists each state's small claims court limit.)

If you win your lawsuit but the fence owner does not remedy the situation, the fence is what is called a continuing nuisance, because its presence continues to harm you. You can sue again and again.

What You Must Prove

When you take your neighbor to court for building a spite fence, you must prove that according to the law, the fence meets the definition of a spite fence.

If you sue based on your state's spite fence statute, the fence must be:

- over the height limit set out in the statute
- built to annoy you, the neighbor (maliciously built), and
- serving no reasonable purpose for the owner.

If you want money from the neighbor, you must also show that you are harmed by the fence, the nature of your harm, and how much money it would take to compensate you for it.

If you sue based on the common law, the fence must be:

- built to annoy you, the neighbor (maliciously built)
- serving no reasonable purpose for the owner, and
- harming the neighbor.

These ingredients cannot easily be separated. For instance, a high useless fence suggests malice on the builder's part. On the other hand, a high fence truly necessary for some reason is not a spite fence, even when the neighbors can't stand each other or the fence does create harm.

Let's look at these elements one at a time.

Motive of the Fence Builder

To be a spite fence, a structure must be "maliciously" erected or maintained. This can be difficult to prove, because most people will not readily admit that an action was malicious—especially in the face of a lawsuit that will turn on their motive. However, there are several ways for a court to determine the fence builder's motive.

Appearance of the fence. The appearance itself of a fence may be evidence of the builder's malicious intent. Often a spite fence looks like a monstrosity, its ugliness being part of the attempt to annoy the neighbor.

There are no laws that control, from an aesthetic point of view, what a person can do with his or her property. That would interfere with the constitutionally guaranteed freedom of expression. But when a simple photograph of the property would produce shock and outrage in an objective observer, the fence itself is probably ample evidence of the builder's malice.

The neighbors' conduct. Sometimes, a court looks at the neighbors' relationship—like a recent fight between them. When there is hostility between the neighbors or an obvious attempt at some kind of revenge, the words and actions of the fence builder may reflect a malicious motive.

A Typical Spite Fence

Close your eyes for a moment and picture a spite fence in your mind. Have it pictured? No matter what you have designed in your imagination, it probably is not nearly as awful as what some neighbors have actually done to each other.

In one spite fence case, the court actually included a picture of the fence with its written decision—most unusual for stuffy law books. If you are ever in your local law library, ask the librarian to help you find volume 273 of the Northwest Reporter. Look on page 660. I will try to describe the picture.

There are two houses side by side, separated by about 30 feet. One house was apparently built very close to the boundary line. The fence erected by the other neighbor appears to be about six inches from this house. It is made of rough boards and is taller than the top of the windows. There is no room to walk between the fence and the house, no room for light and air. Any view from the windows is only of the rough boards. If these houses were along the Atlantic coast, one would assume the owners were preparing for a major hurricane, boarding up against the expected fury of the storm.

But these houses are in a South Dakota town. The only fury involved was that of the neighbors. The fence itself clearly shows malice. This is a typical spite fence.[3]

EXAMPLE: Two Washington state neighbors, a man and a woman, had a disagreement. The man ended his argument with the promise, "Never mind, I will fix you." Soon the fence went up, over eight feet high, made of unplaned wood and standing above the top of the woman's windows. It effectively boarded up the side of her house. After her tenant on that side promptly moved out because she couldn't see in the dark, the neighbor sued, asking that the fence be declared a spite fence.

The judge asked the fence builder what the fence's use was. He claimed that he needed it to keep out children and chickens. On cross-examination, he admitted that he could do this with a five-foot fence. The judge found that "malevolence" was his dominant motive and ordered the fence reduced to five feet.[4]

Usefulness of the Fence

When a fence is challenged in court and it appears to the court that it was erected to annoy the next-door neighbor, it will be ruled a spite fence unless the owner can show that it serves another reasonable purpose. But once a court finds malice, if the neighbor is truly harmed by the fence, the court will look extremely closely at the use claimed by the builder. After all, most people are content with fences from three to six feet high around their yards. The owner must show that the unusually high fence is useful.

Below are some of the most common justifications for an extra-high fence.

Privacy. Privacy in one's own yard is an uncommon treat. Many of us want to enjoy early-morning coffee in a bathrobe. Others may wish to indulge in a midday hot tub respite or swim in a pool with some privacy. Many of us would simply like to sit outside with a good trashy novel without a neighbor's being able to comment on our taste in literature. We just don't like being watched at home.

With today's crowded cities and increasingly tiny properties, outdoor privacy is elusive. Putting up a fence is a reasonable way to get it. Sometimes, a lot slopes steeply, and obtaining privacy means a six-foot fence on one end and a ten-foot one on the other. Or an even higher fence may be desirable if a prying neighbor glues himself to a second-story window every time he hears the lid come off the hot tub.

But if a neighbor is harmed by the fence and complains, the desire for privacy will have to be balanced against the relief for the neighbor, and privacy may not be a sufficient reasonable purpose to prevent the fence from being ruled a nuisance.

Fencing in children or animals. This is probably the most common reasonable use found throughout the country for a proper fence. In the absence of height ordinances or subdivision restrictions, common sense and community norms together decide what's a reasonable height, given what needs to be fenced in or out.

One court has found nine feet to be excessive for the keeping of horses.[5] All courts would surely find that a seven-foot fence is higher than reasonably needed to keep a Pomeranian. Similarly, an eight-foot fence to contain an active two-year-old would be considered unnecessary by most people. This would be true even if the parent argued that he was looking a few years ahead. However, on the theory that two-year-olds grow, a six-foot fence might be found reasonable.

Stopping trespassers. Fences offer protection from intruders. Stopping unwanted people from entering your property is a legitimate use of a tall fence.

> EXAMPLE: A property owner in a California city with no backyard fence height ordinance, was annoyed by a six-and-a-half-foot fence. He sued the builder for erecting a spite fence. At trial, the owner showed that people had climbed over a smaller fence, using the property as a shortcut. The judge agreed that this was a good reason to build a big fence and ruled that it wasn't a spite fence.[6]

Supporting flowers and vines. Roses in full bloom trained up and along a fence are a lovely sight. However, if the fence is unnecessarily high and bothering the neighbor, this use will not be sufficient to keep the fence from being a spite fence and a nuisance.

One owner, actually wishing to block an unsightly house from his view, erected a ten-foot fence and claimed it was necessary for gardening. He said he intended to grow decorative greenery on it, to use it as a trellis. The court said no. Training vines, as a reasonable activity, did not require a ten-foot fence.[7]

Enclosing swimming pools. Enclosing a swimming pool with a fence is not only reasonable but responsible and may be required by law. Maintaining privacy and preventing accidents are both valid purposes for a fence around a pool, if the height of the fence is reasonable.

The presence of a pool, however, doesn't justify any kind of fence the owner decides to build. Consider this creative attempt at a little spite and its result. One neighbor erected what was evidently a lovely wooden fence to enclose his swimming pool, dogs, and shrubbery. It was six feet and four inches tall as it ran along the property. But as the fence approached the next-door neighbor's house, it rose to a height of nine feet and three inches, blocked the house effectively, and then dropped back down to six feet four inches.

The next-door neighbor sued, and the judge ruled that the tall portion alongside the neighbor was a spite fence and ordered it lowered.[8]

Harm to the Neighbor

If someone who wants to annoy a neighbor builds a fence that has no reasonable use, the neighbor must prove one more thing to win a lawsuit under the common law: harm from the fence. If a neighbor is suing under a spite fence statute and asking for money damages, the harm is presumed, but it must be translated into a money amount.

In a spite fence case, the neighbor's harm is the interference with enjoyment of property caused by the fence. The harm is often couched in terms of a loss of light, air, and view. Normally, there is no legal right to light, air, or view. (See Chapter 8.) But in many states, a neighbor may sue the owner of a spite fence for a loss of light, air, and view. This is because a spite fence does not serve a reasonable purpose for the fence owner. In contrast, nonspiteful structures or natural objects like trees do have value for their owner.

The neighbor can show other harm as well, such as loss of rental income and annoyance. (See "How Much to Sue For," below.)

How Much to Sue For

In figuring how much to ask the court to award you, don't be too conservative. If you go to court and present a reasonable figure that represents what you really think your loss is and explain how you arrived at that figure, the judge will respect you for it. It is a welcome relief for the judge to deal with someone who has made a real effort to honestly quantify a loss.

Here are some things to consider when you're trying to put a dollar figure on the harm the fence has caused you.

Deprivation of Light and Air

No one would build a house without windows. We like to be able to look outside. We welcome fresh air to breathe and to eliminate stale or even noxious household fumes. Many of us prefer sunlight to artificial light. A high fence can seriously diminish the enjoyment of our living quarters.

The loss varies greatly according to circumstances, and calculation is not easy. Let's try a little common sense. If your monthly housing cost (mortgage, insurance, and taxes, or rent) is $3000 a month, that is roughly $100 a day. If you have lost light, air, and view for one whole side of the house, $30 a day would seem reasonable as damage.

Light, Air, and View

Most of us have seen (or lived in) a house or an apartment building that is extremely close to another structure. The effect can be a window that opens to reveal nothing but a blank wall. In that situation, we may complain that we have no view, or very little light and air. However, we can't do anything about it legally because the building next door serves a useful purpose, such as housing, office space, even storage. A spite fence is quite different: It hurts us in the same way but serves no real purpose for the owner. (For more on obstruction of view, see Chapter 8.)

What about damage to the yard? Flowers, trees, gardens, and grass also need light, air, and often direct sun to survive. If your prized vegetable garden dies, you have both an increase in your grocery bill and a loss of enjoyment of gardening. Surely, a total amount like $300 would be reasonable for that loss. Did you lose beautiful flowers and the lawn itself on that side? How about $500?

Utility Bills

If your utility bills have gone up because of the neighbor's fence, ask the court for an award to cover your out-of-pocket expense. Be prepared to document the increase.

Loss of Rental Income

You should be able to show the court if the fence made the property unrentable or if, as is more likely, it lowered its rental value. Either way, you can ask for the amount you are out as a result of the spite fence.

Diminished Value of the Whole Property

The property value loss is the difference between the value of your property with the spite fence next door and the value without it. Even if you aren't intending to sell the house anytime soon, you are entitled to this amount if the fence stays up.

A spite fence serves notice to others that there is a neighbor problem, something that can in itself lower the value of the property. If the fence is hideous, its aesthetic impact can contribute further to diminishing market value of the property. If the fence blocks a spectacular view, it has undoubtedly taken thousands off the market value of your house.

Normally you couldn't sue a neighbor for ugliness that lowers your property value. However, if an unlawful act by the neighbor (creating a spite fence) caused your property value to drop, asking for compensation is worth a try. A good real estate appraiser (check online for listings) can help you estimate diminished property value.

Annoyance

Some judges say that they do not consider the neighbor's hurt feelings and embarrassment when evaluating harm in spite fence cases, but others grant money for annoyance.

> EXAMPLE: In a case in Kentucky, an eight-foot solid wall was built one inch over onto the neighbor's property, and the neighbor sued both for trespass and a spite fence. Once the lawsuit was filed, the owner took down the wall, but the neighbor still went to court. The jury awarded the neighbor one cent for trespass and $1,999.99 for annoyance. This case was later sent back for a new trial because the reviewing court considered the amount awarded for annoyance too high under the circumstances.[9]

Probably the best you can do is to understand that it's possible, although tricky, to be compensated for your fence-building neighbor's figurative slap in the face. This seems reasonable; probably the most important effect of a spite fence is psychological. Think for a moment about how prisons use windowless cells as a form of punishment. Suddenly being blocked, shut off by a fence in our faces, can make us feel as if we are in jail in our own houses.

To put a dollar amount on your irritation and annoyance, try this approach: When you get up each morning and look out at the despised spite fence, what do you think? Do you say, "By golly, I'd give $100 to have that thing out of my face"? Feel that way every day? That's $100 a day. You may not get it, but don't shortchange yourself. Just because these amounts are subjective does not mean you can't convince a court they are real.

Other Out-of-Pocket Expenses

Include anything else that has cost you money as a result of the fence. If it has made you physically ill, list your medical bills. Every situation is different, so keep your own accurate account of all out-of-pocket expenses and ask to be compensated for them. ●

Endnotes

1 *Smith v. Morse,* 19 N.E. 393 (Mass. 1889).

2 *Griffin v. Northridge*, 67 Cal. App. 2d 69, 153 P.2d 800 (1944).

3 *Racich v. Mastrovich*, 65 S.D. 321, 273 N.W. 660 (1937).

4 *Karasek v. Peier*, 22 Wash. 419, 61 P. 33 (1900).

5 *Whitlock v. Uhle*, 53 A. 891 (Conn. 1903).

6 *Haehlen v. Wilson*, 11 Cal. App. 2d 437, 54 P.2d 62 (1936).

7 *Bar Due v. Cox*, 47 Cal. App. 713, 190 P. 1056 (1920). Also, for a discussion on trellises as a reasonable use, see *Rideout v. Knox*, 148 Mass. 368, 19 N.E. 390 (1889).

8 *Rapuano v. Ames*, 21 Conn. Supp. 110, 145 A.2d 384 (1958).

9 *Humphrey v. Mansbach*, 265 Ky. 675, 97 S.W.2d 439 (1936).

Dangers to Children: Attractive Nuisances

Youth is wholly experimental.

—**Robert Louis Stevenson**

Children, closely watched or not, stray onto other people's properties sooner or later. Most neighbors have had the experience (and sometimes annoyance) of watching a neighbor child step over the boundary line, ride a bike on the wrong driveway, or take a shortcut through the flower bed. When the trespass is ongoing or vandalism is involved, then it becomes a matter to take up with the parents or even the police.

But there is another concern: The child could get hurt. The problem of trespassing children can become very serious when something on a neighbor's property can cause grave injury.

Many are the parents who have cast wary eyes at neighbors' pools, trampolines, machinery, or stacks of building materials.

Property owners who have something on their property that is both inviting and dangerous to a child have a special legal responsibility to try to prevent injuries to children—whether or not those children were invited onto the property. In many states, this rule is called the "attractive nuisance" doctrine.

The Attractive Nuisance Doctrine

Whether you are a property owner or a neighboring parent who fears an injury, you should be aware that these kinds of situations involve special legal rules:

- When the owner or person responsible for a dangerous condition should realize that children are likely to come onto the property, the owner has a heightened responsibility to prevent harm.
- Children are not expected to fully realize the danger they may encounter.
- If a child can't understand the danger, and the owner fails to reasonably protect that child, the owner will usually be liable for the child's injuries.

For more than a hundred years, the law in this country has placed a special responsibility on people who keep objects on their properties that may attract and cause harm to children. For example, in 1875, a court found a railroad company liable when children played on a railroad turntable and were injured. The court likened a dangerous object children would want to investigate to "bait that attracts fish."[1]

The judge in that case coined the phrase "attractive nuisance" to refer to such objects. Property owners were put on notice that they would be responsible for injuries that resulted from an object's presence. And it doesn't matter that the child comes on the property without permission.

This idea is still alive and well in the law today, although some courts don't use the "attractive nuisance" term anymore. Many judges now refer to this doctrine as the "Restatement Rule," because it is discussed in a book called the *Restatement (Second) of Torts* at Sections 333-339.

What Is an Attractive Nuisance?

An attractive nuisance is a potentially harmful object so inviting or interesting to a child that it would lure the child onto the property to investigate. An unenclosed swimming pool, for instance, or a fountain containing goldfish would be attractive nuisances if they attracted a child onto the property and caused harm.

Ordinary objects used every day can attract and injure children. An idling lawnmower, paint sprayer, table saw—even the family auto—can greatly interest a neighborhood child. Children are also fascinated by construction equipment (as well as any construction site itself), gasoline pumps, excavations, wells, tunnels, dumpsters, and intriguing paths and stairways. A child views objects in a different way than an adult. A grownup might see a freshly delivered truckload of sand as a weekend's work ahead, but a child could find it the perfect mountain to climb or a giant sandbox to investigate.

You may be thinking that almost anything on someone's property could cause harm to a small child. Even a stick in the yard can be picked up and poked into an eye. Yet a stick in the yard is not so unusual or enticing as to draw children over at their peril.

Not every dangerous condition is, legally, an attractive nuisance. Most natural conditions, such as a lake or a naturally steep bank, are not considered attractive nuisances. To be liable for injury, an owner must have created or maintained the harmful object. And even a very small child is presumed by the law to understand some dangers—for example, falling from a height or touching fire. The attractive nuisance doctrine arises when the danger itself or the extent of the danger is hidden to a child.

A property owner's legal responsibility for a child's injuries depends on many factors, which are discussed below. But it always begins with the presence of something enticing to a child who may not appreciate the danger that is present.

Who Is Protected

Very young children are far from the only ones protected by the law. Children old enough to be out and about in the neighborhood on their own are also protected from attractive nuisances. In the past, some courts have limited liability to cases involving children under 14. Today, however, judges are more likely to look at each particular case and each individual child's capacity to understand danger. For example, a court recently found that a 16-year-old boy may not have understood the dangers of exploring an abandoned clay pit, and the owner could be liable when the boy was injured.[2]

Determining Liability

The person who is liable for injury to a child is the one who created or at least maintained the dangerous condition. Usually, that person is the property owner. In some cases, a tenant or someone else could also be liable. (For ease of discussion, we use the term "owner" for the one who is responsible.)

If an owner is sued for an injury due to attractive nuisance, courts almost always ask these questions:

- Should the owner have known that children were likely to come onto the property?
- Should the owner have realized that a serious danger existed?
- Was the danger one that a child might not have understood?

- Was the risk of harm to the child more important than the benefit to the owner of having the dangerous condition?
- Could the owner have taken reasonable precautions that would have prevented the injury?

If the answer to each of these questions is yes, all of the elements of an attractive nuisance have been met, and the property owner will usually be liable for the injury. The court will, however, also consider several other factors, including how easy it would be to eliminate the danger, how important the dangerous condition is to the owner, and the role of the parents in protecting the child.

What does all of this mean to neighbors? That we are responsible for the safety of other people's children? Well, yes, in some situations.

Here are some examples, taken from actual lawsuits.

EXAMPLE 1: A 12-year-old child climbed onto the roof of a building to play and fell three stories to the ground. The court ruled that the owner was liable for these reasons:
  - Children were known to play in the area.
  - The roof itself had an area that was sloped and slippery, something that a child would not notice.
  - It would have been very easy for the owner to lock the door to the roof.[3]

EXAMPLE 2: A 10-year-old child fell three stories from a roof after climbing up and playing on it. The court held that the owner was not legally responsible for the child's injuries because:
  - This owner had no reason to know that children would play on the roof.
  - No hidden danger on the roof itself caused the fall.[4]

Another example shows what can happen in an everyday situation if someone doesn't take that extra step to protect children.

EXAMPLE: During construction of a house, a contractor left wall panels propped against a wall and unattended. An 11-year-old girl, investigating the building site, was injured when the panels tumbled down on her. The court found that there were grounds for a lawsuit because:
  - Children were likely to come onto the building site.
  - The material was left there unattended for days.
  - It could have easily been stacked in a safer manner.[5]

In this case, the property owner did not know about the dangerous condition. The lawsuit was directed against the contractor who stacked the material, the one who created the danger.

Taking Necessary Precautions

The law doesn't require all neighbors to completely childproof their properties. What is expected by the law is simply that people be alert to potential dangers to children. A person creating a danger is obligated to take reasonable steps to prevent harm to those too young to understand that danger.

Following Local Laws

Local laws sometimes regulate objects that are dangerous to inquisitive children. By far the strictest regulations apply to that increasingly common danger, the backyard swimming pool. Many city and town ordinances impose elaborate restrictions on the construction and maintenance of pools and pool areas, including how they must be fenced and what kind of locks are required. When an owner doesn't comply with the regulations, both injury and liability can follow.

> **EXAMPLE:** In Pima County, Arizona, which includes Tucson, local laws require all pools built after 1996 to be enclosed from the street or from neighboring property. In addition, there must be a barrier between the house and the pool, so that no one can walk directly out of the house into the pool area.[6]
>
> When a seven-year-old boy drowned in a neighbor's pool, the court looked at the owner's compliance with the laws. One area of the fence was only four feet high, and a gate was not self-locking; either of these violations could have afforded access to the child. The owner was liable for the tragic death.[7]

Regulations protecting children from pools are similar throughout the country. If you move into a house that has a pool, never assume that the property is totally safe or even that it meets required specifications. It becomes your responsibility to know and follow the law for the protection of others. Likewise, if you are a neighboring parent and are concerned by what you see, check the local laws and inform the owner if there is a violation. You can look up these laws on the Internet, or at your local public library or law library. (Chapter 18 explains how to find local laws.)

Other dangers to children are also addressed by local laws. Almost every town has a law requiring the removal of doors on discarded refrigerators, protecting a curious child from the danger of suffocation. Laws prohibiting barbed wire below a certain height afford protection from the danger of sharp barbs, one that a child might not expect and understand.

Although some laws may not be designed especially with children in mind, following them could well prevent a danger that could attract a child to harm. In most places, for example, old cars and other junk that a child might find a fascinating playground are prohibited under blighted property laws unless they are fenced. (See Chapter 17.) Obeying dangerous dog laws and storing pesticides (and even explosives) according to legal requirements protect neighboring children and reflect responsible ownership.

Using Good Judgment

The best way to avoid tragic consequences to children is to use good common sense. If children live in the neighborhood and something on someone else's property fascinates them, they can be expected to trespass and investigate it if given the chance. If you are the owner, lock it up, fence it, or remove it if you can. If an object is an accident waiting to happen—a ladder propped against a roof or a machine left running— never leave it unattended.

If you are concerned that something on your property may create a danger to children, then it probably does. Many dangerous objects—for instance, swimming pools, wells, and certain machinery—are quite beneficial and even necessary for the owner. Maintaining them with an eye to children's safety should be a very high priority.

If you have objects like these, it would be wise to consult your insurance agent to see what precautions you should take. Don't be surprised if your premiums increase for the pleasure of having a pool, a trampoline, or another object for which the company may require an additional insurance rider. If the insurance company requires a fence, then install it, or you could even lose your coverage.

Advice for Parents

If you are a parent and are concerned about a particular danger, this may be a good time to be a meddlesome neighbor. Find out what local laws apply and voice your concern to the neighbor who is responsible. The person may not be aware of applicable law and may not even be aware that a danger exists. Assume the neighbor would want to know, and offer to help find a solution. (For tips on neighbor negotiations, see Chapter 1.) If a law is being violated and the neighbor won't cooperate, you can contact the appropriate authorities.

Seeking Legal Help

When an injury occurs on someone else's property and it is not severe, the owner's insurance company will probably take care of any medical expenses involved. It also may be possible to sue the owner in small claims court if the amount sought is not more than a few thousand dollars. A few states' small claims courts, however, will not hear personal injury cases. (See Chapter 20.)

But when a child is injured seriously, whether you are the parent or the owner of the property, you will need to consult an attorney. This chapter explains in general terms how the legal concept of attractive nuisance works, but complicated legal questions concerning the child's presence on the property, the maturity of the child, and parental responsibility all bear on an individual case and can only be answered by an experienced personal injury attorney.

Other laws may even come into play. Some states have passed what are called "recreational use laws," which may offer legal protection from liability to a property owner who regularly allows people to use the property for pursuits such as biking, fishing, and hiking. ●

Endnotes

1   *Keffe v. Milwaukee & St. Paul R. Co.*, 21 Minn. 207, 18 Am. Rep. 393 (1875).

2   *Lyle v. Bouler*, 547 So. 2d 506 (Ala. 1989).

3   *Smallwood by Smallwood v. Fornaciari*, 149 Ill. App. 3d 79, 500 N.E.2d 637 (Ill. App. 1986).

4   *Corson by Lontz v. Kosinski*, 801 F. Supp. 75 (N.D. Ill. 1992), aff'd, 3 F.3d 1146 (7th Cir. 1993).

5   *Amara v. Luin*, 725 S.W.2d 734 (Tex. App. 1986); disagreed with by *Koko Motel, Inc. v. Mayo*, 91 S.W. 3d 41, (Tex. App. 2002).

6   Tucson/Pima County, Ariz., Spa/Pool Code § 317.

7   *Johnson v. Harris*, 530 P.2d 1136 (1976).

Rural Neighbors and the Right to Farm

A cow is a very good animal in the field, but we turn her out of the garden.

—Samuel Johnson

During the last several decades, city people have increasingly migrated to rural areas to pursue their modern American dreams. They seek a peaceful place in the country, away from the noise and crime of cities. Many choose homes in modest (or not-so-modest) subdivisions that press into formerly agricultural lands.

This intrusion of urban life into rural life has resulted in an inevitable conflict concerning nearby farming operations. How surprised some neighbors are to wake up one spring morning to roaring machinery, buzzing flies, the stench of manure, and the awareness of pesticides in the air. And how angry many become when they learn that they can't do anything about it.

Ordinary Nuisance Rules

Ordinarily, the law does not allow any neighbor to interfere with another's enjoyment of his own property. However, many states have laws that give farmers a basic "right to farm" without the fear of lawsuits brought by offended neighbors. (See "Right-to-Farm Laws," below.)

In incorporated cities and towns, local laws specifically prohibit most of the common activities that are likely to disturb neighbors. For example, they restrict animal ownership, excessive noise, and conditions that lead to unwanted odors and insects. These are the laws that neighbors have learned to depend on for their protection. (See Chapter 17.) Even when an area is not incorporated and has no town ordinances, county laws usually offer some of the same protections.

In addition to local prohibitions against specific annoying activities, interference with someone's enjoyment of his or her property may be considered a legal nuisance. An offended neighbor can sue the one creating the annoyance for money damages or to have the activity stopped.

Some states define nuisance in their state laws. For example, a California statute says a nuisance is "anything which is injurious to health … or is indecent or offensive to the senses, or an obstruction to the free use of property, so as to interfere with the comfortable enjoyment of life or property. …"[1] Laws in some other states require that the offensive conduct also be unlawful or unreasonable to be considered a nuisance.[2] (For a listing of state nuisance laws, see Appendix B.)

Many states have no statute that defines a nuisance. But even in those states, one neighbor can sue another for creating something that unreasonably interferes with property enjoyment—a legal nuisance. Courts have developed their own standards, over the years, for what constitutes legal nuisance. These standards are very similar to those set out in state statutes.

In the past, courts and legislatures have created exceptions for some necessary but annoying activities to protect them from being considered nuisances. For example, the noise necessary for airports and heavy industry is generally not considered a nuisance—that is, neighbors can't sue successfully over it as long as all zoning and other laws are complied with. But farmers, until recently, could find themselves at the mercy of new and angry neighbors when normal farming operations created offensive conditions that interfered with a newcomer's property enjoyment.

Right-to-Farm Laws

In order to protect farmers from the nuisance laws that usually apply to neighbors, state legislatures have passed right-to-farm laws. These laws create a presumption that existing agricultural pursuits are not offensive enough to create a nuisance to neighbors. North Carolina's law is typical. It declares that an agricultural operation that has existed for a year without being a nuisance is presumed not to be a nuisance even when new neighbors move in. If the farm operations are conducted in a reasonable or non-negligent manner, the new neighbors can't legally complain.[3]

Every state in the nation has adopted some form of a right-to-farm law. (See Chapter 18 for information on where to find your state's laws.) The laws vary slightly from one state to another; for example, California requires that the farm was not a nuisance at the time it began and has been operational for at least three years before it can be protected.[4] California's law also defines the agricultural uses that are protected under the laws. They include (among other activities) cultivating soil, raising livestock and poultry, and preparing crops and livestock for market.

In addition, several states list specific annoyances resulting from agricultural operations that are not considered a legal nuisance to neighbors. The lists include odor, noise, dust, and the use of pesticides—the very conditions that, without the laws, could lead to a lawsuit by a neighbor.[5]

Under the right-to-farm laws, farmers are not completely free to do as they please. The same laws protecting existing farmers also offer some protection for neighbors in the rural area. Farmers in all states must operate in a legal and reasonable manner to avoid being considered a legal nuisance. Some states use the "legal and reasonable" language in their laws; others require "generally accepted agricultural practices."

Some states do not allow a protected farming operation to undergo a large increase in size or operation. Many don't allow farmers to make any substantial changes in what they are doing if they are to remain protected under the right to farm. None of the laws are designed to protect a farmer who does not follow normal procedures or who sets out to deliberately annoy neighbors.

Counties in some states have also adopted their own right-to-farm laws. These local laws not only reflect the state laws but may also include a mediation or arbitration procedure to handle neighbor complaints.

Some state legislatures are adding clauses to their right-to-farm laws that grant more power to counties to restrict particular types of farming activities. Most of these county laws focus on hog farms. They don't address the old complaints of odors and flies but rather the problem of animal waste. Hog waste can create health problems and pollution, so counties are cracking down on increases in the numbers of animals and denying permits for new hog farms.

Before the right-to-farm laws were enacted (mostly during the 1980s), the coexistence of suburbia and farming had not been a happy one. The legal standard used in other situations to stop neighbor annoyances was often devastating when applied to agricultural neighbors. Court decisions abound that resulted in the shutting down of a farmer's operation because it was found to be a nuisance to the neighbors. For example, a group of annoyed neighbors successfully closed a Massachusetts hog farm in 1963 because homes had sprung up around the farm.[6]

Many judges were aware of the unfairness of the law when a farmer was accused of creating a nuisance. Some courts tried to strike a middle ground and ended up applying rules and restrictions that would at least allow the farming operation to continue. A court in Florida, for example, allowed a hog farm to stay in business but placed a limit on how many hogs the farmer could have. The judge also issued instructions on how to store and feed the garbage the hogs were accustomed to eating.[7]

By enacting right-to-farm laws, the state legislatures finally squarely addressed the farmers' legal plight and carved out necessary protection for them from their neighbors.

Turnabout Is Fair Play

After years of urban and industrial triumph over agricultural interests, court decisions began to shift. For example, in Indiana, a hog farmer, instead of being the object of a lawsuit by others, sued a neighboring landfilling operation for creating a nuisance. The farmer claimed that the trucks were disturbing his hogs and was awarded damages for the disturbance.[8]

What Neighbors Can Do

Conflicts between residential and agricultural interests will no doubt continue as our suburbs sprawl into farming territory, although the right-to-farm laws will serve as guidelines for future coexistence with farming neighbors. Being aware of what farming operations are protected and of the rights of both farmers and their neighbors may help prevent unwanted problems.

Investigate the Locality

Before you build your dream house in the country, thoroughly investigate the surroundings. Be aware that the lovely wooded hillside you see from your window may be all that stands between you and a cattle feedlot. If all is well when you visit the peaceful farm next door in February, remember that the scene may look (and smell) quite different in the heat of August. Just because you place your life savings in a rural retreat, you cannot expect to have your farming neighbors make adjustments for you.

Do not assume that because a new subdivision will be large, beautiful, and expensive, farming operations may not be a problem. Use your head and do some checking on your own.

When you purchase property that someone is already living in, the seller may be required to reveal to you any conditions that may create an annoyance. California, for example, requires sellers to give buyers disclosure forms that describe any neighboring problems, rural or urban.[9] The right-to-farm laws are fairly new, and laws requiring developers to disclose the existence of protected neighboring farm operations cannot be far behind. A few counties in California that have adopted local right-to-farm laws now also require sellers to disclose facts about nearby farming operations.

Know the Laws

If you run an agricultural operation or live near one, you should know exactly what your particular state's right-to-farm law allows and what it restricts. You should also check to see if you have a county ordinance on the subject. You can find and read both your state's law and your county's provisions in a law library or on the Internet. (See Chapter 18.)

Just because your farming neighbor is protected by a right-to-farm law, it doesn't mean that you are helpless. If a nearby waving field of corn is replaced with a poultry processing operation, the farmer has probably stepped out of protection and may well have created a nuisance that you can sue over. The same may be true if an existing use of the property is greatly expanded—say, two cows suddenly become a herd of 100—and the state law restricts a substantial increase in operations.

But be aware of an Indiana court decision addressing this question. The Indiana law restricts a substantial change in the type of agricultural operation but does not mention increase in size. When a hog farmer was sued for increasing 29 hogs to 300, he was protected under the right-to-farm law. His operation was found not to be a nuisance, even though it affected the development of an entire residential area.[10]

Get Help If You Need It

The farming laws require that neighbors tolerate annoyances due to normal agricultural operations. But most suburbanites are not well versed in the rules and regulations of standard farming operations. The Department of Agriculture issues regulations pertaining to different types of farming, as do state commissioners of agriculture. If you think that a neighboring farmer has created a nuisance in spite of the right-to-farm laws, you'll want some knowledgeable help from someone who understands the applicable restrictions and knows what farming practices are normal for your area.

As a first step, check with other neighbors to see who else is affected and how severely. You need to know which neighbors are annoyed enough to want to take action. You may also want to get organized to complain.

Many states have county farm agents who may be able to help. In addition to being familiar with customary farming practices, such an agent may also know about local mediation or arbitration procedures that have been set up specifically for these disputes.

Other sources of help include the local or state health department or department of agriculture. These agencies may investigate and solve the problem for you, especially if many neighbors complain at the same time. The appropriate licensing and inspection office for a particular kind of operation—a dairy farm, for instance—should want to know about possible substandard practices and may take action against the farmer.

Using the Courts

As a last resort, under some circumstances, you can still take the farming neighbor to court for creating a nuisance. If you are thoroughly versed in the law and convinced the farmer is in violation, you could consider suing in small claims court for money damages for your annoyance. The amount you can ask for is limited though, usually from $2,500 to $15,000, and a few states' small claims courts will not hear nuisance cases at all. If 20 or 30 neighbors get together and each one brings suit, the amount of money involved could be so substantial that the farmer might well choose to immediately clean up the operation. The money damages you would seek would be to compensate you for annoyance due to odors, flies, or whatever is interfering with your use of property and could be calculated on a daily basis. (See Chapter 20 for more on how to use small claims court.)

Most cases of this kind, however, are far from simple and not easily decided. If you do pursue a lawsuit, you most likely will have to hire an attorney, and you can expect hefty expenses and a lengthy court proceeding. The right-to-farm laws are so recent that courts in most states have not yet addressed many questions concerning them. Experts may have to testify as to what is expected of farmers under the new laws.

Factors other than a neighbor's annoyance may also be present. For example, is water pollution present or probable in the future? Could substandard farming practices have an eventual harmful effect on an entire community? What about situations beyond a farmer's reasonable control?

In 1962, for example, before the right-to-farm laws were in effect, a group of neighbors successfully sued and shut down a dairy farm in California after a flood resulted in living rooms full of manure.[11] One has to wonder how the courts would decide the same case now under the new laws. They might create some kind of compromise to prevent such an occurrence in the future. Or they might even tell the neighbors to go home and clean their houses, because the farmer is protected from a lawsuit.

There are still too many unanswered questions and too many varying circumstances to know exactly what to expect from the courts when a farm is a problem for its residential neighbors. A judge may find that an annoyance you would not have been expected to tolerate in the past is no longer considered a nuisance to you and your neighbors under the right-to-farm laws. As one judge remarked while dismissing a lawsuit against a hog farmer, "We must observe that pork production generates odors which cannot be prevented, and so long as the human race consumes pork, someone must tolerate the smell."[12] ●

Endnotes

1 Cal. Civ. Code § 3479.

2 Okla. Stat. Ann. tit. 50, § 1.

3 N.C. Gen. Stat. § 106-701; (2013 North Carolina Laws S.L. 2013-2014 (H.B. 614)).

4 Cal. Civ. Code § 3482.5.

5 For example, see R.I. Gen. Laws § 2-23-5.

6 *Pendoley v. Ferriera,* 187 N.E.2d 142 (Mass. 1963).

7 *Mercer v. Brown,* 190 So. 2d 610 (Fla. App. 1966).

8 *Sherk v. Indiana Waste Sys., Inc.,* 495 N.E.2d 815 (Ind. App. 1986).

9 Cal. Civ. Code § 1102, and following.

10 *Laux v. Chopin Land Associates, Inc.,* 550 N.E.2d 100 (Ind. App. 1990). Indiana is one of the very few states where several court decisions have been made under the new laws. The written decision in the *Laux* case includes an interesting and fairly comprehensive discussion of how this particular law is expected to be applied for that state.

11 *Wade v. Campbell,* 200 Cal. App. 2d 54, 19 Cal. Rptr. 173 (1962).

12 *Shatto v. McNulty,* 509 N.E. 2d 897 (Ind. App. 1987).

Water

Water, water everywhere,
Nor any drop to drink.

—Samuel Taylor Coleridge

I f you are complaining about water, you probably face one of two
scenarios: Either you have water and don't want it, or you want water
and can't have it. Most often, neighbor problems arise over the first
situation. Many people have experienced the shock of gazing out after a
spring rain and discovering that a prized patio area lies under an unexpected
heap of mud and silt. Many others have heard the dreaded gurgle of an
unwanted pond forming in the basement or a downstairs room.

Whatever the cause of the invading water—a poorly designed
downspout, an improperly functioning sprinkler, or a new ditch next
door—the questions for neighbors are the same: Who is responsible?
Who pays? What can you do?

The flip side of dealing with unwanted water faces the person whose
water supply is somehow thwarted by a neighbor. Suppose your neighbor
diverts the stream you swim in or drills into the water supply for your
well. Because the United States is so big and so diverse geographically,
different areas have developed different legal approaches to these issues.
Where water is plentiful and even excessive, courts are more lenient
toward people trying to protect themselves from it—for example, when
they divert it with a drain or a ditch. And in the arid Western states,
very different laws protect those who need the water.

Natural vs. Man-Made Problems

When one neighbor damages another with water from a man-made
source (pipes and sprinklers, for example), the offending neighbor will
probably be liable. When excessive rainwater is involved, or when water
coursing across land or in a natural watercourse causes damage, finding
fault becomes more difficult. Blanket rules are hard to apply; the outcome
of a dispute depends on its unique circumstances.

This chapter addresses common questions about water and alerts you to your rights. Specific laws concerning water are so vast that one major work on the subject, *Waters and Water Rights*, edited by R. Beck (Michie), consists of seven volumes. You may want to consult this work, which can be found in law libraries. (See Chapter 18 on legal research.)

When the Neighbor Is Liable for Damage

When one person does something on his or her own property that results in water damage to a neighbor, the first person may be legally responsible for the damage. Here are the basic rules.

The Neighbor Was Unreasonable or Careless

Unreasonable action that interferes with a neighbor's use and enjoyment of property is called (in legalese) "creating a nuisance." If your property is harmed, you can sue for compensation for your losses and also ask the court to order the neighbor to stop the action.

> EXAMPLE: Tori arrives home late one evening and finds a saturated floor on the ground level of her house. She frantically searches inside for the source of the water and finds nothing. Then, through the window, she hears a familiar noise—the zip, zip, zip of her uphill neighbor's sprinkler system. Stepping out, she discovers a lake where her patio had been. The neighbors? They are out of town for the weekend.

Sprinklers are not the only culprits, of course. Water from any source has great potential for damage when it gushes from one house to another. Even the lowly garden hose can cause unexpected damage. How many neighbors have forgotten to turn it off? How many have been washing their cars in the driveway when the phone rang? Meanwhile, the water runs across the driveway and into the neighbor's garage, soaking an expensive new tool set.

Keep an Eye on the Kids

Children left unattended with hoses can create unfortunate neighbor problems. It doesn't take long to flood a neighbor's carport or to "fill something up"—like an automobile or an open window. The damage in these cases may seem slight but the principle of liability is the same. The parents will be responsible for the intentional acts or negligence of their kids.

Water pipes also get clogged. They get old. They leak, crack, and freeze. Usually, damage is limited to the unfortunate owner's property. But not always.

> EXAMPLE: A man in Washington, D.C., kept noticing dampness in his house. Finally, one day he walked in to find a room flooded. The source was a broken drainpipe in the bathtub in the house next door.[1] The man had repeatedly complained to his neighbors, who did nothing about it. The neighbors were legally considered negligent because they didn't keep their property in good repair.

The general rule is that owners are responsible for their pipes and for damage they may cause, even if the pipe just wears out or freezes in cold weather. But be aware of a legal complication that can confuse liability. Tree roots, including roots from neighboring property, can damage pipes. In a case in Washington state, a neighbor sued the tree owner next door when the tree roots crossed the property line and crushed his pipes.[2] (See Chapter 4 for a detailed discussion of liability for tree roots.)

Sometimes, neighbors do something that seems perfectly reasonable to them to protect their own property from water but fail to use ordinary care to prevent harm to others. Hostility between neighbors—or even a scramble to small claims court—can result.

For example, when one neighbor blithely goes about solving a problem on his own property without bothering a whit as to the consequences to others, he may be considered to have acted negligently. This, too, can result in a lawsuit.

> **EXAMPLE:** Gus and Ali, next-door neighbors, both have fine vegetable gardens. But Gus discovers that after a hard rain, the water from his gutter downspout is leaving his garden soggy. So he moves the downspout to the other side of the house near Ali's garden, thinking that the excess water will flow between the properties. But after a rain, Ali's vegetables are ruined.

The Neighbor Acted Intentionally

If someone deliberately sends water coursing onto your land, the water is an invasion, and the neighbor is guilty of trespassing on your property. Again, the neighbor is liable for the damage you suffer.

> **EXAMPLE:** Janos soaks his yard above Ida's property heavily once a week. Each time he does it, water floods Ida's den. When she complains, Janos claims he can do what he wants and tells her to go change her own drainage. She can sue for the expenses of cleaning and repair of her carpet and furniture. She can also ask a judge to make him stop the practice—for instance, to make him water lightly every other day, in a more reasonable way.

The Neighbor Broke a Law

Someone who breaks a state, federal, or local law may be automatically liable for any harm that results. For example, federal law prohibits discharging certain wastes improperly. If your property is soaked by an illegal emission, you're entitled to compensation.

These laws also apply to damage to well water. For instance, in New Jersey in 1995, a well was contaminated by underground storage tanks owned by Exxon.[3] The oil company had violated environmental statutes. Damaging a well is usually also a violation of state law. State statutes may automatically place liability for damage and impose a fine.

Sometimes a hapless neighbor can unwittingly destroy a neighbor's water supply. One Georgia man burned gasoline in a waste pit on his property. The residue seeped into his neighbor's well and ruined it.[4]

In a Wisconsin case that ended up in court, several neighbors watched nearby businesses go up in flames one day. One business manufactured fertilizer, and another made insulation materials. During and after the fire, manufacturing material seeped into the ground and into the neighbors' wells. Even though the accidental fire began the process, the neighbors still were able to sue the business owners for destroying their wells.[5] Damage to another's well is an illegal act.

Contaminated Water

If you suspect that water coming onto your property or into your well is contaminated, you'll want to contact your local health department. If the flow is coming from a septic system, local and state rules will regulate the operation and can aid in placing liability. Specific state and federal laws prohibit water pollution and may regulate the drilling of wells. Depending on the type of contamination and the source, you may find yourself dealing with state pollution agencies and possibly the federal Environmental Protection Agency.

Some states have statutes prohibiting one neighbor from damaging another by diverting surface water onto the neighbor's property. Under Texas law, for example, no person may divert or capture the natural flow of surface waters such that the overflow damages another's property.[6]

A Pennsylvania law is designed to protect neighbors from water damage by developers. The law requires any landowner who develops land to take measures reasonably necessary to prevent injury to other property. If water runoff is greater after development and harms a neighbor, the violation is a public nuisance, and the neighbor can sue.[7]

Not all states have laws addressing water damage. You can look in the index of your state's annotated code under "water" to see what's there. (See Chapter 18.)

When the Neighbor May Not Be Liable for Damage

The law does not hold landowners responsible for things they cannot control, including natural events in which they had no part. It may not always be easy to tell, however, whether water damage is from an entirely natural event. Most court cases between neighbors that involve water are the result of runoff and flooding from rainwater. When a severe rain floods your property courtesy of the land next door, liability will hinge on the individual situation and which state you are in.

Surface Water Runoff

As a general rule, a neighbor is not liable for harm caused by the natural conditions of land. If the land lies in such a way that a particular amount of water is dumped onto your backyard every year from rain running off your next-door neighbor's property, it's not legally your neighbor's fault. But what if your neighbor landscapes the property so that the amount of water running onto your yard doubles every year? Your neighbor would say that the change is still caused by the naturally occurring rain, not the landscaping. You would probably prefer to take your neighbor's action into account. It turns out that three different rules of liability govern situations like this. Different states have adopted different rules.

The "common enemy" rule. In the past, many courts treated excessive rainwater as a "common enemy," affecting and damaging property at random. Under this theory, you are expected to take measures to protect your own property from water coursing across the land. Even if one neighbor who lives on higher ground diverts water to prevent flooding and deposits it on you, you are expected to protect yourself from the extra water. Your neighbor is not responsible for damage to your property.

Fortunately for lower landowners, only a handful of courts still claim to follow this theory and those that do have modified the rule.

The "civil law" rule. A number of states follow a rule which is, in theory, the opposite of the common enemy rule. The civil law rule, so called because it comes from Roman law and the Napoleonic code, holds that if a person alters the natural flow of surface waters in any way that harms the use and enjoyment of another property, that person will be liable for that harm. In other words, upper landowner beware. Unlike the common enemy rule, which requires lower landowners to fend for themselves, the civil law rule holds upper landowners liable for any detrimental changes in runoff patterns.

Like the common enemy rule, however, states no longer apply this rule in its strictest form. States have developed modifications and exceptions, and now often judge the behavior of both parties before saddling the upper landowner with the bill. California, for example, expects that both parties will act reasonably, which includes the duty of the lower landowner to take protective steps. If the actions of both sides were reasonable, then the upper landowner will bear the burden.[8] However, if the court finds the lower landowner unreasonably failed to protect his or her land, the upper landowner will not be liable.

The reasonableness rule. Today, in a majority of states, when one neighbor alters the land and damage occurs to another, the neighbor is liable for the damage if the alteration was "unreasonable." If you sue a neighbor over damage you've suffered, judges will want proof that the neighbor did something unreasonable that altered the natural condition and caused your harm.

What to one neighbor appears to be a perfectly reasonable alteration to the land may not seem so at all to another.

> **EXAMPLE:** Salvo and Taki have lived beside each other for several years. Rainwater from both properties has always run off naturally to a ditch behind their houses. Salvo grades his back yard to create a flat patio area. After the project is completed, rainwater and mud flow directly onto Taki's property. Was Salvo's project reasonable? Should Taki be required to protect his own property by putting in a retaining wall? What if he does put in a wall, and then standing water floods Salvo's property?

Judges have wrestled with these kinds of questions for hundreds of years. In 1886, a court decided that although building a house was reasonable, installing a roof without gutters, which caused a neighbor to flood, was not.[9] Gutters and downspouts that send rainwater gushing onto a neighbor's property are also unreasonable alterations to natural flow, and the owner will usually be liable for damages.

What about digging a ditch that redirects rainwater onto someone else's property? One neighbor in Wisconsin who did this caused water to stand and erode the other's retaining wall. He was guilty of intentionally trespassing on the neighbor's property.[10] But if the ditch was absolutely necessary to prevent huge harm, and the damage to the neighbor was slight, there might be an exception. There is also an exception for liability in some situations when the neighbors own waterfront property. (See "Downstream Flooding," below.)

In a 1980 Nevada case in which the development of a new subdivision severely flooded neighbors who were there first (destroying one neighbor's property completely), the court made those who were responsible pay. The judge said that limiting people to only reasonable alterations was necessary for proper urban growth. The developers and the county were found to have acted unreasonably and were liable for the damage.[11]

What is reasonable activity must be decided for each situation.

If you end up in court fighting about this question, you will need a lawyer who is an expert and understands how water cases are treated in your locale.

"Acts of God"

This argument has filled courtrooms for many years. If damage to a neighbor is due to an "act of God," nobody may be liable, or liability may be greatly reduced. And the damaged neighbor is left paying bills out of pocket.

> **EXAMPLE:** Gladys digs a ditch to direct rainwater from her house. A huge and unusual storm dumps ten inches of rain in four hours. The ditch overflows and sends water rushing into her neighbor Henry's yard, flooding his basement.

When Henry takes Gladys to court over his extensive damage, she argues that digging the ditch was a reasonable act, necessary to protect her own property. The particular storm, she claims, was unusually severe—an act of God for which she is not responsible. She shows that the area had never before had such a storm and that she had no way to know it would happen or to prevent the harm. Henry may well be out of luck.

Again, one court has given guidelines. A farmer in North Dakota extensively altered his property for draining and keeping rainwater. During a period of very unusual rain, water on his property overflowed and flooded several neighbors. He argued that the rains were an act of God, but the court did not agree.

To be an act of God, the judge ruled, the rain would have to be unprecedented and extraordinary—something that could not be reasonably anticipated. It would also have to be something one could not protect against. And probably most important, if an act of God and somebody's negligence combined to create harm, the negligent person would be liable. To block a mere mortal's liability, the act of God must be the only cause of the harm. In this case, the farmer not only had to pay for the damage from flooding, but also was ordered to change his land back to the way that it had been.[12]

What the Neighbor at Fault Must Pay For

If water seeps or pours into your house, there may be enormous damage, and the person or entity responsible will face hefty financial liability. Often, either your insurance or your neighbor's will compensate you. But if the cost is huge, and insurance for some reason won't pay or won't pay enough, you may find yourself headed for court.

If your neighbor is liable, you are entitled to compensation for the cost of repairs and replacements, as well as expenses such as having to stay at a motel and perhaps even mental distress. (Mental distress claims, however, are usually allowed only if you have suffered an underlying physical injury.) Any other harm that results from the neighbor's act will increase the liability. For instance, if a patio flooded by a neighbor's runaway sprinkler were to freeze over, and someone slipped and was injured, the owner of the sprinkler would be looking at paying the injured person's medical expenses.

Or if a neighbor contaminates your well, you may have to visit a doctor, dig another well, or obtain water from another source. The neighbor who caused the problem will have to pay your expenses. Damage to a well can also greatly diminish the value of a house. If there is no other source for water, the responsible party will have to pay for the loss in value to the property.

> EXAMPLE: A sump pump gone awry let pollution seep into several neighbors' wells, permanently polluting them. The owner of the pump was found liable and had to pay to the neighbors the difference in the value of their properties before and after the pollution.[13]

If you end up in court, you may get more than money. Time and again, judges order problems to be fixed if fixing them would be relatively easy and inexpensive. Replacing a downspout, clearing away debris, or cleaning out a drain creates very little burden on a property owner. Removing a retaining wall, relandscaping property, or redoing culverts are heavier burdens, so the court will look more closely at alternatives.

If a neighbor has acted maliciously toward you, you can also ask the court for punitive damages, though be warned that most small claims courts don't grant them. This is an extra amount designed to punish someone for malice or reckless disregard of consequences. For example, a neighbor in Vermont built a road and two culverts on his land that resulted in flooding to the property next door. When the damaged neighbor complained, the road-building neighbor built a third culvert that made the flooding worse. He was also abusive to the neighbor and used offensive language with her. When she sued, the court not only compensated her for her damage, but also ordered the neighbor to stop the water diversion and to pay extra money to her as punishment for malice.[14]

What to Do If You Suffer Water Damage

After you have salvaged everything you can and indulged in appropriate hand-wringing, it's time to get to work. Here are some steps to take. (In addition to these suggestions for action, which are specific to water damage, see Chapter 1.)

Find the Source

When your property is flooded, the first thing to do is to find where the water is coming from. Sometimes tracking down the source can be difficult. First, make sure that the water is not coming from someplace on your own property. Depending on what has happened, you'll want to check your own gutters, pipes, appliances, and other possibilities. One way to determine if the water is coming from your property is to check your water meter. Try turning off all water sources—make sure there is no water being used anywhere inside or outside of your home. Wait an hour, then look at your water meter's flow indicator. If it's moving, it means the meter is picking up some water flow, and you may have a leak in one or more of your water pipes or elsewhere in or around your home. Don't be too quick to blame the nearest neighbor.

> EXAMPLE: Leon has fussed for weeks about his neighbor's removal of trees and vegetation in order to build a tennis court. After a heavy rain, his backyard is soggy, and he proceeds next door to blame the neighbor for runoff. Later, when he discovers that his own septic system had backed up, his relationship with the neighbor is already greatly impaired.

Water may appear to be rushing into your yard or house from your neighbor's property next door, but the source may in fact be somewhere else. Someone a block away may have put in a culvert that sends water running over several properties until it finally stops at the lowest point—such as your basement.

Sometimes people who suddenly find their properties saturated by rainwater are not the victims of another's runoff at all. In fact, the reverse is true; their own runoff is blocked. Whether or not the neighbor is liable will depend on the situation. Retaining walls and other objects can block normal drainage. One neighbor in Illinois dumped a load of dirt on his property and found himself in court for blocking his neighbor's runoff.[15] The cause of your water damage could also be debris blocking a storm drain, and the responsible neighbor in that case may be the city.

Call Your Insurance Company

Contact the agent for your homeowners' insurance to find out where you stand and get any advice you can. Insurance in water damage cases is tricky. If the water comes into your home from an inside source—say, from a pipe in the townhouse next door—your ordinary homeowners' insurance should come into play. In some cases, contacting your agent may be all you have to do. Your company may pay for your damage and then go after whoever caused it for repayment.

When the damage comes from outside rising water, even if your neighbor's action caused the problem, you may need flood insurance to involve your own insurance company. However, your neighbor's company may well pay you directly under the liability provisions of the neighbor's policy. The neighbor's insurance company might even force correction of the problem. Many insurance companies demand that a hazard to someone else be removed from insured property; if it isn't, the homeowner's policy will be canceled.

See Who Else Is Affected

This is a blanket rule for almost every neighbor problem: If you are being harmed, someone else may well be also. And remember that when neighbors join together to correct a problem, they become a more powerful force, whether they are dealing with an individual or a city.

Blocked drainage ditches or creeks can affect an entire neighborhood when it rains. Especially when there has been major construction in the neighborhood, several properties may find themselves awash. In parts of the United States where there are distinct dry and rainy seasons (California, for example), a whole subdivision could be constructed between rains. The development could wreak havoc on a large area when the rains finally arrive.

After houses are built and drainage systems installed, the developer may have sold the property and be long gone. However, if the system is faulty and results in damage to others, the developer may still be responsible.[16]

Inform the Neighbor

Tell the neighbor who you think is at fault about the problem. As with most neighbor problems, the person causing the damage is most likely blissfully unaware of any problem at all. Most people will be horrified to learn that their actions have harmed someone else (not to mention that they will also have to pay for it). Invite the neighbor over to see your damage. (For more on how to approach and inform the neighbor, see Chapter 1.)

If you can, try to have some suggestions ready to remedy the problem. You want more than just compensation for your damage; you don't want this to happen again. If rainwater is the problem, see whether you and your neighbor can come up with a solution. Maybe you can do something on your own property that will help. Maybe you and the neighbor can do something together. Water damage is serious business, and there may be a lot of money involved. To protect yourself and preserve peace in the neighborhood, you should even consider the possibility of spending a little money of your own if you have it. If you end up going to court with a legal expert on water law, you will spend a lot more—in money and time.

Educating Yourself

If you own waterfront property, you may encounter literally hundreds of legal questions. For example, does the public have a right to use the beach? What if the water changes course and leaves the property high and dry? What if the water erodes property and deposits it on a neighbor's land downstream?

Water law is not a simple subject—law schools offer entire courses on "riparian law," their term for water rights. You can do some legal research yourself (see Chapter 18 for advice) or consult a lawyer. But be sure that any attorney you consult has knowledge and experience in riparian law—it's an area in which many general practice attorneys are unversed.

As noted above, in some cases your insurance company may take care of your losses for you. And most neighbors will be responsible enough to inform their insurance companies and to cover damage they have caused.

Try Mediation

Neighbors don't belong in court; a lawsuit shatters any possibility of a cordial relationship. Once it's over, neighbors still have to live close by, and they will likely fight again.

Mediation is an extremely effective alternative to court. It allows two neighbors to work out the solution to a problem themselves with the aid of a neutral party, the mediator. You contact the mediator or mediation agency, and they will take it from there. (See Chapter 19 for more on how this works.)

In a water damage case, the neighbor denying responsibility may be terrified of the potential expense. A good mediator can guide this fear into the open, and the neighbors may be able to reach a compromise or an entirely different solution. For instance, it may make very good sense to go in with a neighbor to redirect a ditch rather than spend that money on legal fees.

Sue in Small Claims Court

If you must go to court, choose small claims court if your damage is under the small claims court limit in your state—usually a few thousand dollars—and if your state allows water damage cases in small claims court. (Chapter 20 explains how to use small claims court and lists each state's limit.) However, if you win your case, most small claims courts can only order the neighbor to pay you. The judge can't order the neighbor to fix the problem. You could wait until you are flooded again and then take the neighbor to court again, and rarely, you can estimate future damages and request them, but this is hardly what you want. Find out from your small claims court clerk whether the judge can order anything besides current money damages. If not, you may need to sue in regular court to get the changes you need.

Whether you are asking for money or for an order to make the neighbor fix the problem, you must prove that the neighbor is liable and show the extent of your loss.

Preparation is key to small claims court success. Photographs can help explain a situation to a judge. You also may have to hire an expert—plumber, architect, or engineer—to explain why and how your damage was caused, why the neighbor is responsible, and what can be done to correct the problem. Your neighbor may argue in turn that the damage was caused by a natural condition or by an act of God. You'll want to be prepared to argue against such claims. If your damages are very large or you are dealing with complicated arguments, you will want to talk to a good attorney, and you may have to use regular (not small claims) court.

If your neighbor is arguing that your damage resulted from a natural condition of the land, or that the actions taken were reasonable to protect the neighbor's own property, consider hiring a lawyer and going to regular court. Find a lawyer who understands and practices "water law," and be prepared to pay for this expertise.

Rights to Water

If you and your neighbors share a water source—whether it's well water or the water in a stream or lake—your rights depend on what state you live in. Two quite different systems of rules are in place in different states, and a few states draw rules from both systems.

The Reasonable Use Rule

In most of the country, people who share water must take and use it in a reasonable manner that does not harm their neighbors. What is reasonable is determined on a case-by-case basis. A neighbor who decides to create a private pond from well water or pump it to another property is likely in for a legal battle.

EXAMPLE: A family in Ohio had drawn good water for years from their well until a neighbor began operating a stone quarry. The neighbors both took their water from the same aquifer. After the quarry began operating, the quality of the water declined. Worse, the family's well began to dry up. They drilled a new well and still couldn't find water. They finally moved but couldn't sell the property because of the lack of water.

Two years later, city water became available, and the family connected the property to it. But they still sued the neighboring quarry owner for their damages, and won. The quarry owner had not used the shared well water in a reasonable manner.[17]

Similarly, if you own waterfront (also called "riparian" or "littoral") property, you may make use of lake water in a reasonable manner. Normally, each landowner may use the entire lake. But they may not interfere with use by the other owners.

EXAMPLE: Herbert and his three fishing buddies own adjoining properties on a private lake. They and their families use the lake for fishing, swimming, and general recreation. Herbert retires to the lake property and opens an outboard motor repair shop. Runoff from the shop pollutes the lake. His buddies sue him for destroying their recreational use.

The court will look at whether Herbert's actions were reasonable under the circumstances. Herbert likely will be liable to the other owners for the pollution. (He probably violated environmental protection laws, too.)

Courts try to balance the benefit to one owner against the detriment to the others. In a case in Arkansas, one owner of a recreational lake diverted water from the lake for irrigation. Irrigation is generally considered a reasonable and beneficial use. But the court decided that the irrigation could not be allowed if it destroyed the recreational use of the other owners.[18]

Under the reasonable use system, water must be used on the waterfront property itself. In other words, an owner can't pump the water out and sell it, or pipe it to another place.

Private Land, Public Water

Navigable waters, including many small streams, are regulated by the government and actually owned by the states, along with the land that lies under the water. This gives the public the right to use the waters. But it doesn't give the public the right to use private property adjoining the water unless a special law has been passed concerning a particular area, or an easement to cross the land exists (see Chapter 10).

The Prior Appropriation Rule

Most Western states, where water is scarce, don't require neighbors to share water in a reasonable manner. Instead, they determine rights to water by a method called "prior appropriation." Basically, this means "first come, first served." If you get there first, you are entitled to a government permit to use as much as you need for a particular use. Even a few Eastern states—including Florida, Maryland, and New York— have permit systems in place.

Those who have permits for water use sometimes may use all of it and not be liable to their neighbors.

> EXAMPLE: Regina lives by a babbling brook in Arizona. She wakes up one day to no babble and no brook. Her upstream neighbor has diverted the water for other purposes. Because Arizona uses a permit system, the neighbor may have the right to divert all of the water. (If Regina lived in Georgia or another "reasonable use" state, however, she could probably sue the neighbor.)

Under a permit system, neighbors are unlikely to be caught unaware of what their water rights are. Taking water from common sources and drilling wells is heavily regulated by state and local laws. In California, for example, applications for a well are quite detailed, and the drilling must be done by someone who is a licensed water well contractor.[19] If someone else already has a right to the water you seek, your permit should be denied.

If you live in a prior appropriation state and you suspect that someone is siphoning off or damaging your water, report it to the appropriate official or consult a local lawyer.

Downstream Flooding

An old common law rule in the United States, called the "natural watercourse rule," provides immunity to an upstream owner for damage to lower neighbors. Under this rule, the upstream neighbor can actually alter the water—for example, by adding volume from runoff—and not be liable for flooding the neighbors.

The New Hampshire Supreme Court threw out this rule back in 1862 and decided that someone who causes flooding downstream is liable for the damage if an unreasonable action caused the flooding.[20] But most other courts have been quite slow to make this switch. In neighboring Connecticut, in a case where subdivision development altered a brook and flooded a homeowner's property and garage, the court finally recognized a reasonableness test in 1983.[21]

Courts are shifting to the reasonableness rule for cases involving natural watercourses. When the right case comes along—one with heavy damage and someone probably at fault—judges usually consider the reasonableness of the action that caused the harm.

What is reasonable action on the part of one who damages downstream neighbors? In a case in New Jersey, a developer created surface runoff that increased the volume of a stream and carried away ten feet of a neighbor's property. The court adopted the reasonableness test and suggested balancing the competing interests using general principles of fairness and common sense.[22]

Using the reasonableness test does not mean that a damaged downstream neighbor will always win in court. What is reasonable in any given situation will be decided for that situation.

EXAMPLE: A group of neighbors owned waterfront property on the Reliez Creek near San Francisco. Upstream, the city and state transportation departments had altered the land with a new freeway and rail transportation. Other urbanization had also occurred. All of this resulted in increased volume of runoff into the creek. When severe rains came, the creek spread at some points from its original 40-foot width to 110 feet wide. (You can close your eyes and imagine the property washed away.)

After years in court and who knows how much money, the state supreme court denied damages to the neighbors. The court ruled that the city and state had not been shown to have acted unreasonably, and that both upper and lower owners must act reasonably. In California at least, if the upper person acts reasonably, the lower neighbors must protect their own properties from any potential damage that might result from those reasonable actions.[23]

As you can see, if you face serious problems over water rights and responsibilities, you need the help of a specialist in riparian law. When neighbors can work together to solve the problems, that is the best solution. But if not, you will need expert help. ●

Endnotes

1 *Ackerhalt v. Nat'l. Sav. & Trust Co.*, 244 F.2d 760 (D.C. App. 1956). The damaged neighbor had repeatedly complained about the leak and it wasn't fixed.

2 *Forbus v. Knight*, 163 P.2d 822 (Wash. 1945); *Donner v. Blue*, 187 Wash. App. 51 (2015).

3 *Bahrle v. Exxon Corp.*, 652 A.2d 178 (N.J. 1995), *aff'd*, 145 N.J. 144, 678 A.2d 225 (1996).

4 *Bracewell v. King*, 250 S.E.2d 25 (Ga. 1978).

5 *Scottish Guarantee Ins. Co. v. Dwyer*, 19 F.3d 307 (Wis. 1994).

6 Tex. Water Code Ann. § 11.086.

7 32 P.S §§ 680.13-15.

8 *Keys v. Romley*, 64 Cal. 2d 396, 50 Cal.Rptr. 273 (1966).

9 *Hazeltine v. Edgmand*, 35 Kan. 202, 10 P. 544 (Kan. 1886).

10 *Steiger v. Nowakowski*, 227 N.W.2d 104 (Wis. 1975); *Keller v. Patterson*, 343 Wis. 2d 509 (2012).

11 *Clark County v. Powers*, 611 P.2d 1072 (Nev. 1980); *Fritz v. Washoe County* 376 P. 3d 794 (2016).

12 *Lang v. Wonnenberg*, 455 N.W.2d 832 (N.D. 1990).

13 *Haveman v. Beulow*, 217 P.2d 313 (Wash. 1950).

14 *Powers v. Judd*, 553 A.2d 139 (Vt. 1988).

15 *Dessen v. Jones*, 551 N.E.2d 782 (Ill. 1990).

16 *Keeley v. Manor Park Apts.*, 99 A.2d 248 (Del. 1953).

17 *Wood v. American Aggregates Corp.*, 585 N.E.2d 970 (Ohio App. 1990).

18 *Harris v. Brooks*, 283 S.W.2d 129 (Ark. 1955).

19 Cal. Water Code § 13750.5.

20 *Bassett v. Salisbury Manufacturing Company*, 43 N.H. 569 (1862).

21 *Peterson v. Town of Oxford*, 459 A.2d 100 (Conn. 1983).

22 *Armstrong v. Francis Corp.*, 120 A.2d 4 (N.J. 1956). This is a leading case in the country addressing the reasonable use test for natural watercourses. This means that lawyers in other states present the court opinion to their state courts and argue for adopting its reasoning. Any time you hear a judge say "We agree with *Armstrong*," you know the court will follow the reasonableness test.

23 *Locklin v. City of Lafayette*, 27 Cal.Rptr. 2d 613 (Cal. 1994). The opinion in this case is very long and covers a history of water rights. It also discusses the rules in other states. If you have access to a law library and you are a concerned waterfront owner, it is worth your time to read this case. See Chapter 18; See also *Pacific Bell v. City of San Diego*, 7 Cal.4th 327 (2000).

When Your Neighbor Is a Business

*Labor disgraces no man; unfortunately, you occasionally
find man disgraces labor.*

—Ulysses Grant

Problem neighbors come in all different shapes and sizes. Many of us have to deal with the grouch next door who complains about our trees or with teenagers across the street who blast music at all hours. Then there are those who are awakened every morning before dawn by the shrill beeps of delivery trucks backing up to the grocery store next door or who can never find a parking space because their neighbor teaches yoga classes in her living room.

In many urban areas, residents and businesses must coexist next door to each other or even in the same building. Being able to walk to the grocery store or your favorite deli is a plus and can add value to your property. But a business neighbor can be a nightmare, too. Your problems may stem from a store, a home business, a shopping mall, a nightclub, or even a race car speedway. Your dishes may be rattling day and night as airplanes take off from a nearby airport.

A lot of people do nothing when a nearby business makes them miserable. They feel intimidated or don't know where to look for help. But they do not have to suffer in silence. They often can solve their problems by reading their local laws and learning how to handle disputes with neighbors. We hope this chapter will help.

A basic principle of neighbor law applies to all neighbors, business or otherwise: If you are seriously and significantly harmed by your neighbor's actions, your neighbor is most likely breaking the law. You can seek damages for your harm, and in many instances, you can have the offending activity stopped. You have legal rights, even when your neighbor is a business.

When you are having trouble with a business neighbor, keep in mind:

• Zoning laws are crucial. They control an enormous amount of what goes on in a given area. They may prohibit any business in a certain locale or specify requirements for them. You must understand how they affect you. Other laws may also help.

- Any neighbor who unreasonably interferes with the enjoyment of another person's property is likely breaking the law and may be liable for the harm caused.
- Judges do not like to shut down legitimate businesses and usually won't do it. Be ready to expect a compromise.

Let's look more closely at particular issues relating to business neighbor problems.

Zoning Laws

Most people don't think about their zoning laws until something enters the picture that doesn't seem quite right. At that point, zoning laws can be a real friend to an offended neighbor.

Local Zoning Laws

Zoning laws exist in almost every community in the United States. They are local laws that reflect standard community values by regulating what type of activity is allowed where. Your city's governing body, such as the city council or local board of supervisors, makes zoning laws. In larger cities, a zoning board presides over complaints, hears any requests for change, and enforces the zoning laws. In smaller cities, the body that enacts the laws handles these enforcement matters. Even where a zoning board exists, however, any real change in the law will always be made by the city's governing body.

When you selected your present residence, you probably learned whether the property was zoned for residential single-family dwellings only or whether other uses were allowed, such as residential multifamily dwellings. But did you check the zoning across the street or a block away? Even the property next door to you may fall under different zoning.

Why does this matter? If the other property is zoned for commercial or industrial use as well as residential, the residents will be subjected to fewer restrictions on the types of activities allowed on the premises. Consequently, they can engage in more activities that might affect the neighborhood than they would if their property were zoned residential only.

For example, in Chapter 2 we talk about laws that address allowable decibel levels and quiet-time rules preventing noise during certain hours. These laws vary hugely among different zoning areas.

> **EXAMPLE 1:** Ita and Kari live in a comfortable house on a lovely tree-lined street. The zoning for their entire block is single-family residential and the law imposes quiet times between 10 p.m. and 8 a.m. every day. One day, they are awakened at 6 a.m. by the noise of lawnmowers being repaired next door, with a string of customers down the neighbor's driveway. The neighbor is violating the law.

> **EXAMPLE 2:** Saro and Lola live in a neighborhood protected by zoning. No business is allowed and quiet times are enforced. A block away a nightclub springs to life with music and dancing every night until 1 a.m. Saro and Lola check the zoning for the address of the nightclub and find that it is zoned for commercial and industrial uses. The quiet hour begins an hour after midnight, so the new neighbor is not violating the zoning laws.

These examples show how important it is to check your zoning laws, for your address and surrounding areas. Restrictions in zoning laws may solve your problem, and, if not, they will save you from unnecessary confrontations. For example, the zoning laws in the latter case offer no relief to Saro and Lola. If they call the police to complain, the police will arrive only to tell them that they can do nothing. The police may be annoyed by the call and Saro and Lola may even be a little embarrassed at having called the authorities. Knowledge of the rules could have prevented this outcome.

Even if the nightclub is operating within the guidelines of the zoning law, Saro and Lola, not to mention their other neighbors, may find help from other laws. See "Other Laws Protecting You and Your Property," below.

Watch Out for Variance Requests

You may be sitting snug and secure with your local zoning when a sign goes up down the street announcing a request for a variance. This means a neighbor has asked the zoning board or city council to allow an activity that is not permitted under current zoning. It could be a simple request to place a garage a foot closer to the street and be of no concern to you. But it could also be a request for a commercial license to run a business on the property. Of course, your neighbor's proposal for a business may not affect you either—don't jump to conclusions!—but you should definitely look into the matter.

When someone requests a variance, the zoning board or city council posts a sign on the property stating that a variance request is pending. The request may also be published in the local newspaper. To learn the specifics of the request, you'll have to do a little digging, but not too much. Usually, a call to city hall will tell you what you need to know.

If you don't like what you hear, the first thing you should do is talk to your neighbors. If you find others who oppose the proposed variance, gather names on a petition protesting it. The zoning board or city council will hold a public hearing before voting on the request. Be ready to attend and speak out. Call city hall and find out if you need to present your petition before the hearing and to get scheduled to speak at the meeting. Explain how the change will harm your neighborhood. If enough neighbors complain, the board may deny the request at that hearing.

Where to Find Your Zoning Laws

If you live in a city, the best place to learn about your zoning laws is city hall. You'll be able to read up on the zoning laws and figure out which law applies to your property and any other location that concerns you. A map usually shows in detail what zoning applies where. You may also obtain this information at the public library, but be aware that the law books in the library may be out of date. Also check the Internet. The county courthouse, the public library, or the Internet will house county zoning laws.

If you live in a large urban area, remember that your neighbor down the block could technically be in a different city than you. You may be able to check your own zoning law at Los Angeles City Hall, for example, but have to go to West Hollywood City Hall to check your neighbor's— even if their property is a few houses away. (For more tips on looking up zoning laws, see Chapter 18.)

Zoning Laws Outside Incorporated Towns

Those of you who live outside an incorporated community may have county laws that give you the protection of zoning regulations. We emphasize "may" because many counties simply do not restrict activities in unincorporated areas. And if they do, they often allow agricultural, industrial, commercial, and residential uses to coexist. This lack of regulation greatly appeals to people who want to do their own thing and not have the government poking its nose into their activities. But the lack of regulation can backfire on a neighbor.

> EXAMPLE: Some years ago, author John Grisham (who is also a lawyer) and his family built a beautiful farm outside the city limits of Oxford, Mississippi. The farmhouse itself sits atop a hill and, when it was built, overlooked rolling hills and pastures. A few years later, a large mobile home dealership went up next door. Now, the Grishams have lost their view and they are faced with the very traffic and noise that they had hoped to escape by living in the country. Because of the lack of zoning, this situation could get worse. What is to stop a factory from going up on the other side?

Covenants, Conditions, and Restrictions

If you live in a condo or a community with a homeowners' association, you agreed when you moved in to abide by certain rules. These rules are contained in documents called the covenants, conditions, and restrictions (or CC&Rs). You should have a copy, and a copy should be recorded (on file) at the local courthouse. You can also get a copy from the homeowners' association. The fact that the CC&Rs are recorded means that the restrictions are tied to the land they cover. When the property is sold, each new owner is bound by the rules.

The CC&Rs of purely residential communities have traditionally prohibited any type of business activity within the community. With the growing recognition of telecommuting as a viable work alternative, we see this changing in some of the newer communities. Even when telecommuting is allowed, however, the rules commonly still prohibit any business that is visible, creates traffic, or employs other people.

In these communities, breaking the rules can cause real trouble. CC&Rs usually specify consequences for breaking the rules. The home-owners' association can fine the neighbor, take away his or her privileges (such as use of the common areas), sue the neighbor, or shut down the business. Associations have closed down beauty shops, day care centers, and even an occasional garage sale. Also, one neighbor can bypass the association and sue another directly for breaking the rules.

There are some limits on the power of the association to respond to rules violations. A homeowners' association cannot choose to selectively enforce the rules against only certain homeowners (the lawyerly term is "arbitrary enforcement"). If the association has allowed some businesses in the past, it may not be able shut down a new one that appears.

Home-Based Businesses

Many people complain when they discover that their neighbor is conducting a business at home. They may directly feel the presence of the business through noise or traffic. And they may worry about what the business will mean for the future of their community. The business might disrupt their residential neighborhood, causing a decline in property values. They may also fear that a zoning change is in the wind, which might introduce more unwelcome changes.

> **EXAMPLE:** Jona lives in a residential-only neighborhood. She notices that it's becoming hard to park near her house and that the congestion is worst in front of her next-door neighbor's house. When she asks her neighbor about this, she discovers that the neighbor is running a beauty parlor in her home. Jona is afraid that if the business is not stopped, others will follow. And because of the parking situation, she thinks her property value is already diminished.

Most home businesses are not very intrusive. A computer consultant, for example, who advises an occasional visitor is hardly a problem. But if the same consultant begins teaching classes at home every night, it can change the appearance of the neighborhood.

Local zoning laws and/or city ordinances usually control whether a business can operate at any particular location, including someone's home. In planned residential communities, CC&Rs can govern as well. Both of these are more lenient on home businesses in residential areas if the business is not visible than if the business is obvious—such as a store that is open to the public. A lot of zoning laws don't even address the issue of people working at home unless clients and customers are involved.

State Industrial Homework Laws

A few states have industrial homework laws that prohibit work done at home. These laws were created years ago to address the problem of sweatshops run in people's homes. They are antiquated and are rapidly disappearing. But if you're concerned about a home business and find no recourse in the zoning laws, local ordinances, or your CC&Rs, you might want to look up your state statutes. (See Chapter 18.)

When surrounding property values are not actually affected, regulations on home businesses and offices are often in a gray area and sometimes require interpretation by a court. Usually the key issue is the amount of activity generated by the business and the degree of the neighbor's perceived sense of intrusion. A typical zoning law or regulation will often simply state that the property is zoned for residential use only. How does this apply, for example, to a writer who works at home and lists the home address as an official business address? Let's look at a few general guidelines to help understand the law.

State Laws Protecting Home Businesses

State laws are recognizing our changing times and the fact that working at home is important to many people. The number of U.S. employees allowed to remote work or telecommute has increased substantially in the last few years. According to FlexJobs and Global Workplace Analytics, as of February 2020, 4.7 million U.S. workers (3.4% of the population) work remotely. As a result, we can expect more states to enact laws protecting work-from-home policies. State law will overrule local zoning laws.

Telecommuting not only decreases traffic, but can allow a parent to work and stay at home with children at the same time. And as of the time of this writing, in the wake of the novel Coronavirus outbreak, many tech companies, including Twitter, Microsoft, and LinkedIn have told workers to telecommute to help prevent further spread of this virus.

If You Are the Offended Neighbor

When someone complains, many zoning boards and city authorities will look at the type of the business and its impact on the neighborhood. Local zoning laws may well allow a person to work at home, as long as the work doesn't involve hosting clients or customers in the home. Others forbid inventory storage or increased traffic. Businesses such as the following don't typically bother others and are usually within the law:
- writers, artists, consultants—anyone who is quiet and does not deal directly with the public, and
- hobbies, such as ceramics or woodworking, the products of which are later sold elsewhere.

A more intrusive home business that disturbs the neighbors may violate residential zoning. Activities such as these may cross the legal line:
- clients coming and going all day
- increased traffic on the street
- parking problems for you and other neighbors
- delivery trucks arriving frequently

- a garage or yard littered with inventory
- the making of goods or products that require the use of noxious or toxic chemicals
- signs advertising the business, or
- any activity that you reasonably think decreases the value of your home.

If You Are the Neighbor With the Business

So you want to work at home? The list above provides a good indication of what kinds of businesses are likely to bother your neighbors. You should set your parameters accordingly. Here are a few suggestions that may help prevent problems:

- Make house calls. See your clients at their homes or rent office space part time for client meetings.
- Store your inventory somewhere else. Rent a storage shed.
- Rent a mailbox for heavy mail or deliveries.
- If your neighbors know you are working at home, remind them that your presence during the day could be a safety factor for them—you can keep an eye on the neighborhood.

For more information on how to run a home business without running into trouble with the law or your neighbors, see *Working for Yourself*, by Stephen Fishman (Nolo), and *Legal Guide for Starting & Running a Small Business*, by Fred S. Steingold (Nolo).

Other Laws Protecting You and Your Property

In addition to any zoning laws and CC&Rs that may apply to you, you have other legal rights that protect you from intrusion at the hands of your business neighbor. When a neighbor unreasonably interferes with the use and enjoyment of your property, the neighbor is breaking the law. This is called a private nuisance. When the interference affects an entire neighborhood or the public in general, the activity could be an illegal public nuisance. And a neighbor who harms you or your property through careless behavior could be guilty of negligence. Nuisance and negligence are legal theories created by state law and court decisions that you can use to sue your neighbor.

What does this mean for you? If your neighbor is creating a public or private nuisance or acting negligently, you can do the following:

- You can sue the neighbor for monetary damages; small claims court is a good choice for this. Damages include lack of sleep, inability to work, loss of the use of a portion of your residence (or all of it), legal expenses incurred, and a reduction in your property value (not available if you are a tenant). Some judges will award you damages for mental anguish you have suffered.
- You can ask a judge to order the offending activity stopped. In most states, this will mean going to regular court. A lawsuit will be expensive but may be worth it.

What Is a Private Nuisance?

State laws generally define a nuisance as any activity that interferes with someone else's property. Some states add the words "unreasonably" or "unlawfully." Regardless of the terminology, if you are really being disturbed (in other words, you're not being overly fussy), the neighbor's action is probably unreasonable and is legally a private nuisance. Nuisance is a legal term, but it means exactly what you would think. For instance:

- Have you been kept awake late into the night by noise?
- Are you unable to sit outside and enjoy your yard because of traffic noise and pollution your neighbor has created?
- Have so many cars appeared on the street that you have lost a place to park anywhere near your house?
- Is your property littered with junk left by your neighbor's visitors?
- Has your property decreased in value because of the neighbor's activity?

If so, you've probably been subjected to a nuisance. You can find out how your state law defines nuisance in Appendix B. Be aware that some states do not address the topic in their statutes. In these states, nuisance is a judicially created doctrine, and, in court, it has the weight of a statute. To learn about nuisance in these states, you'll have to read judicial decisions (cases) instead of a statute. (See Chapter 18.)

There aren't a lot of lawsuits these days on nuisance between a residential neighbor and a business. This is partly due to the expense of litigation. Another reason is that most neighbors and businesses settle their problems long before going to court over them. Some old court decisions, however, remain good law and give us guidelines.

> EXAMPLE: Back in 1910, a California homeowner successfully sued a neighboring gas works because of the noxious odors and noise drifting onto his property and into his home. The court stopped the operation and gave the offended neighbor $750 in damages, a hefty amount for the times and a disaster for the company.[1]

In the past, many residential neighbors successfully sued agricultural operations about odors, insects, and noise. But these cases have been overridden by the new right-to-farm laws passed in every state. The laws protect farmers from lawsuits unless they are breaking the law or running substandard operations—quite difficult to prove in court. If your offending neighbor is an agricultural operation, see Chapter 14.

Often the question of interference with your property and whether it is worth going to court is one of degree. Deciding whether to go to court depends on how badly you are being annoyed and whether a judge is likely to find a nuisance. For example, someone who grooms a few dogs a day in a garage may not cause neighbors problems worth a lawsuit. But turn that grooming into a full kennel and a judge could declare it a nuisance and order the owner to shut it down.[2]

And remember, even when you are sure that your neighbor is creating a nuisance, you are better off avoiding court and tackling the problem in other ways. (See "What to Do When the Law Favors You," below.)

What Is a Public Nuisance?

When many neighbors are harmed—sometimes an entire neighborhood—the offensive activity could be a public nuisance. Most states define a public nuisance as one business that threatens the health, safety, or morals of a community. If your business neighbor's behavior creates such a threat, the proper city office can act swiftly to solve the problem. It can fine the business for any harm done, order the activity stopped, and bring suit against the business.

In 2013, the city of Irwindale in California filed a lawsuit against Huy Fong Foods, the manufacturer of the hugely popular Sriracha chili sauce. In order to make its punchy condiment, Huy Fong Foods processed approximately 100 million pounds of jalapeno peppers a year. The city claimed that the odors emanating from Huy Fong Foods' 650,000-square-foot factory constituted a public nuisance to local residents, who complained that the pungent mix of jalapeno peppers and garlic fumes caused a variety of health problems, including headaches, watery eyes, and burning throats.

The city asked the company to install a new filtration system to reduce and dissipate the fumes. After a November 2013 hearing, Superior Court Judge Robert H. O'Brien issued a preliminary injunction, ordering the company to halt operations at its factory and make changes to help lessen the odors. Although the judge found a "lack of credible evidence" linking the stated health problems to the fumes, he stated that the odor was "extremely annoying, irritating and offensive to the senses, warranting consideration as a public nuisance." Eventually, the city of Irwindale and Huy Fong Foods were able to resolve the matter out of court after the company updated the filtration system and made a written commitment to resolve any smell issues identified by the city.[3]

And, in Memphis, Tennessee, a group of neighbors got together and sued to shut down a nightclub. The club was legally zoned but still creating real problems for its neighbors. It was driving down property values in the entire neighborhood because of traffic, noise, and litter. The judge found that it was a public nuisance. He did not close the club but did remove its liquor license.

In general, stopping a business that is harming many people is much easier than stopping a business affecting only one. (See "What to Do When the Law Favors You," below.)

The Negligent Business Neighbor

A different legal theory that you can employ for relief from an annoying business neighbor is negligence. The law of negligence holds that all persons are under a general duty not to act in ways that create an unreasonable risk of harm to others. If someone acts carelessly, or "negligently," and the careless behavior harms you, the person may be liable to you for your harm. You could sue to receive money damages, and, if the carelessness continues, to stop it.

The distinction between nuisance and negligence is often hard to discern because the same person can create a nuisance and be negligent at the same time. The two theories don't always overlap, but sometimes they do. Generally, if a business injures your person or property as a result of careless behavior, it may have acted negligently. If the business interferes with your enjoyment or use of your property, it might be a private nuisance. Negligence normally refers to a single incident: A business's actions caused an accident that injured you or your property. Nuisance, on the other hand, applies to an ongoing behavior that annoys or interferes with you, rather than one that causes a particular, easily identifiable injury.

We have all heard of "slip and fall" cases. Consider the following example.

> EXAMPLE: After a winter storm, the grocer downstairs from you neglects to remove ice from the sidewalk outside the store. On your way to your car, you slip and break your leg. The owner of the grocery may be negligent and have to pay for your medical costs, lost wages, and any other expenses you incur. This is true even though the store itself is not a nuisance.

The difference can be important when you have trouble with a business neighbor. Many judges who would be quite reluctant to declare a business itself a nuisance may be more receptive to finding certain of an owner's actions negligent. This lets the judge order the negligent actions stopped while allowing the business to remain open. The term you use about the activity in the first place could determine whether you are awarded damages for your harm.

The example above pertains to personal injury, but the same principle applies when your neighbor damages your property. In Florida, one neighbor built a retaining wall, which caused rainwater to flood the next-door neighbor's property. The result was negligence.[4] Both of these neighbors were businesses, but the outcome would have been the same if one were a residence. If you are dealing with water damage flowing from a business neighbor, read Chapter 15.

Businesses that act negligently can end up losing heavily in court actions brought by neighbors. In Texas, an underground salt dome facility exploded, damaging many neighbors around it. The court found the facility was a nuisance and acted with negligence, and it awarded the neighbors a huge sum of money.[5]

Additional Help for Tenants

Those who rent their homes, whether a house or an apartment, have most of the same legal rights we have discussed above. As a tenant, you have the right to legal remedies for interference with the enjoyment of your rented property and to request enforcement of other laws that protect you. The only damage that you can't claim is the diminished value to the real estate itself. Only actual owners may seek damages for that. But you can still sue for the other damages listed above.

Probably even more important, you have a powerful tool to help you that owners do not: your lease. All tenants are guaranteed the quiet enjoyment of their rental and safe, healthy, and habitable premises. Many leases and rental agreements echo this guarantee, but the protections are there whether stated in the lease or not. (See Chapter 1 for more details on your rights as a tenant.)

If you lose either your quiet enjoyment of your home or the benefit of habitable premises, you can go straight to your landlord. The landlord is likely to help your cause in order to keep you as a tenant and, if the landlord isn't voluntarily helpful, state or local landlord-tenant law may give you ways to address the problem yourself. If you decide you would rather live somewhere else than fight to make your current residence liveable, you may be able to break your lease without liability for future rent, or even sue the landlord for breach of contract.

> **EXAMPLE:** Como moves into an apartment above two small businesses, a fast-food restaurant and a dry cleaners. He voices concern before signing his lease about odors and noise, even though the lease guarantees a habitable apartment. The landlord strongly reassures him that there is no problem. After a few weeks, Como becomes ill from the dry cleaning fumes, which are masked only by the heavy odor of food from below. His furniture and books are covered with grease.

In a situation like this, a good landlord would act to correct the problem, for instance, by installing a different ventilation system. But if the landlord does nothing, Como can move out without breaching the lease because the apartment is not habitable. The landlord also could end up having to pay for Como's relocation expenses and other damages.

In an apartment complex, you probably have a clause in your rental agreement that prohibits operating a business in your unit. This applies to you and also to your neighbors in the complex. If the neighbor next door starts running a massage parlor with customers coming and going at all hours, the landlord can order the activity stopped or evict the offending tenant.

Expect a Compromise

Before you enter a dispute with a business neighbor, you should understand what you can and cannot expect to happen. Just because the restaurant delivery trucks next door are waking you at 4 a.m. doesn't mean that a judge will simply close the place down.

As we mentioned earlier, judges tend to fashion compromises rather than shut businesses down. Knowing this, you should prepare yourself mentally for the fact that you probably won't be entirely rid of the offender. Consider strategies for a negotiated compromise. That way, you'll have a better chance of having a hand in how the situation is resolved and ultimately being satisfied with the result.

Sit down and make a list of exactly what about the business bothers you—a detailed list. Think about the pros and cons of having a nearby business. Maybe you get mad at the downstairs pizza parlor's noise, but you also love having it there when you are hungry.

Make up your mind about what you are willing to accept from a neighboring business. What matters to you and what are you willing to tolerate? Write out what you believe are acceptable compromises before someone else does it for you. When cases against businesses end up in court, judges can come up with amazing compromises.

> **EXAMPLE 1:** Neighbors of a poultry business sued over odors and insects. The result? The business owners were ordered to clean the place up more often, in order to lessen the offense, but were allowed to remain open.[6]

> **EXAMPLE 2:** A court was faced with the exasperated neighbors of a noisy racetrack. Was the speedway shut down? No. The judge ordered mufflers to be placed on the racing cars to cut down the noise.[7]

What to Do When the Law Favors You

Now that we have covered the laws and regulations for business neighbors, let's get to the nitty-gritty. What steps do you take to stop the problem activity of a business neighbor? Chapter 1 covers in detail how to proceed when faced with a neighbor problem. One suggestion in that chapter applies strongly if you are faced with a business neighbor problem: Keep a written list of what is annoying you, the level of annoyance, and how often it happens. There are additional considerations, especially applicable to business neighbor situations, that we will emphasize here.

Find Out Who Else Is Annoyed

A business neighbor that is disturbing you is likely disturbing others, maybe many others. As we stress throughout this book, it is important for neighbors to band together when faced with a neighbor problem. The more people who complain, the heavier the clout. Before you make any moves, you should get in touch with your neighbors.

Talking to your neighbors is important not just for garnering support but also for figuring out the scope of the problem. When you hear from your neighbors, you might discover that you are the only person affected or that others don't want to complain. You could even learn that the things that drive you crazy don't bother your neighbors in the least. These are all possibilities that you need to know before you act.

How do you find out who is disturbed? Try the following:

- If you know your neighbors, ask them.
- If you don't know the neighbors, or you want to enlarge the numbers as much as possible, put out written notices voicing your concerns and ask for input. You could use a neighborhood listserve or good old-fashioned paper that you hand out yourself.
- Call a neighborhood meeting. This is a good occasion to get to know your neighbors and to find out what they would accept as a solution.

Know the Law

Get copies of your zoning laws, noise laws, CC&Rs, rental agreement—anything that can help you. The law can be extremely useful for rallying support behind your cause. Bring copies of the law to your neighborhood meetings or hand or send them out with your flyers. You'll also need copies of the law at every other step in your fight, from confronting the neighbor to going to court.

Complain to the Neighbor

Amazingly enough, people who are upset with a neighbor often skip this step. What's the point of trying to talk to someone who acts in such an offensive manner? You need to make sure your neighbor knows of the problem. People are often so keenly aware of an annoyance that they can't imagine the offending neighbor doesn't know about it. The fact is, however, that the neighbor who is causing a problem is usually the last to know that there is one.

Many neighbors discover that finding a creative solution to a business dispute is easier than dealing with a single grouch in the house across the street. There are two reasons for this. The first is that most businesses value their reputations and want to be good neighbors. The second is that, when a business is responsible for a problem, an entire neighborhood is often affected, and neighbors have much more power when they complain together.

> **EXAMPLE 1:** In Illinois, neighbors complained about the stench of a large hog farm operation. The farm's operations were protected by a right-to-farm law (see Chapter 14), and the neighbors knew they couldn't shut down the operation. The farm owner, however, did not want unhappy neighbors. In response to neighbors' complaints, he designed a recycling method to decrease odor and turn his hogs' waste into mulch that his neighbors could use for landscaping.[8]

> **EXAMPLE 2:** In Houston, Texas, a neighborhood found itself besieged when a local tennis club began hosting major matches. The neighbors were inundated with heavy traffic, parking problems, and litter. What did the tennis club owners do? They leased parking space in another location and provided free shuttle service for their patrons.[9]

> **EXAMPLE 3:** Owners of a bar in Grand Rapids, Michigan, faced with a group of complaining neighbors, installed insulation to muffle the noise and maintain good neighborhood relations. The bar also moved large events to a different venue to reduce loitering.[10]

Though you may be upset and emotional, it is most effective to complain to a business neighbor in a businesslike fashion. Here are some examples of assertive yet measured ways of alerting business owners to the trouble they have created:

- Present a petition to the owner describing the problem. Hopefully, the petition will be signed by 15, 30, 50, 100 people. Having many names on the petition will draw a lot of attention. It will also tell the owner that you are organized and ready to act.

- Attach to your complaint a copy of the law or regulation that the business is violating. The owner may be blissfully unaware of it and be horrified by the violation.
- Offer a solution to the problem when you present the complaint. Remember the word "compromise." This can make the offending neighbor much less defensive and may actually solve your problem right on the spot.
- Make sure that the person you speak with understands that you have not notified the police or any other authority, and that, if possible, you would prefer to resolve the issue at the neighbor-to-neighbor level. Police visits, calls from authorities, and lawsuits poison neighbor relationships. If this neighbor turns out to be cooperative, you may keep peace among you, which of course is in your best interest.
- If the business is hostile and does nothing, complain again, this time by registered mail. Make sure you keep records of all of your actions. A judge may require them.

Attempt Mediation

Mediation is a process in which opposing parties sit down with a trained neutral person and attempt to work out their own solution to a problem. We almost always suggest it when neighbor problems arise. When neighbors meet even one time with a trained mediator, the success rate for solutions is phenomenal. And both parties should understand that if they refuse to mediate, a court may order it anyway. See Chapter 19 for details about mediation.

Notify the Authorities

When the business clearly won't cooperate, it's time to report any violation to the proper authority. This could be the zoning board, city hall, a landlord, your homeowners' association, or the police. Where you complain will depend on what the particular problem involves. If you have a neighbor violating the zoning laws, you would go to the zoning board or, if there is no board, to the city council. For traffic or noise problems, you probably should use the police. For interference with the enjoyment of your property, you'll take your complaint to court. (See "Go to Court," below.) And if you are a renter, the landlord is the best place to start for any of the above types of problems.

Give the authorities time to act. Don't expect overnight action; they may be swamped. After a reasonable waiting period, report again. Sometimes neighbor problems have a way of finding themselves on the bottom of the stack when it comes to action. How many names are on your complaint? A hundred calls a day to city hall or a landlord will usually get some action.

Go to Court

As a last resort, go to court. Use small claims court if you can. In most states, small claims courts only have the power to impose money damages on a business—they can't order the business to change its behavior in any way.

However, money damages may be sufficient to solve your problem. If each neighbor goes to court individually and asks the court for the maximum amount allowed, the total can be very persuasive. If the business continues to unreasonably annoy the neighbors, you can go back and sue again—and again. Even large businesses tire of being hit in the wallet.

> EXAMPLE: Can neighbors really take on a huge airport for noise and property damage? Neighbors of the San Francisco airport did. They went to small claims court individually and asked for the maximum damage. They got it, and when the airport didn't make changes, they went back. They just hung in there, going back time after time, getting the maximum allowed by the court. The airport began to feel the pinch. Lo and behold, it changed its airplane approach and take-off policies. What a great lesson for any neighbor who feels intimidated.

To find out more on how to use small claims court, and the monetary limits and any content restrictions in your state, see Chapter 20.

Some cases against business neighbors end up in regular court. The maximum damages allowed in small claims court may not even approach what you have lost. We see this in terrible water damage cases in which people have lost their entire properties. Or, you may want a judge to issue an order that a small claims judge can't, such as to modify a practice or close down a business.

If you do go to regular court, be aware that it will consume an enormous amount of your time and cost you big bucks. Even if you prevail and the judge orders the business to pay your legal fees, you will still have spent hours (if not days or weeks) on the effort. Lawsuits eat up time, and the experience is stressful and exhausting.

Ask yourself a few questions. Are you willing to spend the time and the money? Could you go in with others who could share the expense? Do you have a case that you really think you can win?

In the example we used earlier about the race cars, the neighbor had to use regular court to get a judge to order mufflers on the cars. Given that their property values were at stake, this was probably worth the expense.

When the Law Favors the Business

Suppose you search all the laws and regulations that might aid you in stopping an annoying business neighbor and you find nothing. You're stuck with the problem. You think that the law should be on your side but it's not. What can you do?

Publicize Your Plight

Smart business owners recognize that they rely on customers, so it is in their interests to be good neighbors. Call your local newspaper, radio, or TV station. Readers and viewers like human interest stories, and so do reporters, especially when they think they can help. Some media outlets have reporters dedicated to dealing with consumer problems, and if you can get their attention you're likely to make progress.

> **EXAMPLE:** Every morning Zola's yard is covered with beer bottles and debris. The restaurant next door denies that they are in any way responsible. Zola is in her 80s. She gets the local TV station to send a camera crew out and broadcast her problem. Result? Business goes down at the restaurant until they announce that, as good citizens, they will clean Zola's yard each morning. They still claim, of course, that they are not at fault.

Making your problem known in the community can also prevent it from happening to someone else. Earlier in the chapter, we used the example of author John Grisham's plight in which a business was able to spring up and spoil his country haven because of no county zoning laws. Mr. Grisham wrote a letter to the editor of the local newspaper and complained bitterly. His comments angered some people and created sympathy in many others. Now the issue of zoning in his county is a hot topic, on the table for public discussion.

If you decide to go public, you should proceed with caution. Business owners don't appreciate being publicly criticized. In order to save face, a business may stop its offending behavior. But it may also go on the offensive. You could find yourself the target of a negative campaign to match the one you have waged against the business.

Keep an Eye on What Is Happening

Read the news. Stay abreast of what is going on in your area. Keep an eye out for variance requests. If you don't like what you see, get vocal. You must make yourself heard if you want to garner support from others.

We see this quite often when large communities with homeowners' associations take action. Someone applies for a permit to build a mall that will be too close to a given community. The residents come out in force, filling up any town board meetings. The message is very clear and very effective. It is, "We are here. We are enormous. You approve this and we will vote you out of office."

Just a single citizen can make enough noise to educate and gather support from others. Think of all of those people you have read about who were arrested chained to bulldozers or protecting their environment. We don't recommend getting arrested, but we did read about the protest. And the people built support.

Change the Law

If a lawful business activity is bothering you, you don't have to meekly accept it. Remember two facts: The law is not written in stone, and elected officials work for you.

When your neighborhood is threatened, attend your city council meetings. Draft and propose a change in the zoning laws. People do this all the time to meet modern needs. For example, people who live in growing cities and towns have done this to create "historic districts," prohibiting anyone from tampering with the locale.

Want to make real change? Run for office. If you feel strongly enough about zoning laws (or any other matter), serve your city. Just running generates the publicity we discussed above, and serving could help you and your neighbors. ●

Endnotes

1   *Judson v. Los Angeles Suburban Gas Co.,* 106 P. 581 (1910).

2   *Tichenor v. Vore,* 953 S.W. 2d 171 (Mo. App. 1997). The judge completely prohibited the kennel.

3   "Sriracha Lawsuit Dropped," *Los Angeles Times,* May 29, 2014.

4   *Westland Skating Center, Inc. v. Gus Machado Buick, Inc.,* 542 So. 2d 959 (Fla. 1989).

5   *Seminole Pipeline Co. v. Broad Leaf Partners, Inc.,* 979 S.W. 2d 730 (Tex. App. 1998).

6   *Woods v. Kahn,* 420 N.E. 2d 1028 (1981).

7   *McCombs v. Joplin 66 Fairgrounds, Inc.,* 925 S.W. 2d 946 (Mo. App. 1996).

8   William Presecky, "Pig Farm Strives to Breathe Easy with Suburbs: Hog Waste Turned into No-Odor Compost," *Chicago Tribune,* April 13, 2005, at p. 1.

9   "Neighbors Don't Love Tennis Site's Popularity," *Houston Chronicle,* Nov. 15, 2003, p. A31.

10 Gary Morrison, "Bar Takes Action After Complaints," *Grand Rapids Press,* July 22, 2004, at p. 1.

Other Common Neighbor Issues

One man's trash is another man's treasure.

—Proverb

The most frequent causes of serious neighbor disputes—trees, fences, boundaries, easements, and noise—are covered in separate chapters in this book. This chapter describes other common problems—problems so common, in fact, that most cities and towns have laws (ordinances) covering these issues. If you find yourself faced with one of the issues described in this chapter, find your town's ordinance, which may also describe how to get the city's help resolving the problem. See Chapter 1 for a detailed, step-by-step guide to resolving any troublesome neighbor situation.

Blighted Property

Blighted property is property that has been allowed to fall into a state of disrepair. Owners violate local ordinances when their property creates a danger to others or is such an eyesore that it reduces the value of surrounding property.

Junk or Art?

An extremely upscale neighborhood on Long Island, New York, was the location of a dispute when one neighbor decided to decorate the grounds of his spacious estate with what he called "art." His neighbors called the decorations "discarded bathroom junk." Yes, we are talking about toilet bowls, urinals—you get the idea.

The "artist's" next-door neighbor finally got fed up and sold his 11-bedroom mansion to media mogul Rupert Murdoch. No word on whether Mr. Murdoch complained about the artworks, but recently, a homeowner in Lakemoore, a Chicago suburb, found herself at the losing end of a similar complaint when a judge upheld the local village ruling that she could not use toilets as planters in her front yard.

Some ordinances contain a long list of items not allowed on property, such as structures (including fences), windows, driveways, sidewalks, and retaining walls that are broken, deteriorated, or defaced with graffiti. An uncaring neighbor can be forced to repair the unsightly mess or face a fine. Check your city's ordinances for a blighted property ordinance, which should also include instructions for how to file a complaint.

Weeds, Rubbish, and Garbage

Most towns prohibit high weeds, rubbish, and garbage on property and often lump them together in one ordinance. Communities may consider these health problems because they encourage the breeding of insects and rodents or because they are fire hazards. The city can fine a person for a violation or clean up the property and bill the owner. When necessary, the city can also get a judge's order for the owner to keep the premises clean from then on.

Some laws address weeds alone. They prohibit the kinds that bother neighbors the most, such as weeds that are downy, wingy, poisonous, or noxious to the community. An ordinance may require a property owner to keep the premises clean and sanitary and the yard neat and orderly. Most towns also require property owners to keep the sidewalks in front of their property clean.

The complaint process is different in different locations. In some cities, a person accused of violating the law against weeds and rubbish is entitled to a hearing, and the city council makes a decision on the matter. If the city council upholds the violation, the property owner is given a short time to clean up the premises before the city does it and sends a bill.

Loud and Offensive Language

Most noise ordinances prohibit loud and boisterous conduct. (See Chapter 2.) If your neighbors are fighting and screaming, they are probably also violating state or local disorderly conduct laws, which means they can be arrested, fined, and jailed. A neighbor can call the police, who will usually warn the person first and then may write a citation or make an arrest. Some local ordinances also prohibit "rude, obscene or insulting remarks" that could create a breach of the peace.

Drug Dealers

When someone sells illegal drugs, it is ordinarily a matter for the police. But many police departments are overburdened and unresponsive to citizen complaints about neighborhood drug dealing.

Some frustrated neighbors have banded together to try to get the dealers out. They have brought individual small claims court lawsuits against owners of properties where drug dealing and other associated crimes flourish—and they have won. Because the small claims court limit in most states is $2,500 to $15,000, clusters of such claims can quickly add up.

In 1989, 19 neighbors plagued by the crime, noise, and fear generated by a crack house in Berkeley, California, won $2,000 each in small claims court (the California small claims maximum at the time) against an absentee owner who had ignored their complaints for years. In San Francisco, a similar rash of small claims suits cost a landlord $35,000. Soon after the verdicts, both landlords evicted the troublesome tenants.[1]

Many cities have passed laws aimed at getting drug-dealing tenants evicted. The laws both make it easier for landlords to evict drug-dealing tenants and also punish landlords who sit by while drug dealing takes place on their property. In Los Angeles, for example, the police department can notify landlords when tenants are arrested or convicted of drug-related offenses. In Pasadena, California, a landlord who refuses to evict the tenants after a request from the city can be fined up to $5,000.

Local governments are also rigorously enforcing laws that allow them to sue landlords to have premises declared a public hazard or nuisance. In New York City and other places, owners have been fined and buildings have been closed down.

Landlords can even lose their property altogether. Federal or local law enforcement authorities can take legal action to have housing used by drug dealers seized and turned over to the government, even if the owner's part in the crime is merely to ignore it. In 1988, the San Mateo

County, California, district attorney brought just such a suit against the owner of a 60-unit drug haven in the city of East Palo Alto. The owner was fined $35,000 and had to shut the building down and pay tenants' relocation expenses.

Registered Sex Offenders (Megan's Law)

If you have children, you are no doubt concerned with their safety. Chapter 13 dealt with dangers to children that can arise on a neighbor's property, but there are also dangers that can arise from neighbors themselves. Megan's Law is the name given to the 1994 Federal law— signed into law by President Bill Clinton in 1996—that requires persons convicted of violent sexual offenses and sexual offenses against children to register with law enforcement wherever they live. All states have adopted some form of Megan's Law, although each individual state can decide what information will be made available to the public and how it will be provided.

Law enforcement uses the information to keep track of the registrants and to alert the community when they feel notification is warranted. Most states have created their own Megan's Law websites, where anyone can search for offenders by location or name and get information on that person's record and whereabouts, and sometimes see a photo.

Be Careful How You Evaluate and Use Megan's Law Information

Megan's Law databases are notoriously inaccurate and often mistake one person for another. The criminal offense you discover may not be relevant to whether the neighbor you're checking on is really a threat to your family. For example, in some states consensual intercourse between minors—called statutory rape—is an offense for which a person must register. Make sure you have accurate and complete information before you take any action based on Megan's Law research (other than possibly warning your child to stay away from the neighbor).

Notification procedures and the public's right to access vary widely. A few states are "wide open," meaning that they allow local law enforcement to notify neighbors of the presence of sexual offenders and make the information available to anyone who chooses to access the database. Some states don't permit notification but do allow open access, and some do the reverse, allowing law enforcement to release the information only if they deem it necessary or permitting public access only to certain individuals or officials. Finally, many states permit access and notification only to certain individuals and officials with a need to know.

The U.S. Department of Justice maintains a National Sex Offender Public Website where you can search for registered offenders at www. nsopw.gov. In addition, each state maintains a website with information on its Megan's Law database and instructions on how to access it. Simply type "Megan's Law [your state and/or postal code]" into a search engine query box. Or, go to www.klaaskids.org and choose the Megan's Law link, which will take you to a page with links to every state and a summary of each state's provisions.

Animal Problems

Most towns have several ordinances designed to deal with problems created by animals—or more accurately, by irresponsible animal owners.

Noise

Noise ordinances often single out barking dogs, but dogs are sometimes regulated in separate ordinances indexed under "Dogs" or "Animal Control." Wherever the laws are found, they usually limit the length of time a dog may bark, or the frequency of the barking allowed. The watchdog down the street that barks at intruders, or even occasionally at passersby, is within the law. But the owner of the pooch next door left out to howl at the moon all night is not. (See Chapter 2 for more guidance on problems with noisy neighbors.)

Leash Laws

Almost all towns have leash laws, requiring dogs to be under restraint when they are off the owner's property. Sometimes these are called "running at large" laws. A neighbor can report a loose dog, and the city will pick up and impound the animal and fine the owner.

Some areas regulate cats, as well, insisting that they be registered and wear collars.

Pooper-Scooper Laws

Most people are familiar with pooper-scooper laws. These require the owner of an animal to immediately remove and dispose of an animal's droppings when the animal is away from the owner's premises. Even without a specific law to handle this annoying problem, a neighbor whose yard is the target still has rights.[2]

Number of Animals

Local ordinances often limit the number of animals allowed per household to two or three adult animals. These laws are designed to cut down on noise, odors, and health problems. Someone who is determined to keep more animals may have to buy a special kennel license from the city.

Although dog and cat owners are the animal owners most likely to be affected by these laws, they are not the only ones. Ordinances also limit the number of ducks, pigeons, and chickens on property within the city limits. Raising pigeons is a common hobby in some urban areas, and the laws regulate not only how many pigeons a person can keep, but also how close the coop can be placed to a neighbor's property.

Roosters have created problems for years for neighbors who are not early risers. Many towns simply prohibit owning them due to their frequent crowing; others allow hens but not roosters; still others limit the number any one person can own. When there is no limit on the books, too many roosters in your neighbor's yard can be unlawful if they interfere with the use of your property. This is called a private nuisance.

In one Mississippi case, a court found that 19 roosters created a nuisance and ordered the owner to keep no more than two.[3] If the problem is only one rooster on your neighbor's property, ask the owner to please keep it in the dark until a certain hour. If this doesn't work, take a look at your noise laws, especially the quiet time requirements—the law may be on your side. (See Chapter 2.)

With the recent rise in backyard chickens, local governments are passing new regulations and city ordinances governing hens. Many of these ordinances have a number of restrictions and specific requirements for coops and other approved enclosures.[4]

Types of Animals

Other farm animals, such as pigs, hogs, goats, and horses, are usually not allowed within the city limits. The rules are very different outside the city limits, of course. (See Chapter 14 on state laws protecting farmers from complaints.)

Some cities exempt Vietnamese potbellied pigs from their rules against pigs. At least one court has found that a potbellied pig is not necessarily a nuisance as a pet.[5] This was a case brought by a homeowners' association. Homeowners' associations tend to be powerful opponents in court, so a win by one owner is a rarity.

Licenses and Special Permits

Dogs must usually be licensed, and special permits are often required for exotic or dangerous animals. If a dog is ruled dangerous—usually because it has injured someone—then the owner must get a special permit and buy liability insurance.

Regulations may also cover the keeping of bees, both by requiring a permit and limiting the location of hives.

Secondhand Smoke

Secondhand smoke is a growing problem, especially between neighbors in multiunit apartment buildings or condominiums: Smoke can seep under doorways and make its way through wall cracks, open windows, open doorways, and ventilation systems. If you're a nonsmoker and live in the same building as a smoker, there may be absolutely no way to protect yourself from your neighbor's secondhand smoke. Indeed, the United States Surgeon General has concluded that eliminating smoking in indoor spaces is the only way to completely protect nonsmokers from secondhand smoke exposure.

According to the National Centers for Disease Control, the National Center for Environmental Health, and the Division of Emergency and Environmental Health Services, secondhand smoke contains more than 4000 chemicals, 250 of which are harmful to human health and more than 50 of which are known to cause cancer.[6]

Medical experts also agree that exposure to secondhand smoke can cause disease and lung cancer in nonsmoking adults. It can also cause sudden infant death syndrome or "SIDS," bronchitis, pneumonia, and ear infections in children. For children that suffer from asthma, secondhand smoke can trigger more severe and frequent asthma attacks.

Nonsmoking laws in government buildings, hospitals, restaurants, and bars are becoming more and more common. As of April 2013, 81.3% of the U.S. population lives under a ban on smoking in workplaces, restaurants, and/or bars by a state or local law.[7] But until recently, if the smoke wafting into your house, condominium, or apartment from your neighbor's cigarette bothered you, all you could do was move out. The situation is changing, however. As a result of the growing awareness of the dangers of secondhand smoke, more states, local governments, landlords and condominium associations are adopting smoke-free policies for a variety of locations, including condominiums and other multiunit dwellings. Nonsmokers bothered by their neighbors' smoking may find that they can now take action.

Enforce No-Smoking Clauses

If the smoke that disturbs you comes from someone who rents, find out whether the other tenant's rental agreement contains a no-smoking clause; these clauses are becoming more common. If it does, then the tenant is violating the lease and may be evicted if you notify the landlord. (See "Additional Rights If You're a Tenant (or Your Neighbors Are)," in Chapter 1.) If the troublesome smoker lives in a planned development or a condominium with covenants, conditions, and restrictions (CC&Rs) that prohibit smoking, then either you or the homeowners' association may take legal action against the smoker. (See "Subdivision Rules," in Chapter 1.)

Sue Your Neighbor

Even if the smoker doesn't live under a no-smoking restriction, you may find a court to be sympathetic if you sue the smoker for creating a private nuisance (interfering with your ability to use and enjoy your property). Some states, including Utah, define a private nuisance to include tobacco smoke that drifts into any occupied residential unit from another residential or commercial unit, so long as the second-hand smoke is injurious to health, offensive to the senses, or an obstruction to the free use of property. A nuisance may provide the basis for a lawsuit as long as the smoke drifts in to the neighbor's unit more than once in each of two or more consecutive seven-day periods.[8]

> EXAMPLE 1: A Florida court awarded $1,000 to a nonsmoker after she successfully argued that her condominium neighbor's smoking was trespass, a nuisance, and violated her right to quiet enjoyment (see "Additional Rights If You're a Tenant," in Chapter 1). The nonsmoker and her family suffered health problems as a result of the smoking and sometimes had to sleep elsewhere when the smoke from the neighboring condominium was particularly dense.[9]

EXAMPLE 2: A jury in Boston decided that a heavy-smoking couple could be evicted from their rented loft, even though smoking was allowed in their lease. The landlord gave them seven days' notice to move out after several neighbors complained about smoke smells wafting into their apartments. The couple fought the eviction by arguing that the smoke from their apartment spread as a result of faulty air-conditioning systems, but the landlord prevailed.[10]

Check Your State and Local Laws

At least one state—Utah—now includes tobacco smoke in its statute defining a private nuisance. Specifically, second-hand smoke is a nuisance in Utah if it drifts into any residential unit from a home or business more than once a week for at least two consecutive weeks and if it interferes with the neighbor's "comfortable enjoyment of life or property." The only exception is if the neighbor signed a lease, restrictive covenant, or purchase agreement waiving his or her right to sue a neighbor for causing a nuisance by smoking. Under Utah's law, an annoyed neighbor may sue the smoker directly and may sue the landlord in some cases if the smoker is a renter.[11]

If your state laws don't have useful prohibitions against secondhand smoke, you may find some relief on a local level. Many cities and counties now prohibit smoking in outdoor parks, other common areas, and within multiunit housing. For example, in Belmont, California, a 2007 ordinance prohibits smoking in multiunit buildings in any units that share a floor or ceiling with another unit.[12] Similarly, a 2011 Sonoma County, California ordinance prohibits smoking in multiunit dwellings, including common areas and all existing units of multiunit residences.[13] Penalties include fines of up to $100 for the first offense, $200 for the second offense, and $500 for each additional offense within one year. Any person that violates the code more than three times within one year is guilty of a misdemeanor.

As of February 2019, over 101 California municipalities have instituted smoke-free housing policies; 63 of these counties and cities have passed strong, comprehensive bans on smoking in multiunit housing.[14] California is currently considering a statewide ban on smoking in multiunit dwellings. Because of the increased awareness of the health risks posed by secondhand smoke, many states and municipalities are likely to follow suit.

To learn more about smoke-free laws and policies in your state, check the American Lung Association website at www.lung.org.

Vehicles

Old broken-down cars in the yard are an unwelcome sight to neighbors and are usually a violation of local law. A typical ordinance requires any disabled car to be either enclosed or placed behind a fence. Some limit the parking of RVs and disabled cars to 72 hours, unless they are enclosed or out of sight. Almost all cities prohibit leaving any vehicle parked on a city street too long—often, more than 72 hours.

Good Will to You, Too

Six neighbors in Little Rock, Arkansas, celebrated the 1993 Christmas season in court. They sued to stop a couple in their midst from throwing the switch on their annual Christmas light display, which consisted of a million red lights. The display included glowing Santas, reindeer, Mickey Mouse, and a 40-foot-high revolving globe.

The neighbors charged that the giant display not only bathed the entire area in red, but also created bumper-to-bumper traffic. Sightseers blocked the neighbors' driveways and covered their lawns with trash. The festive couple with the lights pointed to freedom of speech and religion.

The court found the display to be a nuisance and ordered it toned down. But the story has a happy ending. The light show (now expanded) has found a new home at Disney World.

When someone in the neighborhood brings it to their attention, some towns will tow away a vehicle that has been parked for too long. And the relatives in their RV, who have been visiting across the street for the past year, could pay their next visit to a judge.

Drones

Some of the best questions about neighbor issues come from readers, friends, and colleagues. Last year, a friend asked me what she could do about a neighbor who was flying a drone into her backyard. In searching for the answer, I discovered that the law is still playing catch up with the fascinating technology of drones.

A drone—also referred to as an unmanned aerial vehicle (UAV)— is basically a flying robot. To start, UAVs were used primarily by the military for intelligence gathering and as weapons platforms. They've also been used by firefighters for search and rescue surveillance and by local police departments for traffic monitoring. In 2013, Amazon announced that it would use commercial drones for delivery services.

Today, the personal use of drones is also fairly common. You can go online and purchase a small, remote-controlled drone, equipped with a high definition Wifi camera for as little as $50.00. According to the Consumer Technology Association, approximately 3.4 million drones were sold nationwide in 2019, representing just over $1 billion in profit—this figure is up from 1.1 million drones in 2015.

As a result of this new, highly accessible technology, there has been a rise of complaints about drones entering and hovering over private property, causing unwanted noise and even recording neighbors' activities. In the last few years, federal, state, and local governments have begun passing legislation aimed at restricting the use of drones. Although these laws are evolving rapidly, here is a basic overview on where things stand today.

Federal Regulations

In August 2016, the Federal Aviation Administration (FAA) issued regulations which state that private citizens can own and fly drones.[15] But these laws apply to smaller drones that weigh less than 55 pounds and are operated for commercial and governmental purposes. The laws are fairly limited, and prevent people whose privacy or property is intruded upon by a drone from bringing a civil tort lawsuit. However, the FAA rules don't prohibit individuals from bringing trespass or invasion of privacy lawsuits and using FAA violations as evidence in court. In 2018, the FAA adopted additional rules for the recreational use of drones. For more information on these rules, check the FAA website at www.faa.gov/uas.

Local and State Laws

If you're having issues related to your neighbor's use of a drone on your property, you'll need to search for helpful local laws. (See Chapter 18, Legal Research). Many states, cities, and towns have passed laws regulating the use of drones. Between 2014 and 2016, Beverly Hills, Los Angeles, Chicago, and West Hollywood adopted their own drone ordinances, which include requirements that govern both distance and time of use.[16] For example, in Los Angeles, operators can fly their drones only during daylight hours and not higher than 400 feet above the ground. In Chicago, drones must remain a certain distance away from sensitive areas, such as schools.

Trespass and Invasion of Privacy

If you come into contact with a drone in a public area, like a local park, where you have a limited expectation of privacy, it's unlikely you'll be able to file a grievance. But if a neighbor's drone is in your backyard, taking pictures of you while you're sunbathing, you can consider filing a suit for trespass and/or invasion of privacy. You'll need to check your state statutes to determine what you need to show for both of these claims and to see if there are any specific laws that address the use of drones in your area. For example, in 2016, California passed a law, known as its "Paparazzi Law," that makes a person liable for invasion of privacy if that person purposefully navigates a drone onto another person's private property without consent.[17] This law specifically applies when both of the following are true:

- The drone's user entered the private air space in order to record audio or video of the person or property.
- The conduct was offensive to a reasonable person.

Private Nuisance Claim

If your neighbor's repeated use of a drone in your yard is interfering with your use and enjoyment of your property, you may want to consider filing a lawsuit for private nuisance. The sound or simple presence of a drone hovering in your space could amount to a private nuisance. Check Appendix B to see if your state has specific laws that define a private nuisance —some states require the conduct also be unlawful or unreasonable.

Whatever legal remedy you choose to pursue, you should approach a drone issue in the same manner as you would any other neighbor issue we've covered in this book. To start, find an appropriate time to have a chat with your neighbor and explain what's happening. Ask that it stop. If it continues, be sure to document each event, by taking a video of the drone while it's hovering in your yard and keeping a journal or calendar of the dates, times, and locations of the incidents. If necessary, send a letter asking that your neighbor consider mediation to resolve the dispute, and include any laws or CC&Rs that your neighbor may have violated. If all else fails, you may need to file a lawsuit to make it stop.

Outdoor Lights

Some cities where houses are located fairly close together have enacted laws protecting people from a neighbor's glaring lights. These laws prohibit directing an outdoor light in a neighbor's direction. ●

Endnotes

1 "Neighbors in West Use Small Claims Court to Combat Drugs," *N.Y. Times,* Oct. 17, 1989, at A16.

2 You can find answers to many dog problems in the book *Every Dog's Legal Guide: A Must-Have Book for Your Owner,* by Mary Randolph (Nolo).

3 *Lambert v. Matthews,* 757 So. 2d 1066 (Miss. App. 2000).

4 City of Champaign, Illinois allows a maximum of six hens and no roosters (Code of Ordinances, Chapter 7, Section 7-19); Saginaw, Texas prohibits roosters, but allows up to three chickens by permit and with the use of a pen or coop (Chicken Ordinance No. 2018-05); San Francisco, California allows no more than four chickens (S.F. Health Code Article 1 Section 37, Keeping and Feeding of Small Animals, Poultry, and Game Birds).

5 *Gebauer v. Lake Forest Property Owners Ass'n, Inc.,* 723 So. 2d 1288 (Ala. Civ. App. 1998).

6 "Healthy Homes Manual, Smoke Free Policies in Multiunit Housing," published by the CDC and the National Center for Environmental Health.

7 American Nonsmokers' Rights Foundation.

8 Utah Code Ann. § 78B-6-1101.

9 *Merrill v. Bosser,* No. 05-4239 COCE 53 (Broward County Ct., June 29, 2005).

10 "Jury Finds Smoking Grounds for Eviction," *Boston Globe,* June 16, 2005, p. B1.

11 Utah Code Ann. §§ 78B-6-1101 and following.

12 City of Belmont, Cal., Municipal Code § 20.5-3, Ordinance Number 1032.

13 Sonoma County Code §§ 32-1–32-23.

14 "Basic Overview of All Local Smokefree Multi-Unit Housing Ordinances," The Center for Tobacco Policy and Organizing, www.center4tobaccopolicy.org.

15 Small Unmanned Aircraft Rule (Part 107).

16 FAA Reauthorization Act, § 249.

17 Beverly Hills Mun. Code § 5-6-604; Los Angeles Mun. Code § 56.31; Chicago Mun. Code § 10-36-400; West Hollywood Mun. Code Ch. 9.30.

18 Cal Civ. Code § 1708.8.

Legal Research

Learn, compare, collect the facts.

—Ivan Pavlov

Whether you are preparing for a neighborly meeting, heading for small claims court, or about to hire a lawyer, you need to know what the law is on your dispute. No deep or mysterious powers are required. Usually, all you'll need to know is how to find the local ordinances, state statutes, or judicial opinions that speak to your particular problem. Sometimes, researching the law doesn't even mean a trip to the local library: City and county agencies and offices can often give you good advice and information. For example, a zoning or planning office may answer questions about fence height restrictions or building permits.

This chapter gives basic guidelines for using the Internet and libraries to locate answers to neighbor law questions. If you wish to delve more deeply into the law, Nolo publishes a comprehensive book called *Legal Research: How to Find & Understand the Law,* by Stephen Elias and Susan Levinkind.

Local Laws

Much of the law affecting neighbor relations is local, passed by a city council (or board of selectmen) or a county board of supervisors.

Finding Local Laws

Local governments have staked out turf on the Internet. Sometimes this presence is nothing more than a not-so-slick public relations page, but other sites may include large bodies of information, including local ordinances available for searching and downloading. Most cities' and counties' websites follow these formats:

- **county:** www.co.<county name>.<state postal code>.us
  Example: www.co.alameda.ca.us
- **city:** www.ci.<city name>.<state postal code>.us
  Example: www.ci.berkeley.ca.us.

Your state website also may have links to cities and counties.

If your city's website does not include the text of local ordinances, you may be able to find local laws on one of these sites:

- State and Local Government on the Net (www.statelocalgov.net), and
- the Municipal Code Corporation (www.municode.com).

You can also use a Google search (www.google.com). For tips on using Google to search for local ordinances, see "Finding State Laws on the Internet," below.

If you don't have success with the Internet, your local laws may be available at your local public library or the city or county law library (usually located near the courthouse).

Neighbor Law Topics Covered by Local Laws

- animals
- blighted property
- building codes
- fence appearance
- fence height
- fence location
- garbage
- noise
- protected trees
- sick trees
- trash
- view obstruction
- weeds
- zoning

You can also try getting a copy of local ordinances from the relevant city or county office or special district. For example, the zoning board may give you a copy of your town's zoning ordinances; your regional water district may have copies of local water usage ordinances. These departments usually charge a small fee to cover photocopying costs.

Using an Index or Table of Contents

Once you have the codes in hand or on screen, look for your topic in the index, if there is one, or in the table of contents. Be prepared to look under several different terms. Some indexes are not as helpful as they should be. For instance, if you have a dangerous tree problem, you may not find anything under "danger" or "tree." Keep looking. Try "sick trees," "hazardous conditions," "nuisance," or even "miscellaneous."

If the index doesn't get you anywhere, read the table of contents. If you are looking for building height restrictions or fence regulations and there is no entry under height or fence, check under zoning laws.

For example, if your downhill neighbor plans a large house addition that will block your view, you probably won't find anything in the codes to help you under "view." Look instead at the building code and the zoning restrictions. You'll want to check for any building height restrictions, road setback rules, and any law that limits the ratio of building area to that of the total lot. If you find an ordinance limiting a building to 55% of a lot and your neighbor's proposed addition will exceed the legal limit, you have a good shot at stopping the project.

Make Sure the Law Is Current

Once you've found the law you need, make sure it hasn't been changed or repealed. If you're reading an ordinance online, the source will tell you what year's version of the law you're looking at. If you're not sure it's current, you can call the city or county clerk's office and ask when the law was last amended.

At the library, check the front or back of the book of ordinances for updates, and ask the librarian when the library received its most recent update. Public libraries are sometimes out of date, in which case you can call the city or county clerk's office.

State Statutes

Some situations that affect neighbors are regulated by state laws, passed by the legislature.

Finding State Laws

The easiest way to find a copy of a statute is if you already know its citation—that is, the number of the specific statute. For example, the appendixes in the back of this book list the citations to many state statutes on neighbor law issues. If you don't know the statute's citation, there are both Internet and print resources to help you find statutes on a particular subject.

Neighbor Law Topics Covered by State Laws

- adverse possession
- boundary fences
- damage to trees
- disorderly conduct
- easements

- nuisance
- right to farm
- spite fences
- trespass

If You Know the Citation

Citations to state statutes normally refer to the title (or volume) and section numbers. The three examples shown in the figure below are typical.

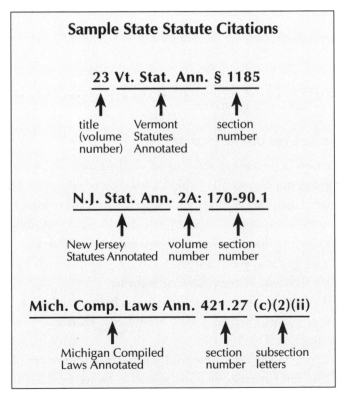

Figure 1

Some states' laws are divided up into several different topical sections. In such states, like New York and California, citations look like those shown below.

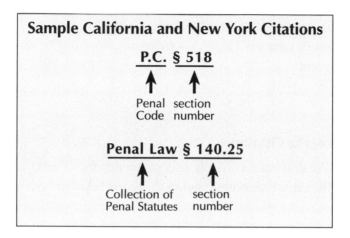

Figure 2

When you know the statute's citation, then you can use the Internet or a local law library to get a copy.

Finding State Laws on the Internet

Every state now maintains its statutes on the Internet. The websites vary in their format, but almost all of them allow you to search for statutes by topic, keyword, or citation. Start your search with Nolo's legal research pages (www.nolo.com/legal-research), which will guide you to your state's website containing laws and other legislative materials.

If your state's official website does not allow you to search by topic or keyword, then try one of the following websites:

- FindLaw (www.findlaw.com). From the home page, click Search Cases & Codes, then click U.S. State Laws, then select your state link.
- The Cornell Legal Information Institute (www.law.cornell.edu) lets you search for statutes by topic as well as by name. The "search by topic" feature is under the "Law by Source or Jurisdiction" section of the website.

> ## Finding Your State's Website
>
> Every state has its statutes on the Internet. State websites usually use the following format:
>> www.<state postal code>.gov
>>
>> Example: www.ca.gov
>
> Within the state's site, look for a link to Legislature or Laws.

Finally, another online search option is Google (www.google.com), far and away the best nonlegal search engine on the Internet. If you are searching for a law on Google, try using any combination of the following elements in the search box:

- keywords that identify the law. For instance, if a law increases the penalty for damaging a neighbor's tree, try entering the terms "tree," "damage," and "penalty."
- your state's name, so that the search engine won't give you an Illinois law while you are in Texas
- the word "law" or "statute"
- if possible, the literal name or number of the law, in quotation marks, or
- the year that the law was passed, if you know it, so you don't get an out-of-date law by the same name.

Finding State Laws in the Library

If you don't have Internet access, you can find state laws in your local public law library, which is usually located in or near the courthouse. Try looking in the government listings of the white pages under Law Library. If that fails, call the clerk of the local court for information.

Once at the library, use the "annotated" version of the statute book if possible, because that version includes additional information that will help with research. These books also have subject indexes or tables of contents that you can use to find statutes on particular topics. For example, if someone has cut down your tree, you'd look under "trees." Nothing useful there? Try "timber" or "trespass"—anything you can think of. For next-door neighbor problems, always check under "adjoining landowners." Sometimes finding a particular state statute is easy. But sometimes, depending on the subject and the particular state, it can take quite a bit of time and patience. A few states have pretty bad indexes.

Make Sure the Law Is Current

Once you've found the law you need, make sure it hasn't been changed or repealed. If you're reading an ordinance online, the source will tell you what year's version of the law you're looking at. At the library, check the front or back of the book of statutes for updates. Just look for the number of the law in the update material. If nothing is there under that number, it means there has been no change. If you find a change, it replaces the law printed in the hardbound volume. If there is nothing but the word "repealed" after the number of the law, the law printed in the hardbound volume is no longer in effect.

Reading and Interpreting a Statute

When you find a statute on your subject, read it carefully. Remember that the laws are written by lawyers, many of whom seem unable to write in plain English. (How wonderful it would be if other states could learn from North Dakota. That state not only has a good index, but the laws are clearly written in a style that puts other state statutes to shame.)

Figure 3 shows a page from a volume of state statutes. This state law on spite fences is from the annotated laws of Massachusetts. Let's look at the different pieces of information on the page:

❶ the topic of the statute

❷ the section number of the statute

❸ the name of the statute

❹ the text of the statute

❺ historical information including when the statute was enacted (1887), modified, and so on

❻ a listing of reference materials that discuss the statute

❼ a subject index of cases interpreting the statute

❽ a citation to a case discussing the statute, and

❾ the page number of the book in which the statute appears.

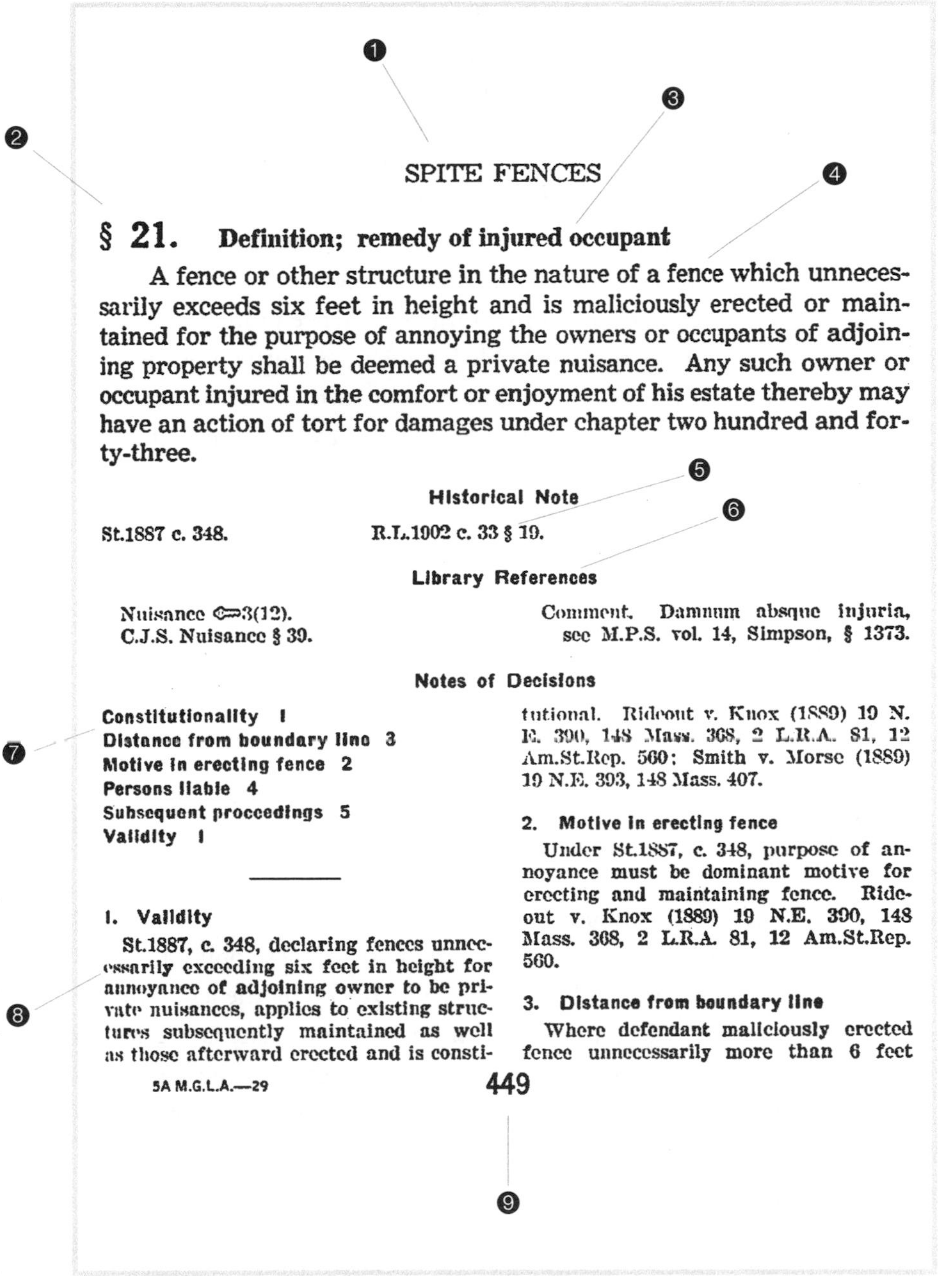

SPITE FENCES

§ 21. Definition; remedy of injured occupant

A fence or other structure in the nature of a fence which unnecessarily exceeds six feet in height and is maliciously erected or maintained for the purpose of annoying the owners or occupants of adjoining property shall be deemed a private nuisance. Any such owner or occupant injured in the comfort or enjoyment of his estate thereby may have an action of tort for damages under chapter two hundred and forty-three.

Historical Note

St.1887 c. 348.   R.L.1902 c. 33 § 19.

Library References

Nuisance ⟜3(12).
C.J.S. Nuisance § 39.

Comment. Damnum absque injuria, see M.P.S. vol. 14, Simpson, § 1373.

Notes of Decisions

Constitutionality 1
Distance from boundary line 3
Motive in erecting fence 2
Persons liable 4
Subsequent proceedings 5
Validity 1

_____

1. Validity

St.1887, c. 348, declaring fences unnecessarily exceeding six feet in height for annoyance of adjoining owner to be private nuisances, applies to existing structures subsequently maintained as well as those afterward erected and is consti-

tutional. Rideout v. Knox (1889) 19 N. E. 390, 148 Mass. 368, 2 L.R.A. 81, 12 Am.St.Rep. 560; Smith v. Morse (1889) 19 N.E. 393, 148 Mass. 407.

2. Motive in erecting fence

Under St.1887, c. 348, purpose of annoyance must be dominant motive for erecting and maintaining fence. Rideout v. Knox (1889) 19 N.E. 390, 148 Mass. 368, 2 L.R.A. 81, 12 Am.St.Rep. 560.

3. Distance from boundary line

Where defendant maliciously erected fence unnecessarily more than 6 feet

5A M.G.L.A.—29

449

Figure 3

Sometimes you'll want to read a judicial decision interpreting a particular statute—for example, if the phrasing of the statute is unclear or if you want to know how the court applied the statute in a particular situation. To find cases interpreting a statute, check the listings after the text of the statute in an "annotated" version of your state's statutes in the law library. In the example here, the cases follow the heading "Notes of Decisions."

In the annotated code, one-sentence summaries of court cases that interpret the statute directly follow the notes on the statute's history. (See Number 8 on Figure 3, above.) Some statutes have been interpreted by the courts so many times that the publisher includes a little index to the case summaries, which are organized by issues raised by the statute. (See Number 7 on Figure 3, above.) It is often difficult to tell from such a brief summary whether or not a case is in fact relevant to your problem. Fortunately, the summaries also contain a case citation that allows you to look up the case and read it for yourself. It is essential that you read the case itself and not just rely on what it says in the annotation.

Annotated statutes are generally not available online except for a fee. At Westlaw (www.westlaw.com), you can pay a fee by credit card and then enter the citation for a statute and receive a list of all court cases discussing the law.

Case Law

A judicial "opinion," "decision," or "case" is a written opinion of a court, ruling on one or more issues of a particular lawsuit. These opinions are called case law. Often, they interpret the laws created by the legislature, which is why you may need to read them. Even if your state laws address a particular topic, the language of the law may not give you a clear-cut answer to your dilemma. If you find a particular statute that looks as if it will help you, it's always helpful to know how courts have actually interpreted the law.

You may need to read a judicial decision for another reason, too. Although most neighbor relations issues are addressed either by local law or state statute, some issues are governed entirely by the courts. When there are no state statutes or local ordinances to help you, you may find help in what's called the "common law." The common law is the body of law that is entirely developed by the courts through their written decisions.

Neighbor Law Topics Covered by Court Cases	
• boundary lines	• negligent behavior
• boundary trees	• nuisances
• encroaching trees	• other next-door neighbor
• hazardous trees	(adjoining landowners) questions

Finding Cases on the Internet

Unfortunately, the full text of many judicial decisions is not available online unless you're able to pay a (usually reasonable) fee.

Free Research Sites

The best free resource for finding state cases online is FindLaw (www.findlaw.com). Even FindLaw, however, doesn't have a complete database of cases from every state. And FindLaw's database consists of case summaries, not the text of actual decisions. However, a FindLaw search may give you the names and citations of cases you want to read, and you can then use another resource (a fee-based website or your local law library) to read the entire case.

To use FindLaw's service, you first must click on the tab that says "For Legal Professionals." Then click on "Cases & Codes," then find your state. You can search by state and by topic (including property law), or you can search the text of FindLaw's summaries for keywords of your choosing.

Another free resource for finding cases online is the court website for your state. Most state courts have their current or recent cases available online free of charge, but you'll only find cases decided in the past two to 12 months. Another limitation is that most court websites allow searches only by party name; keyword or topical searches are not usually available.

The best way to find your state's court website is to use one of the following sites, which provide direct links to state cases:

• Cornell Legal Information Institute (www.law.cornell.edu), or

• FindLaw (www.findlaw.com).

You can also try a basic Google keyword search to find a case. Try typing any combination of the following elements in the search box:

- one or both names of the parties to the case. You can search with the "v." abbreviation, as well—for example, typing "Israel v. Carolina Bar-B-Que" will get you a copy of a 1987 South Carolina case stating that a tree owner may have to pay for damage caused to his neighbor's property by his tree.
- one or more terms that describe the subject matter of the case. For example, typing in "spite fence" and "Rhode Island" yields a 2002 Rhode Island case in which one neighbor sued another for planting trees that blocked her view.
- the year of the case
- the name of the court that heard and decided the case, and
- the word "case" or "court."

Fee-Based Research Sites

If you can't find what you need for free, you'll need to try a site that charges for access to cases. A good place to start is VersusLaw, a fee-based system for finding both current and past (archived) state and federal cases. VersusLaw (www.versuslaw.com) offers state and federal court opinions that range from the most recent to those decided 75 years ago.

At $18.95 a month, VersusLaw is the most reasonably priced of all the online sources of archived cases. You don't have to subscribe for more than a month at a time, so if you are a one-time researcher, you can buy just one month of solid online research.

You can get a good sense of how VersusLaw works by using its "Guest Research" utility. Just provide some basic personal information and you will be able to browse the search facilities and create a search. If your search brings up some links to cases that meet your search criteria, you'll have to subscribe to go further. So, no free lunch here, but an opportunity to familiarize yourself with this service.

One of the great features of VersusLaw is its online help. The Research Manual and FAQs (links to both appear on the search page) are written in plain English and provide the best research support we've encountered on the Internet.

Other fee-based legal research sites include Westlaw (www.westlaw.com) and LexisNexis (www.lexis.com).

Understanding Case Citations

A case's "citation" is like its address: It tells you exactly where to locate the published opinion. A citation will tell you the name of the case, the book it is published in, which court decided the case, and the year it was published.

Court cases are published in books called "reporters." There are two kinds of reporters: One publishes just the court cases from a particular state; the second includes cases from a group of states in the same book. A case's citation will usually give you information about where to find the case in either the state or the regional reporter.

Let's take an example: You find a citation for a case stating that a tree owner may have to pay for damage caused to his neighbor's property by his tree. The case citation is *Israel v. Carolina Bar-B-Que, Inc.*, 292 S.C. 282, 356 S.E.2d 123 (Ct. App. 1987). This tells you the name, the two different reporters the case is published in, plus the court and the date. Here's how to decode the information:

- The case name is Israel versus Carolina Bar-B-Que, Inc. (who sued whom). The first reporter information, 292 S.C. 282, means the case is published in volume 292 of the South Carolina Reporter, at page 282. Abbreviations for particular reporters are listed in the front of the volumes of reporters.
- The second reporter information, 356 S.E.2d 123, tells us the case is in volume 356 of the Southeastern Reporter, 2nd Series, at page 123.
- The court that published the opinion: We know the case is from South Carolina, because the South Carolina Reporter publishes only cases from that state. We can see that the case comes from a Court of Appeals of South Carolina from the "Ct. App." language in the parentheses.
- The date is 1987.

Finding Cases in the Library

Even if you start your legal research on the Internet, you may find yourself needing a law library, especially if you're looking for case law and are unable or unwilling to pay a fee for searching. Your city or county has a public law library, which is usually located near the courthouse. Try looking in the government listings of the white pages under Law Library. If that fails, call the clerk of the local court. In the law library, you can read the full text of court cases once you know the citation (see "Understanding Case Citations," above), or use reference materials to find cases on particular subjects.

Ask the librarian to point you to some reference books on neighbor issues or to a general legal encyclopedia. These books can give you background information and may also mention cases that will bear on your situation.

Legal encyclopedias. Some states have their own; if yours doesn't, use a national one, such as *American Jurisprudence* (called *"Am. Jur."* for short). Like regular encyclopedias, these books are arranged alphabetically by topic. The encyclopedia articles discuss how courts have ruled in actual court cases.

Some encyclopedias have more than one series; you want the most recent. For instance, the current series of *Am. Jur.* is *Am. Jur.* 2d. Also be sure to check the back of the books for more recent updates (called pocket parts).

Figure 4 shows a page from *Am. Jur.* 2d, discussing uncertain boundary lines—in this example, neighbors setting a boundary by building a fence. You can see the short summaries of court decisions that follow each issue that is raised. Let's look at the different sections of the page:

❶ the volume you're currently reading

❷ the topic

❸ the section number within that topic

❹ the name of the section

❺ explanatory text

❻ citation to a relevant case

❼ the page number, and

❽ a cross-reference to A.L.R., a set of volumes whose full name is *American Law Reports*, where you'll find another article about this topic.

American Law Reports is another national compilation of court decisions, books, and articles published concerning all areas of the law. *A.L.R.* also comes in several series—the 5th is the latest—and has updated material in the back. *A.L.R.* has separate index volumes that list the topics in alphabetical order.

BOUNDARIES

mutual acquiescence and recognition by the adjoiners is essential to practical location, provided that there is, at the time of the location, a disputed, indefinite, or uncertain boundary line between the adjoining owners.[11] A practical location of a boundary line has been said to be simply an actual designation on the ground, by the parties, of the monuments and bounds called for by the conveyances,[12] and it has also been said that when a disputed or uncertain boundary line is fixed by practical location it is binding, not by way of transfer of title, but by way of estoppel.[13]

§ 88. Erection of fence.

Where there is doubt and uncertainty as to the location of the true boundary line[14] between adjoining landowners, they may agree that a fence may be the division line between their lands.[15] To constitute the fence the boundary line it is not necessary that the agreement be express; it may be inferred from or implied by the conduct of the parties, especially where the fence is acquiesced to as the boundary line for the period of the statute of limitations.[16] It has

---

11. Drury v Pekar, supra, quoting Kincaid v Peterson, 135 Or 619, 297 P 833.

The practical location of a boundary line can be established in any one of three ways: (1) the location relied upon must have been acquiesced in for a sufficient length of time to bar a right of entry under the statute of limitations; (2) the line must have been expressly agreed upon between the parties claiming the land on both sides thereof and afterward acquiesced in; or, (3) the parties whose rights are to be barred must have silently looked on, with knowledge of the true line, while the other party encroached upon it or subjected himself to expense in regard to the land which he would not have done had the line been in dispute. Fishman v Nielson, 237 Minn 1, 53 NW2d 553.

12. Wells v Jackson Iron Mfg. Co. 47 NH 235.

Boundary lines may be determined by physical indications of the lines on the ground accepted by the parties over a period of time. Fallone v Gochee, 9 App Div 2d 569, 189 NYS2d 363, app den 9 App Div 2d 699, 191 NYS2d 560.

The actual location of a deed may be satisfactorily established, not only by the natural objects found on the ground, but by the fact that all the parties who knew the facts and were interested in the land located the deed in a certain way. Kenmont Coal Co. v Combs, 243 Ky 328, 48 SW2d 9 (holding that location of deed by grantor and his grantee, subsequently acquiesced in for more than 30 years, could not be disputed).

13. Adams v Warner, 209 App Div 394, 204 NYS 613, quoted with approval in Drury v Pekar, 224 Or 37, 355 P2d 598.

14. Uncertainty of or dispute as to the location of the true boundary line is essential in order that a fence built on a line agreed as the boundary line may operate to preclude the parties from later claiming a different boundary line. Vowinckel v N. Clark & Sons,

217 Cal 258, 18 P2d 58; Pederson v Reynolds, 31 Cal App 2d 18, 87 P2d 51; Blank v Ambs, 260 Mich 589, 245 NW 525; Talbot v Smith, 56 Or 117, 107 P 480, 108 P 125. Annotation: 170 ALR 1146.

But it is not necessary that there should be an actual dispute between the parties regarding the true division line; it is sufficient if it appears that they were uncertain as to the true line and therefore agreed to a designated and certain boundary upon which they constructed a fence and occupied and cultivated or improved their respective portions to that division fence for more than the statutory period. Martin v Lopes (Cal App) 164 P2d 321, superseded 28 Cal 2d 618, 170 P2d 881.

When the real boundary line between contiguous landowners is known to them, neither of them may acquire title by acquiescence beyond such line by merely building a fence upon the other's property and cultivating and claiming the land to that point, since title to land by acquiescence is founded on an agreement when an uncertainty exists as to the true line. Martin v Lopes, supra.

15. An oral agreement fixing an uncertain and disputed dividing line of lands, and execution thereof by the building of a fence thereon, is not in violation of the statute of frauds, since the parties do not thereby undertake to acquire and pass title to real estate, but merely fix the location of the boundary of the land that they already own, the purpose being to identify their several holdings and make certain that which they regard as uncertain. Holbrooks v Wright, 187 Ky 732, 220 SW2d 524.

Generally as to oral agreements fixing boundary lines, see §§ 78 et seq., supra.

16. Hannah v Pogue, 23 Cal 2d 849, 147 P2d 572; Roberts v Brae, 5 Cal 2d 356, 54 P2d 698; Kandlick v Hudek, 365 Ill 292, 6 NE2d 196.

Annotation: 170 ALR 1145.

Figure 4

Books on particular subjects. Books on particular topics are most helpful for gaining an overall perspective on a subject and also for getting more citations to court cases in your area. Consider the following:

- For property questions, a huge series of volumes called *Powell on Property* covers topics such as boundaries, easements, and adverse possession in detail.

- For questions on nuisance (such as encroaching tree branches) and negligence (such as allowing a dangerous tree to fall), see *Prosser and Keeton on Torts* (a single volume).

- For information on problems between next-door neighbors, look at a recent book called *A Practical Guide to Disputes Between Adjoining Landowners—Easements*, by James H. Backman and David A. Thomas. This large loose-leaf volume covers many subjects of concern to next-door neighbors, is updated periodically, and lists court cases for most states.

Because all of these books are written for lawyers, they are predictably full of frustrating legal jargon. However, if you approach them with a little patience, you can learn a lot about a particular subject.

Reading a Case

A court case contains a lot of information before you even get to the court's actual opinion. Let's look at an example. You find a case that says that a homeowner was not able to collect money for damage caused by a neighbor's healthy tree. The case is *Turner v. Coppola*, 102 Misc. 2d 1043, 424 N.Y.S.2d 864 (N.Y. Sup. Ct. 1980). Figure 5 shows a copy of this page. Let's look in depth at what you see there:

- ❶ the name and volume of the reporter (collection of cases) you're reading
- ❷ the page number
- ❸ the official citation for the case
- ❹ the name of the case
- ❺ the name of the court
- ❻ the date the opinion was decided
- ❼ a summary of the case, including what this court ruled, and
- ❽ a topic and key number.

864   424 NEW YORK SUPPLEMENT, 2d SERIES

"8. The instruction and supervision given * * * were so negligently given as to result in the * * * injuries sustained."

No other factual averment was made by plaintiff which in any way indicates a basis for his conclusion of negligence (*Koppers Co. v. Empire Bituminous Products, Inc.*, 35 A.D.2d 906, 316 N.Y.S.2d 858); and, such is not satisfied by a mere repetition of the complaint without factual evidence upon which to impose liability upon the movant (*Golding v. Weissman*, 35 A.D.2d 941, 316 N.Y.S.2d 522).

Defendant, Senior's motion is granted.

102 Misc.2d 1043

Barbara G. TURNER, Plaintiff,

v.

Caroline COPPOLA, Richard Petersen, Minna Petersen and Freda Amster, Defendants.

Supreme Court, Special Term, Nassau County, Part I.

Feb. 13, 1980.

Plaintiff, who alleged that branches on defendants' trees encroached on plaintiff's property, caused cosmetic damage to her garage and prevented her lawn from receiving adequate sunlight and that twigs, branches and buds from the trees constantly fell on her property, brought action for omnibus relief. On defendants' motion to dismiss complaint for failure to state cause of action, the Supreme Court, Nassau County, Special Term, B. Thomas Pantano, J., held that: (1) the trees were not a "nuisance per se," in such a sense as to sustain an action for relief; (2) complaint did not state cause of action for relief from private nuisance; (3) plaintiff did not have a cause of action in trespass; (4) plaintiff did not

have a cause of action in negligence; but (5) plaintiff could protect herself by self-help consisting of a reasonable cutting of branches to extent that they invaded her property.

Motion to dismiss complaint granted.

1. Nuisance ⟸1

Essence of a "private nuisance" is interference with the use and enjoyment of land amounting to an injury in relation to a right of ownership in that land.

See publication Words and Phrases for other judicial constructions and definitions.

2. Nuisance ⟸3(1)

In light of fact that defendants' trees, whose branches allegedly encroached on plaintiff's property and from which twigs, branches and buds were alleged to have constantly fallen onto such property, were not poisonous or noxious in their nature, the trees were not a "nuisance per se," in such a sense as to sustain an action for relief.

See publication Words and Phrases for other judicial constructions and definitions.

3. Nuisance ⟸42

Right to recover damages from overhanging branches depends on presence of actual injury to plaintiff or plaintiff's property.

4. Nuisance ⟸48

Complaint, in which it was alleged that branches on defendants' trees encroached on plaintiff's property, caused cosmetic damage to her garage and prevented her lawn from receiving adequate sunlight and that trees, branches and buds from the trees constantly fell on plaintiff's property, did not state cause of action for relief from private nuisance. RPAPL § 871.

5. Nuisance ⟸3(1)
   Trespass ⟸10

If an invasion of plaintiff's interest in exclusive possession of his land also deprives him of use and enjoyment of the land, trespass and nuisance would jointly arise, so long as the interference causes

Figure 5

The West Publishing Company has given thousands of discrete issues of law their own "key numbers," ordered under topic headings. The topic and key number of a particular rule can be used to find other cases on the same point.

All published cases begin with this kind of introductory information. Once you have gone over the introduction, it is time to read the opinion itself. Never depend on what a reference book, or even the case summary, tells you an opinion says. The people doing the research for these books are only human, and occasionally summaries are very misleading.

Make Sure the Case Is Still Valid

Once you've located a case that addresses the issue you're interested in, you'll want to make sure the case is still valid (that is, hasn't been overturned or reversed by another court decision) before you give a copy to your neighbor or a small claims court judge, for example. You can make sure a case is still good law by using an online service called KeyCite, which is available from Westlaw (www.westlaw.com). KeyCite requires you to register and use a credit card to pay approximately $3.75 for each search, which will tell you whether the case has been overturned. For your money, you also get a complete list of all cases that refer to the case, which may lead you to additional cases on the subject you're interested in.

You can check a case's validity using books in the law library—it's an arcane process called "Shepardizing." For instructions, see *Legal Research: How to Find & Understand the Law*, by Stephen Elias and Susan Levinkind (Nolo). ●

C H A P T E R

19

Mediation

A long dispute means that both parties are wrong.

—**Voltaire**

One of the most troublesome aspects of neighbor disputes is that they can fester for years. One neighbor becomes angry, the other retaliates, the first neighbor adds fuel to the fire, and the dispute escalates. Sadly, it is not uncommon to find neighbor quarrels that have gone on for years where the people can't even agree on how it started. If one neighbor actually sues another, the lawsuit drains not only money and time but usually ends any possibility of salvaging a friendly relationship. Then the neighbors continue to live side by side, sometimes not speaking ever again, more often finding something else to fight about.

Happily, there is a way out of this problem—it's called mediation, and, in one form or another, it's probably available in your community. Today, many judges commonly order disputing neighbors into mandatory mediation after they get to court. Far better for the neighbors to arrange it early on by themselves, and to avoid ever darkening the doors of the courthouse.

What Is Mediation?

Mediation is a process in which the people involved in a dispute sit down and find their own solution with the help of a mediator. A mediator is a person who is neutral to the dispute and has training in techniques to get people talking.

Mediators are not necessarily lawyers; in fact, many are not. Some undergo hours of intensive training in mediating disputes. Many are volunteers, which helps enormously in keeping costs down. Often a mediation service provides disputing neighbors with a panel of several skilled people to hear and guide them.

The job of the mediator is to help keep the neighbors focused and reasonably civil, to allow the presentation of each person's side, and to suggest compromise. The mediator has no power to impose a solution or order any action. If the neighbors reach an agreement, the mediator helps put it in writing, so everyone can remember exactly what was agreed.

It's amazing how well neighbor dispute mediation works. Unlike a court of law, each neighbor comes in not to win at any cost, but simply to be heard and to work at a solution. The fact that no judge or arbitrator can impose a decision greatly reduces the need to posture and shade the truth. The mediator's expertise helps, but usually most neighbors are tired of the quarreling and really would prefer peace in the neighborhood.

Another great feature of mediation is that, unlike a court proceeding, where only matters relevant to the dispute can be considered, anything can be discussed in a mediation session. Often, the result is that hidden problems, not even mentioned at first but at the heart of the dispute, emerge. For example, a dispute over a tree may really have its roots in a perceived slur about one neighbor's race, religion, or taste in motorcycles.

How to Find a Mediator

If you live in an urban area, you will probably have little trouble finding a mediator. The small claims clerk at the courthouse, the county law librarian, or the police may have a list of free community mediation services. For example, in San Francisco, an organization called Community Boards provides free mediation services on a neighborhood-by-neighborhood basis. In some East Coast cities, the Society of Friends has provided mediation services for many years. And in other areas, state or city funds support local mediation (dispute resolution) centers. You simply call the center and, in many cases, a mediator will contact your neighbor for you.

In any planned unit development or subdivision, the homeowners' association may offer mediation services to its members. If there is no neighborhood or community mediation service where you live, contact your local or state bar association. The American Bar Association has put its support behind mediation in recent years. Many attorneys volunteer as mediators through their local bar associations.

Private mediators are listed in the yellow pages of the phone book. Some lawyers may also mention mediation services in their telephone book listings under "attorneys." If you choose a mediator at random like this, find out first what the mediator's training is and how much you'll be charged. Some nonlawyer mediators may charge fees as high as $100 an hour, but if they are good, the expense will be far less than a lawsuit. Lawyer-mediators will charge at lawyer rates.

In areas that do not yet have organized mediation services, a troubled neighbor can still arrange for mediation of a dispute. All it takes is someone who is respected by both parties, who can remain neutral, and who is willing to help. A respected member of the neighborhood or of the clergy, a retired cop—you can probably think of someone who would be willing to help you and a neighbor work out a problem.

How Mediation Works

When choosing mediation, the disputing neighbors decide that they are willing to try to work something out themselves. Usually, one neighbor contacts the dispute resolution center and asks for help. A mediator contacts the other neighbor and attempts to get that neighbor to agree to participate in mediation. Mediators are very skilled at helping disputing neighbors to realize there is nothing to lose by such a meeting. The neighbors make no obligation beyond agreeing to sit down together in the same room with the mediator. Often the mediator has his or her own set of procedures. For example, sometimes a mediator wants to meet alone with each disputant before the mediation session.

At the mediation session, the neighbors may feel comfortable attending alone or may bring someone with them. Typically, each neighbor has a turn to explain how he or she sees things, with the mediator sometimes asking questions. It is the mediator's job to try to keep the neighbors from interrupting each other and guide them toward a dialogue. In some instances, a mediator also explains relevant laws, but the neighbors don't have to follow the solution the law sets out; they are free to make their own agreement. If an agreement is reached, the mediator helps puts it into writing.

Let's take an example.

Mary and John have been next-door neighbors for years. In the last year, John has begun to complain bitterly about the debris in his yard from Mary's oak tree. Mary does nothing. John gives veiled threats about cutting down the tree. One day, they have harsh words over the tree, and Mary warns him to leave her property alone.

John doesn't say anything more but turns up the volume on his TV when he watches late-night movies. And he moves his TV closer to a window on Mary's side of the house, which he leaves open a few inches. When Mary complains, John just smiles and does nothing.

A few weeks later, while watering her yard, Mary just happens to place the sprinkler too close to the property line, wets down John's tools, and soaks his cactus garden. John says nothing but begins parking his car right at the edge of Mary's drive so it's hard for her to turn into her driveway and even harder to see traffic when she pulls out. (Does this sound familiar to anyone?)

Mary and John no longer complain; they no longer speak. One night when the TV keeps Mary awake, she calls the police, claiming John is in violation of the local noise ordinance.

A cruiser pulls up, and the war goes up a notch. The police talk to both of them (with all of the neighbors watching, of course). Fortunately, a perceptive officer senses that there is more going on than one loud television set. He hands them both the name and address of a free local mediation project with offices at the local courthouse. Although it's a voluntary program, the officer gets both Mary and John to somewhat reluctantly agree to try it.

Mary and John are interviewed separately by the mediator, who takes notes in each session and prepares a tentative summary of the complaints. A date is scheduled for them to meet together. John, who lives alone, attends alone. Mary, upset over a confrontation with John, takes along her son, Bill, for support. Here is what happens.

Mediator: Thank you for coming. We will do this in an orderly fashion, with one complaint at a time. Mary, please begin by telling us what is happening. John, please do not interrupt; you will have plenty of time for your own story.

Mary: I don't really know why I am here. The only problem is that John here has suddenly begun turning up the volume on his TV at all hours and I can't get any sleep. I just want him to turn it down, or off.

Mediator: You told me earlier that John is also blocking your driveway and threatening your tree.

Mary: That too. I don't know what has happened. We used to get along, but then he started acting like a real jerk.

John: Jerk? Who's a jerk? You're the one who ruined my tools.

Mediator: Slow down. Let's start by keeping language as civil as possible. It's fine to be mad, but calling each other names won't help. Also, John, let Mary tell her story first in as much detail as she wants. Then it will be your turn.

Mary: I don't mind dealing with the tools. I was just watering my yard. There must have been a surge of pressure. I'm not the kind of person to deliberately harm someone else's things. [pause] I didn't mean to ruin any tools. John has just made me so angry.

Mediator: Mary, I have written down three complaints that you have about John: his loud television set, his blocking your driveway, and his threatening your tree. Would you like to add anything?

Mary: No. That's about it, and that's enough.

Mediator: John, you have the floor.

John: I never was going to hurt her precious tree, even though it drives me crazy. Living downwind from that thing with all the leaves it sheds is a nightmare. But the real problem here is Mary. She ruined $200 worth of my tools and destroyed my garden. I should be taking her to court.

Mediator: What about the loud television?

John: It's my house, and I can watch TV anytime I please. Besides, noise doesn't seem to bother her when she's throwing those loud parties.

Mary: Parties? What parties? (This is the first time she has heard this and she is surprised. She thinks back for a moment. The only party she had this year was her annual Christmas open house. It didn't seem loud, even though it did go a bit late. And John knew he wouldn't be invited this year, after he had been so nasty.)

Mediator: Just a minute, Mary. John, let's talk about the tree, the oak in Mary's back yard. You say it is driving you crazy?

John: I've never seen so much debris in my life. I dread the fall when I'll have to spend all of my time raking up the leaves.

Mediator: How long have you two been next-door neighbors?

Mary and John: For ten years.

Mediator: During the past years, have you had any trouble before?

Mary: No. [pause] In fact, John has been a good neighbor in the past. I don't understand what is wrong. He used to like my tree; he even raked the leaves in my yard sometimes when he raked his. Now all he does is complain. I won't allow my tree to be harmed. And John, I have never had loud parties.

John: There just seemed to be so many more leaves last year. I can't rake as well after my back surgery. I can't do much of anything anymore. (He thinks maybe he should have told Mary about his back, and maybe asked her son, Bill, to do the raking. He realizes that he does still like the tree.)

Mary: Surgery, what surgery? When did you have surgery? Why didn't you tell me? I'm your next-door neighbor.

At this point the anger over the television and the tools is subsiding. Both Mary and John are beginning to see the trap they have made for themselves with their quarrels. They both are beginning to want out of the hostilities.

The mediator suggests that they make an agreement between them covering the issues that have caused their disputes. With the mediator's help, they draft one in writing, so they will have it for future reference.

And yes, Bill started raking the leaves and John was invited to the next Christmas party. Corny? Not really. This is not nearly as emotional as some neighbor disputes. The real problem is usually lack of or missed communication.

Of course there are times when mediation doesn't work. Sometimes, one neighbor just flatly refuses to participate in the process. Other times, the neighbors storm out, unable to agree, and head straight to court. There are also situations when it appears that only one neighbor is completely at fault and there is no room for compromise. Even when this seems to be the case, the mediator can be on the alert for hidden problems. They can pop out just as they did with John and Mary, letting the settlement process begin.

For a more detailed discussion of mediation and a list of national and state-specific mediation organizations, see *Mediate, Don't Litigate,* by Peter Lovenheim (Nolo), available as a downloadable eGuide at www.nolo.com.

Sample Mediation Agreement

AGREEMENT

Mary Malone and John Jasper, in an effort to settle their differences and live peaceably, make the following agreement:

- The entire oak tree in Mary's back yard is to be trimmed and thinned every three years, cost to be borne by Mary.
- Any branches of the oak tree over John's property may be cut at his expense at any time, if he chooses.
- There will be no loud television playing that disturbs the other. If John watches TV after 11 p.m., he will use earphones or move the TV from the wall on Mary's side of the house.
- At least a three-foot clearance will be left between John's car and Mary's driveway.
- Watering of lawns will be done with care and attention to each other's property.
- Any parties will be held at a reasonable time and without excessive noise.

In the case of any future dispute, Mary and John agree to talk to each other, with or without a mediator, to try to solve the problem amicably.

Mary Malone   *March 15, 20XX*
―――――――――――――――   ―――――――――――――――
Mary Malone   Date

John Jasper   *March 15, 20XX*
―――――――――――――――   ―――――――――――――――
John Jasper   Date

Small Claims Court

A successful lawsuit is the one worn by a policeman.

—**Robert Frost**

When all lines of communication between neighbors are severed and a legal dispute remains, consider using small claims court. You can do this yourself, without a lawyer, and avoid the expense and delay of regular court.

What Is Small Claims Court?

Small claims court is a local court where you can go to sue a person who has caused you damage. In a few areas of the country, this court is called by other names such as "justice" court or "pro se" court. Wherever you live, one of these courts should be available to you.

The hallmark of small claims court is that it's cheap and easy to file a case, and court procedures have been simplified to the point that attorneys are not necessary and in many states not even allowed. The hearing before the judge, magistrate, or commissioner (sometimes a volunteer lawyer) usually happens quickly and the decision is made on the spot or in a few days.

The amount you can sue for is limited, usually no more than $2,500 to $15,000. The chart below lists the limits for every state. These limits increase regularly, so double-check the amount with the court clerk if you decide to use this court.

You may well want to use small claims court even if your losses are higher than the amount you can sue for, because of the attorneys' fees and the enormous amount of time required to use regular court. For example, if you have a $6,000 claim and a lawyer will take a third of what you win as a fee, you could use a small claims court with a limit of $3,000 and still come out ahead, once the delay and expenses are figured in.

Also be aware that a few states, including Hawaii, Montana, and New Jersey, place restrictions on what type of lawsuits a judge will hear in small claims court. These restrictions may limit lawsuits only to landlord-tenant disputes or to personal injury claims.

Small Claims Court Limits

Most states raise their small claims limits frequently. Also, in some states, the small claims court limits—and the types of cases that may be brought—vary county by county and/or city by city. If you plan to sue in small claims court, ask the court clerk for up-to-the-minute information on your local court's claims limit and procedures.

State	Amount	State	Amount
Alabama	$6,000	Montana	$7,000
Alaska	$10,000	Nebraska	$3,600 through 6/30/2020
Arizona	$3,500	Nevada	$10,000
Arkansas	$5,000	New Hampshire	$10,000
California	$10,000	New Jersey	$3,000
Colorado	$7,500	New Mexico	$10,000
Connecticut	$5,000*	New York	$10,000 city courts****
Delaware	$15,000	North Carolina	$10,000
D.C.	$10,000	North Dakota	$15,000
Florida	$8,000	Ohio	$6,000
Georgia	$15,000*	Oklahoma	$10,000
Hawaii	$5,000*	Oregon	$10,000
Idaho	$5,000	Pennsylvania	$12,000
Illinois	$10,000	Rhode Island	$2,500
Indiana	$6,000***	South Carolina	$7,500
Iowa	$6,500	South Dakota	$12,000
Kansas	$4,000	Tennessee	$25,000*
Kentucky	$2,500	Texas	$20,000 as of 9/1/2020
Louisiana	$5,000*	Utah	$11,000
Maine	$6,000	Vermont	$5,000
Maryland	$5,000	Virginia	$5,000
Massachusetts	$7,000**	Washington	$10,000
Michigan	$6,000	West Virginia	$10,000*
Minnesota	$15,000	Wisconsin	$10,000*
Mississippi	$3,500	Wyoming	$6,000
Missouri	$5,000		

* No limit in certain landlord-tenant or eviction cases.
** No limit for property damage caused by motor vehicle.
*** $8,000 in Marion County.
**** $3,000 town or village courts.

Most small claims courts can award only money. If you want a judge to order your neighbor to do something, such as remove a fence or stop an obnoxious noise, you will probably have to use regular court. But keep in mind that a lawsuit asking for money can get a neighbor's attention, even though the court can't directly order the neighbor to solve the problem. And if you are suing for a nuisance—for instance, a noise problem—you can sue more than once. As long as the neighbor doesn't correct the problem, you can sue again and again. Check with the small claims court clerk to find out whether you may use small claims court to ask the judge to order your neighbor to do something (or stop doing something).

Preparing for Small Claims Court

You must know the law before you go in front of a small claims court judge. If you are using a state statute or a local ordinance, have a copy of it available to hand to the judge. If you are relying on a court opinion, you must be certain that a more recent court decision or statute hasn't changed the law. (Read Chapter 18.)

Gather your written evidence, including photographs, estimates for repairs, and copies of letters.

Ask the small claims court clerk about any special procedure that you need to follow before you file, such as writing a demand letter for the money to the person you are suing. Some courts require proof that this has been done before you can file a lawsuit. In some states, small claims courts have free advisors who will give you information and help you prepare for court.

Go down and watch a few small claims court cases before your case is scheduled, so you will be more comfortable and know what to expect.

For help preparing and presenting a suit in small claims court, read *Everybody's Guide to Small Claims Court,* by Ralph Warner (Nolo). For access to small claims court information and rules, go to the Small Claims Court section of Nolo's website, at www.nolo.com, under the heading "Rights & Disputes."

Small Claims Court Pointers

- Be organized.
- Know the law.
- Be brief.
- Be polite.
- Be comfortable. Go down to court a few days before your hearing and watch the proceedings so you will know what happens.

How Small Claims Court Works

Let's take an example of a simple neighbor dispute and follow it through the small claims court process.

In his back yard, Steve has a spreading black walnut tree of which he is very proud. Ralph, who lives next door, does nothing but gripe about the tree: too many leaves, too much shade, and the tree kills his flowers. One day Steve comes home and discovers that the tree has been cut down. Sally, his neighbor across the street, tells him that she saw Ralph doing the cutting and assumed he had permission. Steve takes photos of the damage and notifies the police and his insurance company. The insurance company informs him that his policy doesn't cover damage to trees. Steve calls a local nursery and learns that they can put in a good-sized but smaller tree of a different kind for $900. He learns to his disappointment that he can't have another black walnut tree because a local ordinance has declared them harmful and prohibits planting new ones. The cost of removing the old stump will be an extra $200. He obtains a written estimate from the nursery.

The next step for Steve is a trip to the law library, where he looks up his state statutes on trees. He finds that under his state law, a person who willfully cuts down another's tree is liable to the owner for triple the amount of damages. He makes copies of the statute and writes this letter to Ralph:

Sample Demand Letter

Dear Ralph,

   Last Thursday, October 2, 20xx, you deliberately and without permission cut down my black walnut tree. Instead of trying to resolve any problems you had with the tree in other ways, you waited until I was not at home, deliberately trespassed on my property, and destroyed the tree.

   I am enclosing the state law concerning your action and an estimate of my repair and the replacement cost of a smaller tree. I will never be able to have another black walnut tree.

   As you can see, my actual damage is $1,100. The law says that you owe me triple this amount or $3,300. I demand that you pay this amount to me immediately or I will pursue legal action.

Yours truly,

Steve Shapiro

Steve Shapiro

Ralph does not reply. Steve knows from doing research that because the tree can't really be replaced, he could use regular court and base his losses instead on the diminished value of his entire property. This would put his damages as high as $5,000 or $6,000. But he also knows that a lawyer may charge a third of the money award as a fee and that the case could take about two years.

In Steve's state, the small claims court limit is $3,500. What he really wants is a good-sized new tree and he wants it now. He considers the lawyer's fees and the time it would take to use regular court. He decides to do it himself, use small claims court, and ask for the limit—$3,500. He proceeds to the small claims clerk, fills out the papers, and pays a small filing fee. A hearing is scheduled within three weeks.

Steve sits down and writes out:

- what happened
- what the law is, and
- how much money he should be paid and why.

He gathers the few documents he will want to use: the police report, the pictures, the estimate, a copy of the statute, and a copy of his letter to Ralph. He calls Sally and gets her to agree to go to court with him and testify. He makes a few notes on a card so he won't forget anything.

That week, Steve goes down to the small claims court for a few hours and watches some actual cases, learning what to expect and how to proceed. Now he's ready.

The Hearing

Clerk: The next case is *Steven Shapiro vs. Ralph Rogers*. Please step forward.

Judge: Good morning. Mr. Shapiro, will you please begin?

Steve: Your Honor, on October 2, my neighbor Mr. Rogers cut down my black walnut tree in my back yard. He did this deliberately and without my permission. Here is a picture of the tree that he cut (hands the judge the picture). I asked Mr. Rogers to pay me for the damage he caused and he did not respond (hands the judge a copy of the letter, which the judge reads).

Judge: Go on, Mr. Shapiro.

Steve: Here is the estimate from a nursery for $1,100 for removing the stump and replacing the tree with a smaller tree of a different kind (hands the judge the estimate).

I am asking for $3,500 because our state statute provides for me to receive triple the amount of my damages (hands the statute to the judge), plus the value of my property has been diminished.

Judge: Mr. Shapiro, how do you know Mr. Rogers was the one who cut down the tree?

Steve: Your honor, this is Sally Smith, who saw what happened.

Judge: Ms. Smith?

Sally: Your honor, I saw Mr. Rogers cut down Mr. Shapiro's black walnut tree, the one in the picture.

Judge: Thank you. Mr. Rogers, what do you have to say about this?

Ralph: Your honor, the tree was an absolute nuisance. The leaves and sticks were all over my yard and the tree poisoned my flowers. Black walnut trees are so harmful that they have been outlawed in this town (hands a copy of the local ordinance to the judge). I complained several times to Mr. Shapiro and he did nothing about it. The tree was an illegal tree and I was within my rights.

Judge: Well, Mr. Rogers, this local ordinance prohibits planting any new black walnut trees. This tree was legal when it was planted, so the fact that black walnuts can't be planted now isn't relevant. Under the laws of this state, any limbs that were hanging over your own property and bothering you were a nuisance and you had the right to cut them back to the property line. But you did not have a right to go over and cut down the tree. Did you cut it down?

Ralph: Yes I did, and I didn't think I was doing anything wrong by taking the law into my own hands. At least the thing is gone and I can enjoy one autumn without all those leaves and grow my flowers.

Judge: Thank you. You will get my decision in a few days by mail.

The decision was for Ralph to pay Steve $3,500.

Some of you are thinking that Steve should have had Ralph arrested and thrown into jail. In some states, this would have indeed been an option. If you think a neighbor has committed a crime, you can notify the police. They will decide whether the neighbor can be charged. ●

State Statutes on Injury to Trees

Note: The statutes provided in this book are simply a starting point for your research. If you don't find the information you're looking for in these appendixes, you should look for all applicable statutes in your state or speak with an attorney to make sure there are no exceptions that may apply in your particular case.

These states have statutes providing for injury to trees.

Alabama	Ala. Code Ann. §§ 35-14-1 to 35-14-3; 9-13-60
Alaska	Alaska Stat. Ann. § 09.45.730
Arizona	No directly applicable statutes; however, the owner should be able to sue for actual damages and trespass.
Arkansas	Ark. Code Ann. §§ 18-60-102, 5-38-203
California	Cal. Civ. Code § 3346; Cal. Penal Code § 384a
Colorado	No directly applicable statutes; however, the owner should be able to sue for actual damages and trespass.
Connecticut	Conn. Gen. Stat. Ann. § 52-560
Delaware	Del. Code Ann. tit. 25, § 1401
District of Columbia	D.C. Code Ann. § 22-3310
Florida	No directly applicable statutes; however, the owner should be able to sue for actual damages and trespass.
Georgia	Ga. Code Ann. § 51-12-50
Hawaii	No directly applicable statutes; however, the owner should be able to sue for actual damages and trespass.
Idaho	Idaho Code Ann. §§ 6-202, 18-7008, 18-7021
Illinois	740 Ill. Comp. Stat. § 185/2
Indiana	No directly applicable statutes; however, the owner should be able to sue for actual damages and trespass.
Iowa	Iowa Code Ann. § 658.4
Kansas	No directly applicable statutes; however, the owner should be able to sue for actual damages and trespass.
Kentucky	Ky. Rev. Stat. § 364.130
Louisiana	La. Rev. Stat. Ann.§ 3:4278.1
Maine	Me. Rev Stat. Ann. tit. 14, § 7552; tit. 17, § 2510
Maryland	Md. Code Ann. [Nat. Res.] § 5-409

Massachusetts	Mass. Gen. Laws Ann. ch. 87, § 11; Mass. Gen. Laws Ann. ch. 242, § 7; Mass. Gen. Laws Ann. ch. 266, §§ 113, 114
Michigan	Mich. Comp. Laws. Ann. §§ 600.2919, 750.367, 750.382
Minnesota	Minn. Stat. Ann. § 561.04
Mississippi	Miss. Code Ann. §§ 95-5-10, 97-17-81, 97-17-83, 97-17-89
Missouri	Mo. Rev. Stat. § 537.340
Montana	Mont. Code Ann. § 70-16-107
Nebraska	Neb. Rev. Stat. § 25-2130
Nevada	Nev. Rev. Stat. §§ 40.160, 206.015, 527.050
New Hampshire	N.H. Rev. Stat. §§ 227-J:8, 227-J:8-a, 539:9
New Jersey	N.J. Stat. Ann. §§ 2C:18-5; 4:17-9 to 4:17-10
New Mexico	N.M. Stat. Ann. §§ 30-14-1 to 30-14.1.1; 68-2-17; 68-2-22 to 68-2-23
New York	N.Y. Real Prop. Acts. Law § 861
North Carolina	N.C. Gen. Stat. §§ 1-539.1, 14-128, 14-135
North Dakota	N.D. Cent. Code Ann. § 32-03-30
Ohio	Ohio Rev. Code Ann. §§ 901.51, 901.99
Oklahoma	Okla. Stat. Ann. tit. 21, §§ 1768, 1773; Okla. Stat. Ann. tit. 23, § 72
Oregon	Or. Rev. Stat. §§ 105.810, 527.260, 527.990
Pennsylvania	18 Pa. Const. Stat. Ann. § 1107
Rhode Island	R.I. Gen. Laws §§ 11-44-2, 34-20-1
South Carolina	S.C. Code Ann. § 16-11-520
South Dakota	S.D. Codified Laws Ann. § 21-3-10
Tennessee	Tenn. Code Ann. § 43-28-312
Texas	Tex. Nat. Res. Code §§ 151.051, 151.052
Utah	Utah Code Ann. § 78B-6-1002

Vermont	Vt. Stat. Ann. tit. 13, §§ 3602, 3606, 3606a
Virginia	Va. Code Ann. §§ 18.2-140, 55.1-2835, 55.1-2836
Washington	Wash. Rev. Code Ann. 64.12.030
West Virginia	W.Va. Code Ann. §§ 61-3-48, 61-3-48a, 61-3-52
Wisconsin	Wis. Stat. Ann. §§ 26.05, 26.09
Wyoming	No directly applicable statutes; however, the owner should be able to sue for actual damages and trespass.

The following states have no directly applicable statutes; however, the owner should be able to sue for actual damages and trespass.

Arizona	Hawaii	Kansas
Colorado	Indiana	Wyoming
Florida		

State Statutes on Private Nuisance

Common Law Definition

The following states have statutes that follow the common law definition of private nuisance. Typically, they define nuisance something like this: "Anything which is injurious to health, indecent or offensive to the senses, or an obstruction to the free use of property, so as to interfere with the comfortable enjoyment of life or property."

Alabama	Ala. Ann. § 6-5-120 (slightly different language)
Alaska	Alaska Stat. § 09.45.255 (slightly different language)
California	Cal. Civ. Code § 3479
Georgia	Ga. Code Ann. § 41-1-1 (slightly different language)
Idaho	Idaho Code Ann. § 52-111
Indiana	Ind. Code Ann. § 32-30-6-6
Iowa	Iowa Code Ann. § 657.1
Kentucky	Ky. Rev. Stat. Ann. § 411.550
Minnesota	Minn. Stat. Ann. § 561.01
Montana	Mont. Code Ann. § 27-30-101
Nevada	Nev. Rev. Stat. § 40.140
Utah	Utah Code Ann. § 78B-6-1101
Washington	Wash. Rev. Code Ann. § 7.48.010

Conduct or Condition Must Be Unlawful or Unreasonable

In these other states, conduct must be unlawful or unreasonable to be defined as a nuisance.

New Jersey	N.J. Stat. Ann. § 2C:33-12 (limiting public nuisance)
New Mexico	N.M. Stat. Ann. § 30-8-1 (limiting public nuisance)
North Dakota	N.D. Cent. Code Ann. § 42-01-01
Oklahoma	Okla. Stat. Ann. tit. 50, § 1
South Dakota	S.D. Codified Laws Ann. § 21-10-1

Note: The states not listed above have no statute but use the common law definition of nuisance. ●

Boundary Fence Statutes

These states have statutes providing for joint expense and maintenance of division fences.

Alabama	Ala. Code Ann. § 35-7-3
Arkansas	Ark. Code Ann. § 2-39-105
California	Cal. Civ. Code § 841
Colorado	Colo. Rev. Stat. § 35-46-112 (for agriculture or grazing)
Connecticut	Conn. Gen. Stat. Ann. § 47-49
Delaware	Del. Code Ann. tit. 25, § 1304
Hawaii	Haw. Rev. Stat. §§ 664-21, 664-23
Idaho	Idaho Code Ann. §§ 35-103, 35-105
Illinois	765 Ill. Comp. Stat. §§ 130/3, 130/4
Indiana	Ind. Code Ann. § 32-26-9-3
Iowa	Iowa Code Ann. § 359A.1A
Kansas	Kan. Stat. Ann. § 29-301
Kentucky	Ky. Rev. Stat. §§ 256.020, 256.030 (by agreement)
Louisiana	La. Civ. Code art. 685
Maine	Me. Rev. Stat. Ann. tit. 30-A, § 2952
Massachusetts	Mass. Gen. Laws Ann. ch. 49, §§ 4–13
Michigan	Mich. Comp. Laws Ann. § 43.53
Minnesota	Minn. Stat. Ann. § 344.03
Mississippi	Miss. Code Ann. § 89-13-1
Missouri	Mo. Stat. Ann. § 272.060
Montana	Mont. Code Ann. § 70-16-205
Nebraska	Neb. Rev. Stat. § 34-102
New Hampshire	N.H. Rev. Stat. Ann. 473:1
New Jersey	N.J. Stat. Ann. 4:20-7 (for pasturing or keeping animals)
New York	N.Y. Town Law § 300 (unless agreement or no animals for five years)
North Dakota	N.D. Cent. Code Ann. § 47-26-05
Ohio	Ohio Rev. Code Ann. § 971.02 (unless agreement; lots within municipal areas exempt)

Oklahoma	Okla. Stat. Ann. tit. 60, § 70
Oregon	Or. Rev. Stat. §§ 96.010, 96.020
Pennsylvania	29 Pa. Cons. Stat. § 41
Rhode Island	R.I. Gen. Laws § 34-10-9 and following (unless agreement)
South Dakota	S.D. Codified Laws Ann. §§ 43-23-1–43-23-2 (unless agreement or no livestock for five years; also local option)
Tennessee	Tenn. Code Ann. § 44-8-202
Utah	Utah Code Ann. § 4-26-102
Vermont	Vt. Stat. Ann. tit. 24 § 3802
Virginia	Va. Code Ann. § 55.1-2821
Washington	Wash. Rev. Code Ann. § 16.60.020
West Virginia	W.Va. Code § 19-17-6 (livestock)
Wisconsin	Wis. Stat. Ann. § 90.03 (farming or grazing)
Wyoming	Wyo. Stat. Ann. § 11-28-106

Index